More praise for **whatever it takes**

"An eloquent collection . . . Individually, the essays and poems are technically precise and revealing and passionate. Together, they form a much-needed resource that gives voice to female athletes, summarized by one sportswoman's call: 'The barriers fall. Now we can play.'"

—*Kirkus Reviews*

"Thoughtful and thought-provoking, this collection celebrates the power of sport in the lives of women. The voices you hear are fresh, funny, and triumphant."

—Lauren Kessler
Author of *Full Court Press*

"Beautifully wrought narratives . . . The athletes' voices speak with clarity and authority."

—Margaret Carlisle Duncan
Department of Human Kinetics
University of Wisconsin—Milwaukee

"For the growing ranks of women who will fulfill their dreams in the sport world, this insightful collection is a must read."

—Jean S. Cione
Player for the Rockford Peaches in
the All-American Girls Professional
Baseball League

about the editors

Joli Sandoz has played, coached, and written about sports since her first plunge off the starting blocks in 1961. She teaches at The Evergreen State College in Olympia, Washington.

Joby Winans was a varsity collegiate athlete who now competes in road races and masters track and field. She works as a training and organizational development professional in Tacoma, Washington.

also edited by joli sandoz

A Whole Other Ball Game: Women's Literature on Women's Sport

whatever it takes

WOMEN

ON

WOMEN'S

SPORT

Edited and with an introduction by

Joli Sandoz and **Joby Winans**

farrar, straus and **giroux**

new york

Farrar, Straus and Giroux
19 Union Square West, New York 10003

Introduction and compilation copyright © 1999 by Joli Sandoz and Joby Winans
Distributed in Canada by Douglas & McIntyre Ltd.
Printed in the United States of America
Designed by Debbie Glasserman
First edition, 1999

Library of Congress Cataloging-in-Publication Data
Whatever it takes : women on women's sport / edited and with an
    introduction by Joli Sandoz and Joby Winans. — 1st ed.
        p.   cm.
    Includes bibliographical references.
    ISBN 0-374-52597-8 (alk. paper)
    1. Sports for women.   I. Sandoz, Joli, 1952–   .   II. Winans,
Joby, 1952–   .
GV709.W52 1999
796'.082—dc21   98-31855

Cover art:
Large photograph copyright © MyWire
Small photographs, from left: © The Picture Book/Photonica, © The Picture
Book/Photonica, © Susan Meiselas/Magnum Photos, © White/Packert/The
Image Bank, © Reuters/Micahel Leckel/Archive Photos, © Hirz/Archive Photos,
© Reuters/Jeff Topping/Archive Photos

To sportswomen!
—js

To my first team,
the Armstrong/Winans family.
—jw

And to the athletes of the future;
especially Hannah and Jake,
whom we fondly envision
wearing identical uniforms
as they compete side by side.
—js and jw

*What changes when a woman
becomes an athlete?
Everything.*

Mariah Burton Nelson, 1994

contents

Introduction   **3**

Pulling No Punches (from *Kill the Body: The Head Will Fall*)   Rene Denfeld   **12**

Summer Showdown   Pat Griffin   **22**

Women Play Football   Theodora Sohst   **28**

Killer Instinct   Anne Alexander   **30**

Next Game   Nancy R. Nerenberg   **33**

Never   Maxine Kumin   **39**

Remembering Stella Walsh   Grace Butcher   **41**

Awesome Women in Sports   Ruth Conniff   **52**

O Promised Land!   Anonymous   **61**

Smells Like Team Spirit: Portrait of a Rank Season   Holly Morris   **62**

They're Pooling Their Power   Shawn Hubler   **75**

The Value of Girl's Basket Ball   A Kokomo High School Student   **78**

A Peaches Fan for Life   Susan E. Johnson   **79**

American Past Time   Barbara Crooker   **88**

In Praise of Bush Leagues   Michelle Brockway   **89**

Camper of the Year   Carol Bergman   **93**

Recognition   Kim Schaefer   **100**

From *A Wheel within a Wheel*   Frances E. Willard   **102**

Grandmothers Nowadays Play   Theodora Sohst   **108**

My Mother, My Rival   Mariah Burton Nelson   **109**

Of High-tops and Home Plates   Deborah Abbott   **113**

Swimming and Writing   Maxine Kumin   **118**

Green Afternoons   Barbara Davenport   **127**

From *Swimming the Channel*   Sally Friedman   **137**

MVHS X-Country Team   Debra Pennington Davis   **143**

Privilege   Leila Green   **144**

Dawn Staley (from *Venus to the Hoop*)   Sara Corbett   **146**

I Ching #17 Following   Karen Zealand   **151**
   (The Discus Thrower)

Dreams on Ice   April Martin   **152**
A Swimming Lesson   Jewelle Gomez   **156**
The Athletic Girl   Anne O'Hagan   **160**
Precious Medals   Anna Seaton Huntington   **163**
Wheelchair Flying   Carrie Dearborn   **165**
Baseball Is about Playing   Wendy Patrice Williams   **167**
From *An American Childhood*   Annie Dillard   **175**
Sikes Room, Princeton Boathouse   Sandra J. Chu   **177**
Coming Home   Joli Sandoz   **179**
Learning to Swim at Forty-five   Colleen J. McElroy   **195**
Seconds   Teresa Leo   **197**
Sidelines   Amy Irvine   **211**
Turning It Up   Betsy Crowfoot   **218**
Losing Baseball, the 1950s   Susan Eisenberg   **229**
Memoirs of a Would-Be   Ann Geracimos   **230**
   Swim Champ

Sneakers   Alisa Solomon   **243**
Q: Why Do You Want to Race?   Grace Butcher   **252**
   A: Because My Name
   Comes Apart

Ernestine Bayer   Linda Lewis   **257**
Solo Shoot
   (from *In These Girls,*   Madeleine Blais   **260**
   ***Hope Is a Muscle*)**

What Goes Around,   Frances K. Conley   **262**
   Comes Around

By Atoms Moved   Diane Ackerman   **268**
From "The Revolutionary Bicycle"   Anonymous   **269**
Ready, Wrestle   Helen Vozenilek   **270**
Up for the Count   Louise A. Smith   **275**
Tournament-Tough   Barbara Beckwith   **280**
Longing and Bliss   Megan McNamer   **290**
Bench Press, or Becoming   Leslie Heywood   **298**
   a Girl Again

From *Pilgrim at Tinker Creek*   Annie Dillard   **306**

Contributors' Notes   **309**
Permissions   **319**
Acknowledgments   **323**

whatever it takes

introduction

What does sport mean to girls and women? "The signal," writes Ann Geracimos, "for life to begin." Since the first female ballplayer circled the bases at Vassar College in 1866, sportswomen have taken their athletic experiences to heart.

Whatever It Takes gathers for the first time women's personal nonfiction writings focused on their participation in competitive sport. In these pages, sportswomen shape their own athletic legacy, taking *themselves* seriously, if no one else will, and making their own meanings.

For women in sport, meaning-making leads to dilemma. Words and ideas used to understand self and experience derive from a larger context: in this case, an athletic tradition almost exclusively shaped to define "masculine" and build "men." And cultural pressures have kept most women's writings on the subject from being widely read, or circulated very long in print. So, of necessity, we began this project by asking questions. What is it like for a woman to wrestle? To box? To learn to race a motorcycle? What does victory mean to women? What do today's girls think as they lace up their Sheryl Swoopes sneakers on their way to shoot hoops with the guys? What did the first woman *ever* to step onto a basketball court think, back in 1892? And what strengths have they drawn, during their nearly one hundred and fifty years in competitive sport, from themselves and each other?

It struck us as odd—and, finally, insupportable—that after a combined total of more than fifty years as athletes and coaches, we simply didn't know. Sportswomen's inner game customarily plays out in a silence so complete that we couldn't recall taking part in even one locker-room conversation about it. Why is this? Do women just not care?

For answers, we turned first to the public record: printed and broadcast stories of sport. At the library we quickly discovered that U.S. women have indeed written about their experiences in physical activity and competitive sport, though historically they've most often advocated for their right to play. The literally hundreds of articles, books, personal essays, and poems we read became for us an education in what we'd never heard told: women's long, fiery hardiness—fueled, it seemed, by the unquenchable joy of being physically active—in the face of outright opposition.

Obviously, we'd misunderstood the situation. Women certainly do care about sport; they've fought in print for their right to physical fitness and physical games since at least 1790. Along the way, they've also chronicled their athletic experiences, at times reflecting publicly on what those experiences meant to them.

The kicker is that hardly anyone noticed. In the big picture, a woman in an athletic uniform, to borrow Julie Phillips's perfect phrase, creates "a disturbance of the social order."[1] Sportswomen simply are not, and haven't really ever been, among sport's more acceptable stories.

For decades widespread conventions proscribed U.S. sportswomen's very presence in gyms and on playing fields. Though the strength of these prohibitions varied across social class, race, time, and geographic location, their authority forbade many girls and most women any sport participation; even those who were able to play for the most part found themselves confined within certain limits of "ladylike" behavior.

Narrow conceptions of gender roles, even as total numbers of female athletes grew in fits and starts across the country, continued to deny women an important part of athletic experience: their inclusion in meaningful public stories. Americans tend to use sports symbols and myths to help define and give life to shared cultural values. When the well-known exemplars of courage, success, and grace under pressure are all or mostly male—from Babe Ruth to Sammy Sosa and Mark McGwire—where does that leave girls and women? At home, apparently, shut into their own "lesser" and often-forgotten scripts.

In her essay in this collection, Susan E. Johnson describes what it meant to her as a girl to cheer for the Rockford Peaches, one of ten teams in the All-American Girls Professional Baseball League (AAGPBL). The images she absorbed during the early 1950s, of highly competent competitive action on her hometown field, gave her nothing less than a future: "a womanhood," she writes, "that attracted me, that I could imagine myself into."

Four decades later, it took recognition of the AAGPBL by the National Baseball Hall of Fame at Cooperstown in the form of a permanent exhibit, six books of women's baseball history, and the release of the movie *A League of Their Own* to convince most Americans that females had ever played the game at all. Rockford reserve infielder Helen Waddell Wyatt called the process "resurrection."[2] But forty years of widespread disregard robbed athletes like Peaches first-sacker Dottie Kamenshek—whom Wally Pip, player of the same position for the New York Yankees in the 1920s, called "the fanciest fielding first baseman I've ever seen—man or woman"[3]—and generations of female would-be major-league all-stars of the chance even to dream of ongoing national recognition. Sadly, little girls who grew up away from the AAGPBL's Midwestern playing grounds, as we did, missed out on learning from female professional ballplayers what the luckier Johnson describes now as the conviction that "women can do anything."

Historian Susan Cahn identifies the conflicting understandings of women's capabilities and of athleticism as the "tension" which makes sportswomen's cultural presence so troublesome, once it is known. Athleticism, she points out, has been generally thought of as male and masculine, hence not at all proper for the respectable, "normal" female.[4] This has led to a host of compensatory efforts to present female athletic physicality as "feminine." Although the AAGPBL received good coverage in local newspapers, for example, editors balanced game accounts with feature stories about players' home lives. League organizers, almost all men, thought a feminine image would sell best; players wore uniform dresses on the field and read advice manuals on how to dress and apply makeup.

Today, things have changed . . . and they haven't. Women's basketball uniforms often look a lot like the baggy, functional outfits worn by the men. But as a society, we're still not talking much about what sportswomen accomplish. The two of us graduated from high school during years (1969 and 1970) when fewer than one in twenty-seven female U.S. high school students played competitive sport. Today that number is one in three.[5] Nationally, the ratio of stories in print media and television newscasts about sportsmen compared to those focused on sportswomen remains, as it has for a quarter of a century, at roughly ten to one[6]—despite the fact that today 39.5 percent of all high school athletes and 37 percent of all college athletes are women.[7]

In addition, few of the stories available present sportswomen as they actually are; instead the media continues to shape women's truths to fit the long-outworn femininity frame. The cover photo for the first issue of *Women\Sport*, *Sports Illustrated*'s short-lived 1997 magazine for women, depicted a perfectly groomed, very pregnant woman in a basketball jersey standing sideways to the camera, one hand across her swollen belly. The other hand, made vivid by a multi-diamond ring, lofted a basketball. Star player Sheryl Swoopes agreed to be photographed, she reportedly said later, because she didn't want anyone to think she felt ashamed of being pregnant. Of course she had no reason to be. But the juxtaposition of a woman's pro-basketball uniform and such obvious "womanhood" on the cover of a national sports magazine sent a very ambiguous message about the status of women and their relationship to competition and athleticism. We're here, it seemed to shout. But we're still married and mothers. No reason to worry. We're not really changing a thing.

At the time of the photo, Swoopes had a sterling athletic record. She scored 47 points in the National Collegiate Athletic Association (NCAA) title game while leading Texas Tech to the 1993 championship, was the first woman to have a basketball shoe named after her, played basketball around the world for the U.S. national basketball team, and earned an Olympic gold medal. Until her unexpected pregnancy, the new Women's National Basketball Association touted her as its guiding star. But the article inside the magazine framed Swoopes as domestic, just a homebody who spurned the game's "subtexts." It ended, in fact, with the sentence "Play the game, play it hard, and eventually a man will take notice."[8]

Unfortunately, the Swoopes photos and story are not an isolated instance of the diminishment of world-class women to domestic stereotypes. They represent a continuing pattern researchers have identified during several decades of study. As another case in point, media critic Gina Daddario observed that during the 1992 Olympics reporters repeatedly referred to stellar speed skater Bonnie Blair as "America's little sister" and our "favorite girl next door." One television commentator apparently even described Blair as "smooth as peanut butter on ice and as sweet as jelly off." In 1992 Blair, twenty-eight years old, was an exceptionally skilled, experienced, and visibly powerful world record holder and the winner of five Olympic gold medals.[9]

Old habits die hard. At stake is the male-oriented focus of sport, and more. Editors and producers who choose to run stories which valorize men while ignoring, belittling, or distorting truths about women buttress the social power structure that "proves"—in a rigged game—females to be inferior to and reliant on males. The consequences are enormous. By keeping her in her place, for example, such tales keep a woman out of sport's boardrooms. In 1972, women coached more than 90 percent of women's collegiate teams and administered an equal percentage of women's sport programs. Just twenty-four years later, in 1996, 47.7 percent of the coaches of NCAA teams for women were female (compared with 1 percent of coaches of men's teams); women administered only 18.5 percent of women's programs, while 23 percent had no female top brass at all.[10] Myths about women's lack of competence and experience in sport supported, after a 1972 federal law resulted in more funding being channeled into sports for girls and women, a simple and continuing power grab.

Emphasis on domesticity and heterosexual appeal works at a different but equally insidious level, by communicating that these surface attributes are more important than accomplishments sportswomen display in equal measure with sportsmen: intelligence, courage, hard work, integrity of play, ability to collaborate, and grace under competitive pressure. Popular sports stories, in other words, typically emphasize what keeps current gender-based power arrangements in place, the idea that what matters about sportswomen is whatever serves and pleases men. In effect, such images acknowledge that female athletes exist, but continue to confine them within narrow bounds.

The daily reality of many female athletes' lives has moved a step or two away from the conventional picture. And that's exactly the point. Why don't writers and photographers portray sportswomen as the strong and competent women they actually are? Continued widespread misrepresentation denies women the same cultural recognition, respect, and power enjoyed by sportsmen. And at the deepest level, where inner passion and power are born, such images can—are perhaps meant to—keep girls and women off balance, out of touch with their own inner reality. Such depictions too often prevent women's unambiguous experience of their own nascent power, undercutting their ability to make their own meanings and understand their own significance apart from the false and denigrating messages of a male-centered culture. And so such fabricated stories limit, finally, athletic women's abilities to be wholly themselves, excellently and without equivocation.

Given the circumstances, a woman who writes honestly about competitive sport commits a courageous and revolutionary act. Where the cultural understandings of "athlete" and "physicality" are tied to "male"—and where few grant public significance to women's personal experiences—the pressures on female writers to stay safely within conventional constraints are enormous. Pulitzer Prize winner Maxine Kumin swam competitively for Radcliffe College in the 1940s. She tells us here in her essay "Swimming and Writing" that the swimmer in a poem she wrote in the late 1950s, although generated by her own experiences, appears as male. Kumin "did not think [then] the average reader would be willing to invest much emotion in a female competitive swimmer."[11]

As we sent out our call for manuscripts, we weren't entirely sure what would happen. We asked for writing with "edge, passion, and depth." What would we get? In "Learning to Swim at Forty-five," poet Colleen J. McElroy notes that in writing, as in swimming, "You must learn to labor under the threat of air lost / Forever and hold fear close to you like a safety net." Another contributor, Mariah Burton Nelson, has written elsewhere of feeling in the early 1980s that she had to invent how to write about personal experiences in women's sport because so little was then being published on the subject. Even in 1999, would more than a few women feel safe enough, trust themselves and us enough, to be willing to make their personal stories part of the public record?

The more than two hundred responses amazed and delighted us. Their open exuberance, intensity, and, yes, pain surpassed our largest hopes. The works women sent us, written primarily since the 1970s, eschewed charm-school ambiguity and evasion. We found a passing reference to women's pleasure in sport during our library research, for example, Minna Smith's brief description in 1885 of women's inner connection to strenuous physical exercise—the "fascination of using one's strength" (slipped into an otherwise factual article about women's adult tricycling to explain why Mrs. Bonnett of Elizabeth, New Jersey, persisted in riding outdoors when the temperature dropped below 0°F).[12] By 1993, the occasional phrase had become Anne Alexander's entire essay on the joys of bicycle racing, entitled "Killer Instinct." Famous women's rights activist Elizabeth Cady Stanton's rather mild observation in 1882 that "a canter on horseback is more desirable, for pale cheeks and cloudy brains, than an anxious hour over a cook-stove"[13] had transmuted into Pat Griffin's public recounting, in an essay first published in 1995, of the thrill of challenging a male bully from the pitcher's mound. Each told sportswomen's, as distinct from sport power's, personal story. In the end, we chose a mix of old and new nonfiction pieces (and added a few poems) for this volume honoring women's long enjoyment of sport. The tests we used were these: the writer's success at communicating the significance she finds in her engagement with sport, and each piece's potential to nurture gender revolution.

Sportswomen take themselves seriously enough today to tell their stories out loud. It's time for the rest of us to listen. Here's the fact, as recorded by writer and two-time Olympian Anna Seaton Huntington: most female athletes are—and always have been—well beyond caring "what they look like, sound like or smell like . . . as long as they cross the finish line first."[14]

Across that line lie women's rights to be fully who we are and to tell it like it is. Don't bet against us. Sportswomen are athletes, trained to succeed. We're ready to do whatever it takes.

—**Joli Sandoz and Joby Winans**

notes

1. Julie Phillips, "A New Season for Women's Sports," *Ms.*, July/August 1997, 86.
2. Susan E. Johnson, *When Women Played Hardball* (Seattle: Seal Press, 1994), xvii.
3. Ibid., xxiii.
4. Susan Cahn, *Coming on Strong: Gender and Sexuality in Twenti-*

eth-Century Women's Sport (New York: The Free Press, 1994). See especially the introduction and chapters 1, 7, and 9.

5. Women's Sport Foundation, "Women's Sports Facts," August 12, 1997. Available http://www.lifetimetv.com/WoSport/stage/TOPISS/html/women_ssportsfacts.html#highschool.

6. Women's Sport Foundation, "Women's Sports Facts," August 12, 1997.

7. Gina Daddario, *Women's Sport and Spectacle: Gendered Television Coverage and the Olympic Games* (Westport, Conn.: Praeger, 1998), 17, 19.

8. Alexander Wolff, "United No More," *Women l Sport*, Spring 1997, 62.

9. Gina Daddario, "Chilly Scenes of the 1992 Winter Games: The Mass Media and the Marginalization of Female Athletes," *Sociology of Sport Journal*, vol. 11 (September 1994), 282.

10. R. Vivian Acosta and Linda Jean Carpenter, "Women in Intercollegiate Sport: A Longitudinal Study. Nineteen Year Update, 1977–1996." Available from http//www.lib.uiowa.edu/proj/ge/Acosta/womensp.html.

11. Since "400-Meter Freestyle" Kumin has written several significant poems in the female persona about women's experiences in sport.

12. Minna Caroline Smith, "Women as Cyclers," *Outing Magazine*, June 1885, 318.

13. Elizabeth Cady Stanton, "The Health of American Women," *North American Review*, December 1882, 512.

14. Anna Seaton Huntington, "What Women Athletes Are Really Like," *Glamour*, January 1996, 96.

pulling no punches (from *kill the body: the head will fall*)

RENE DENFELD

The first time I entered the Grand Avenue boxing gym, a few of the men jumping rope stopped to watch me. As I crossed the floor, a petite twenty-six-year-old with gym bag in hand, they seemed mildly shocked to see a woman enter their world.

Having been forewarned that there wasn't a women's locker room, I arrived in workout clothes—old shorts and a T-shirt. Feeling naked and ill at ease, I paused and looked around. The boxing ring—with soft elastic ropes and a stained canvas floor—dominated the small gym. A few fighters beat on heavy bags that dangled from chains, making a *huff, huff* noise as they threw their punches. Over the stench of old sweat and leather, I smelled something else, too, as ripe and healthy as cut fruit. It was the smell of *fresh* sweat, the kind that comes in an invigorating downpour.

Boxing gyms are not health clubs where you go just to exercise. You go to learn how to fight. The dues you pay include the cost of a trainer, usually an older man with a lean body and battered hands.

Within five minutes of entering the gym I was paired with trainer Jess Sandoval, an ex-pro fighter in his seventies. Dressed in slacks and an open-collar, short-sleeve shirt, Jess still looked dangerous and fierce. He didn't seem too thrilled about training a woman.

Stuttering shyly, Jess led me to a spot before the mirrors. I later learned that what sounded like poor pronunciation was actually caused by an old throat injury. He told me to warm up, then walked away. Stupefied and self-conscious, I did some half-hearted stretches until he returned to begin what turned out to be a long, painstaking process—teaching a woman how to throw a punch.

Gently, over and over, Jess would form my fist correctly, show me the proper alignment of the shoulder, move my body to show me the perfect form. I didn't know the first thing about hitting. I would tuck my thumb inside my fist—a good place to get it broken, said Jess. I would throw a punch as if my arm were made of rubber, fall off balance, and blush like a fool. I would stare at my feet as if they were two small animals. I tried to move them in the precise, clean steps that Jess demonstrated, in the perfect balance that every fighter must learn, but what I produced was a pathetic shuffle. Meanwhile, beside me an old man shadowboxed gracefully, his feet seeming to float above the floor. Finally Jess, his face full of sympathy, told me I could stop and go home.

As I look back now, I think that I must have been brave even to go in there. But at the time it was almost a lark. Bravado, not courage, carried me through. The real courage would come later, when I actually stepped into the ring. It was then that I found out how terrified I was by the thought of being hit. And it was then that I discovered how gratifying it could be to meet my fear and grapple with it.

I didn't take up boxing to make a political statement about women. As a writer, I was looking for something to get me out of the house. Boxing seemed like fun and offered the bonus of physical fitness. I hoped it would help me quit smoking. Eventually, it did.

I soon found that boxing was not going to be anything like a hobby or a spare-time endeavor. My experience in the gym led me to question some of my most basic assumptions about aggression and, in the end, about myself.

Today we recognize that women can be just as smart, just as ambitious, and just as good at math and science as men are. Yet women who are attracted to contact sports like boxing are still perceived as oddities, even traitors to their sex. More than one female acquaintance has suggested that I box to get male attention or that I surely suffer from high testosterone levels.

Seeing a woman use her fists still makes a lot of people uncomfortable. But if women have never seemed as openly aggressive as men, perhaps it's simply because we haven't been allowed. I could never have become an amateur boxer, for example, if it hadn't been for a crucial court decision won by a teenage girl named Dallas Malloy only weeks before I first entered the gym in 1993. Until that year, amateur boxing was off-limits to females. Angry at being shut out of amateur boxing—the more respected Olympic side of the sport—because she was a woman, Malloy filed a complaint against United States Amateur Boxing Inc., which regulates the sport. The judge ordered USA Boxing Inc. to rescind its ban and allow women to compete against one another. A scant two years later, in 1995, about five hundred women were registered as amateur boxers. And for every woman registered to compete, there were probably a dozen in the gyms training.

In my first months competitive matches seemed very far away, but after several false starts, Jess and I began to make progress. At first when I made mistakes, he wouldn't yell at me the way he did at the men. Over time, though, I think he began to forget that he was dealing with a female. Sometimes he'd reach out, reflexively, to pat me on the behind, only to freeze his hand inches from my tush.

Outside the gym I was running more and more miles to build up my stamina. In the gym I worked in front of the mirrors, on the double-end bag, on the speed bag. I worked until my shirt was soaked through, until the sweat ran down my legs, and I would go home as lathered as a hard-run horse.

I worked out, and I learned. I learned that boxing technique may run counter to human instincts (which in a confrontation are to kick, hit out wildly, cringe, or run in big, batty circles). I learned that everything you do in the gym—everything—is taking you one step closer to the ring.

In shadowboxing you watch yourself in the mirror. At the heavy bags, slugging at seventy pounds of dangling weight, you practice hitting hard as well as hitting with proper form. In front of the double-end bag (which the Mexican fighters call the crazy bag, because the more you punch it, the harder it is to hit), you learn accuracy.

Lead with your left fist, Jess would say. This is the jab, used to pepper your opponent's face. The jabbing left doesn't always hit hard, but it keeps your opponent away, confuses her. The straight right hand is a power punch, which I've only recently begun to fully grasp (at first I was too stiff to throw my weight into it and hit "like a girl"). Arch the left arm and you have a left hook, which is a punch I'm much better at, using the leveled forearm to quickly deliver a series of blows (as Jess softly chants: "Like a cat, like a cat").

In boxing you learn to use your body as a weapon. There is no ball, no bat, no lines on the floor, no goal post or hoop. Most of the costumes, rituals, and excuses of other sports have been trimmed away. What is left is unavoidably frank, exquisitely real. The violence of a boxer is not the violence of a mugger or rapist. Fighters are not filled with rage, out of control, or driven to hurt. People unfamiliar with boxing often see a fight as a flurry of emotion, a sport of bloody conquest. But emotion is the boxer's enemy. Fights are calculated, impersonal. Punches are timed. The aim may be to pummel your opponent, but this goal coexists with a profound respect. You agree to hit each other, as equals, in this safe place, with no hard feelings.

The first time I got into the ring to spar, my knees were shaking. Jess fitted the damp, smelly leather helmet neatly over my head and ears, leaving my face exposed. Next he laced on the fourteen-ounce training gloves. They felt foreign on my hands, heavy and bulky, and I flexed my fingers inside their sweaty interiors, feeling the empty spaces.

With the gloves on I was as helpless as a baby. I couldn't blow my nose, wipe the sweat out of my eyes, or do anything else requiring fingers. Jess popped in my mouthpiece, and I composed my face, shuffled my feet, and tried not to let anyone know just how scared I really was. The men gathered around. They watched, mouths agape at the novelty of a woman entering their ring, until the coaches began bellowing, "Get back to work."

Octavio, the seventeen-year-old boy who had been picked as my sparring partner—he weighted only 118 pounds—was already in the ring, shadowboxing to loosen up. The bright gym lights glinted off his muscled arms and narrow shoulders. A heavy leather belt (for crotch protection) fitted snugly over his trunks, cupping his groin. Under the shadow of his helmet, his face—with heavy lips and brown eyes—looked blank in concentration.

There was only one thought in my mind: I am going to get hit.

The idea frightened me more than I had imagined. Now that I realized—at gut level—that getting punched was unavoidable, I ran smack into twenty-six years of social indoctrination. I was afraid I would freeze. I was afraid it would hurt. I had visions of women being hit in the movies: cringing, helpless, pleading.

Jess gave me a careful, considering look. Then he pointed his head toward the ring. I climbed through the ropes and stood on the gritty, unfamiliar canvas.

I raised my fists. The gloves, padded, loomed like red balloons in front of me. For a second I couldn't remember if I had my fists turned properly. My mind went blank: I couldn't remember anything of my training. I took a deep breath. Okay. Here goes.

The bell rang. My sparring partner looked up at me from under his helmet, bit his lips, and crossed himself. He shifted forward slightly, his legs moving under the long trunks. I forced myself forward, uncertain, my feet numb and clumsy.

My training returned: I threw a few jabs.

Nervously, he responded. A stinging jab to my nose. Overexcited, I lunged at him, trying to hit him with my jab, throwing wild rights. He slapped me politely on the ribs, landed a few more jabs.

And I thought, That doesn't hurt so bad.

Somehow that realization was more exciting and fulfilling than I could ever have imagined. I was being hit by a man. But I wasn't falling to pieces. I was going to be okay.

I hit him back as best as I could, opposing his skill with my perseverance. Bobbing and weaving across the ring, breathing rapidly through our mouthpieces, we flicked jabs, rights, and body blows. I was going too fast, getting too wound up. Jess made a soothing sound from the side of the ring.

Octavio and I kept eye contact the entire time. Even in the heat of battle—how curious, that tempestuous term for what turns out to be so quiet, almost peaceful—I noticed little things: his eyelashes, the shadow by the cusp of his nose. A bubble of mucus appeared under his left nostril. We were both prickly with heat, our chests ragged with breath. Our faces were scant inches away from each other, close enough to kiss.

Thwack. I saw that coming, the right, and still walked into it. When you get smacked in the nose like that, it's quick, stunning—painless in an odd way and yet deeply disturbing. Desperate, I plowed into him, and he captured my arms in a quick clinch, turned me deftly against the ropes, and spun me out again. Jess made a snorting, derisive noise from the side of the ring. I barely had time to feel like a fool (I would learn how to store these moments for later self-castigation) before we were hitting each other again.

I now calculated time only in blows. A jaw-rattling left hook to my chin. A surprisingly stunning straight right, a jabbing left peppering my face. Later I became aware of how much he was babying me—how light the punches actually were. At the time they seemed more than enough. Boxers call my reactions being glove-shy: the sense of shock at being hit, not because you feel pain but because your privacy has been invaded. You close your eyes and involuntarily wince. You're in body shock.

Only through sparring do you eventually lose your glove-shyness, learn to look straight into your partner's eyes and not blink when you get hit.

I became aware of a stitch under my ribs, of sweat trickling under my helmet, of my nose running. I could hear all the sounds of the gym—Jess giving calm advice from the side of the ring, someone hitting the heavy bag, guys conversing in quiet tones, the ten-seconds-to-go buzzer—yet at the same time it seemed the world had narrowed down to just us, two bodies pitted against each other. I got through with a strong right hook to his rib cage and felt a rush of hot pleasure when I saw his eyes blink in startled pain.

When the bell rang we stopped immediately. We didn't grin at each other and slap our gloves together. That would come later. But we did smile, shyly. And I walked out of the ring as if I were floating. I had done it.

My face was tender, and later it bruised slightly. I lay on the couch that evening, nearly bursting with pride, seraphic with exhaustion.

Before that first sparring match, I had never competed physically with a man before, and certainly not on such intimate—and equal—terms. Octavio was far more skilled than I, but mostly because he had been training longer. I fought my first real match against a woman who could punch harder than Octavio—harder than most men, in fact. And in February 1995, after fifteen months of going to the gym, I found myself among the first women to compete at a Golden Gloves tournament in Tacoma, Washington.

The Tacoma Athletic Commission Golden Gloves was one of the largest tournaments on the West Coast, attended by a crowd of several thousand as well as the local TV news and a crew shooting for ESPN. The skill level of the male competitors, many of whom had trained and competed for a lifetime, was years beyond that of my opponent, Sandra, and of mine. We fought our hearts out, though.

I learned later that Sandra worked as an aerobics instructor and had trained at a boxing club in Washington state. But we didn't chat before the match; in fact we avoided each other, barely exchanging hellos. There is something too uncomfortable about being friendly to your opponent before a fight. Not because you need to build anger—I had none—but because there is just too much anxiety.

Adrenaline carried me through the fight but kept me from having any sense of its continuity. What I was left with, afterward, was overexposed snapshots of memories. I remember climbing through the ropes, the sudden sense of the lights dimming, the referee signaling us to touch gloves. I remember looking into my opponent's face, and then the bell ringing. For the rest of the bout my eyes never left hers. The fight itself was bizarre, with the crowd yelling, the lights, the metallic taste of anxiety. I'd fought in other matches, but this was the first time I began to understand my own boxing as a style, rather than just crude effort. A style Jess teaches: Go in crouched, throw lots of hooks, never relent. Always keep the pressure on.

But Sandra happened to be a left-hander, which changes everything. I knew I should be throwing the right hand more, since southpaws are vulnerable to the right, and to follow with the left hook. When the bell rang after the first round I went back to my corner nearly sick with nerves. Jess rinsed my mouth and caustically told me that I "looked better in the gym."

His words had the intended effect: feeling wounded, I was off the stool and into the fight the moment the bell rang, and desperate not to fail.

I barely remember what punches I threw or the order of the combinations. I do remember one moment when my opponent was backed toward the ropes, her head tilting back from a jab, and my left glove was swinging up to make contact, in a hard hook to the side of her chin. Her head went reeling and the crowd made the sound reserved only for a good punch.

This time when I went back to my corner, Jess was pleased. He told me to win the next round, and then pressed his hand comfortingly on my chest.

When the third bell rang I was already off my stool, shifting my feet. All I really remember is moving forward. When I felt as if I was tiring, finally, toward the end of the fight, I told myself, "This is it, keep going," and I extended those fists again, punching madly, hitting in final frustration and fear of loss.

Back in my corner Jess was telling me to smile, to look good, to look as if I'd won the fight. He unlaced the gloves and took off my helmet, and then I was being led into the middle of the ring for the decision. I could only stare at the canvas, filled with dread, as the referee firmly gripped my wrist, his other hand around the wrist of my opponent.

The announcer, holding the little slips of paper from the judges, began opening his mouth to announce the decision. I heard the echo-chamber sound of the microphone booming over the crowd, before my nerves made everything go blank. And then my hand was being raised, and as I became aware of what that meant, a wild, exultant excitement broke over me. My rib cage lifted with joy. I don't think I have ever felt such pleasure.

Not long ago an interviewer asked me if I believed women should be able to compete against men in the ring—for real, for titles. My response was an immediate "Yes, of course." Not just because women in boxing are marginalized by lack of competition but because I believe that women can compete with men, and even win.

Maybe not this year, I said, or even this decade. But someday a woman, trained correctly from an early age, will attain the skills needed to compete against men on the professional level. Especially at the lower weight classes.

Recently I sparred with a twelve-year-old girl who came into the gym with her father and brothers, all actual or aspiring boxers. They entered in a crowd, six at least, of which she was simply one more—one more set of legs warming up, one more body in a row practicing jabs across the wide wooden floor. Her dad watched over her just as he did his sons, giving her advice that sounded no more critical or protective.

As I watched the family enter, I realized that the girl felt an affinity not with the other women in the gym but with her brothers. They were the ones she immediately turned to between rounds, her helmet lowered through the ropes so she could receive advice and be lovingly cuffed.

It is here that I find evidence of a different kind of young woman: an evolution from my mother's day to mine, and beyond. Unlike the older women of the gym, these girls don't remember when women didn't compete with men. Unlike women of my age, who grew up in tumultuous times when social and legal change clashed with old views, the messages they hear aren't as contradictory, as imbued with insecurity. These girls seem fierce, unafraid of wrangling with the boys. They have an indefinable foundation, a core belief in their abilities, which is deeply appealing in its artlessness. They don't care what I think. I'm already a relic, a dinosaur, who can offer them nothing.

As I left the gym one night, the father of the twelve-year-old glanced up at me as I passed, and I paused for a second, halfway around the corner by the door.

His daughter was now in the front of the room. The neon light of dusk poured through the plate-glass window, capturing everything in soft, chalk-colored air. Dressed in long trunks and a wide, oversize T-shirt, her hair in a thick braid, she was shadowboxing across the floor. Not a phantasm or a passing fad, she seemed solidly rooted, snapping punches through the milky air. If I turned the corner of that gym today, I would expect to see her there: shadowboxing with silver feet, delivering devastating punches to imaginary enemies.

A woman. A fighter.

summer showdown

PAT GRIFFIN

When I think of growing up in Maryland, I think of summer and baseball: hazy, hot days spent playing games that ended only when everyone was called home for dinner. When there weren't enough players for a full game, we played work-up or hot box or some other game we made up. Our gang had a core group who always played together. Kerry, Steve, Wayne, Billy, and Tom are the guys I remember most. Nine or ten other guys played with us, too, but not every day. We were all in fourth, fifth, or sixth grade, and we all wore blue jeans, T-shirts, and sneakers. We had a special way of rolling the bills of our baseball caps, too, so that they rounded in just the right way.

I was different from the rest of the guys on two counts: I was a lefty and I was a girl. I expected no special treatment, though, and got none. I didn't need it. I could hit, catch, and throw as well as any of the guys, and I wasn't afraid to dive for a line drive or slide into the catcher. That seemed to be all that mattered. I had rules for myself, though, things that I didn't do that the guys did. I didn't fight, spit, or cuss. That seemed to be enough to preserve my female identity among all those boys.

I was a baby dyke, too, though I had no words then to describe what I knew to be true about myself. It was the late 1950s, after all, and I had never heard the word "lesbian." I just had this sense that I was different from friends in my Girl Scout troop and that I wasn't quite what most adults expected me to be. I staged little rebellions against those pressures of femininity intended to herd me into a frilly pink box: When my mother made me wear a new dress to my grandmother's

Christmas party, I insisted on wearing my new Hopalong Cassidy two-gun holster set over it. When I was given dolls for my birthday, they became hostages that I rescued in heroic fantasy games.

My major rebellion was being an athlete. From early on I had a gift for sports, which developed into a passion for baseball. The closest I came to being fully me in that Donna Reed world of the 1950s was on the baseball diamond. And so I played ball with the guys, my sexuality expressed through the sensuality of athletics: the crack of the ball on the bat, the thwack of the ball in my glove, the taste of sweat on my lips, the stretch of muscle, and the joy of a ball well hit or an impossible catch made.

The guys and I spent many hours together playing inning after inning in the hot sun on a field we carved out of a corner of Mr. Cronin's horse pasture. We built a backstop out of chicken wire and old barn boards we got from Tommy's dad. Kerry and Steve's mom made us canvas bases filled with sawdust. My dad cut us a regulation-sized plywood home plate. We played so much that we wore base paths in the grass. Our field felt like Griffith Stadium to us, Washington Senators fans all.

Since we played together nearly every day, we were comfortable with one another. We knew who the hotheads were and who were the peacemakers. We had our clowns and hot dogs and the crybabies who whined about every little scrape or bump. We knew who could hit the ball the farthest and who the best fielders were. Some guys always brought the bats and others brought the balls.

On one of those soft summer days, our gang was well into a game. A lot of us were playing that day, and our usual ragging and baseball chatter ricocheted comfortably around the field. Kerry had just caught a fly ball in left field for the last out of the inning when Bay Quinn showed up wanting to play with us.

As well as we knew one another, we knew Bay hardly at all. When he bent under the barbed wire fence and walked onto the field, we all got quiet. We watched as he took a last drag on his cigarette and flicked the butt over the fence. We had never played ball with him. He was in junior high school, a "big kid" to us. He wore his hair like Elvis Presley, greasy and slicked back. (Our guys had crew cuts and I had pigtails.) He had the sleeves of his white T-shirt rolled up to show his well-developed biceps, and a pack of Camels bulged at his left shoulder. Instead of sneakers, Bay wore shiny track spikes that glistened in the sun like sharks' teeth. We'd heard rumors about him driving without a license and getting into trouble with the police. It was simple, really: Bay Quinn was older, tougher, and a hood. We had to let him play, because none of us had the nerve to tell him we didn't want him around.

He ended up on the other team, since they had been one player short. Everyone was a bit subdued as we resumed play, but things loosened up a little after we got back into the game—until Bay came up to bat.

I was pitching that day. Bay stepped up to the plate and took two vicious practice swings, his bat whipping through the still summer air. As he settled into his stance, he looked toward the pitcher's mound. He smiled at me over his shoulder and flicked his bat back and forth. The smile was not friendly. It said, Get ready to duck. I'm going to take your head off. As he dug the toes of his shoes into the dirt, I watched the stiletto points of his spikes shine through the dust he kicked up. Finally, he was ready. The chatter from my team was tentative: "Come on, Patty, kiiiiddd, put it in there, babeee."

I rocked, kicked, and threw the ball. Bay twitched his bat, stepped into the pitch, and swung mightily. I expected to hear the crack of wood on leather. What I heard was leather on leather. The ball was in Steve's catcher's mitt. Strike one. Bay looked at his bat in disbelief, spit in the dirt behind him, and dug himself in again. This time he wasn't smiling. I took the throw from Steve and looked back at Bay. I rocked, kicked, and threw again. It was a meatball, right down the center. He went for it with everything he had, caught a piece, and fouled it off over the fence behind home plate. Bay swung so hard, he had to prop himself up with his bat to keep from going down. Strike two.

He reached down and rubbed dirt onto the bat handle. When he stepped back into the box, he snarled at me, "No girl is striking me out." I felt my jaw tighten and I thwacked the ball into my glove a couple of times. I had never felt like this before. This had become more than a simple pickup game, more than a play that would unfold and be forgotten by the next day. Though I didn't completely understand why, I knew that whatever happened next was important: something was on the line here for both Bay Quinn and me. All the guys felt it, too. The field was quiet.

I tugged at the bill of my cap. I smacked the ball into my glove one last time, then gripped it, fingers light across the ball's seams. I looked at Steve's mitt, held up as my target. I didn't look at Bay. I could feel him there at the plate, radiating waves of hatred toward me. I stretched, rocked, kicked, and threw the ball as hard as I could. Bay's face contorted with anticipated effort and he swung so hard, I could hear his bat whistle through the air. Steve stood up as he threw the ball to third base and yelled, "Awright, Patty, kiiid!" Strike three.

I had struck Bay Quinn out! I wanted to jump up and smack my fist into my glove and yell something to celebrate, but Bay's glower and hissed cuss words warned me not to. Instead, I turned to second base and grinned at Wayne. Striking someone out had never felt so sweet. Bay Quinn was outraged that a girl had struck him out. None of the guys in my gang had ever acted like that. If I struck them out, it was just like when anyone else struck them out. With Bay, it was different, and I felt mean and superior in a way I'd never felt before after a good play. I had this giddy sense of triumph. Bay Quinn taught me something that day: I learned to appreciate the special malicious satisfaction there is in beating a guy who considers himself my better just because he's a guy.

The game continued. Bay had lost some of his power to intimidate, and we slid back into our comfortable chatter with only a small awareness now of the stranger among us.

Bay came up to bat twice more before I left the game. On his second trip to the plate, I struck him out again. Actually, to be fair, Bay struck himself out. His first swing was another attempt to put the ball in the next county. His second and third swings were more tentative and a little late. By then, he was so worried about striking out that he made himself do it. It didn't matter what I served up as long as it was near the plate. Before he left the batter's box this time, he spit toward the pitcher's mound and shot me a look of pure hate. The second strikeout felt as fine as the first. I even risked a smile at him this time, probably a mistake, in retrospect.

The third time Bay came up, the sun was going down and the game was losing steam. It was almost suppertime and we were ready to load up our bikes and head home. Bay dug his spikes into the dirt and looked grimly determined to get a hit. He swung at the first pitch late and hit a short fly ball that fell into the outfield just behind first base: a single, nothing more. Tommy came in from right field and took the ball on the hop. I ran to cover second, since at this point we were short a couple of players. Tommy made a routine throw to me, as we all expected Bay to hold on first. He didn't.

I stood on second base with the ball in my glove and watched with horror as Bay rounded first and, picking up speed, headed straight for me. My first thought was that it was a crazy thing for him to do. I had the ball. There was no way he'd safely make it into second. Then, with a flash of fear, I realized that he didn't care about being safe. Bay Quinn had turned into a locomotive steaming down the base path, spikes flashing in the late-afternoon sun, and I was on the tracks. Bay wanted to hurt me.

I suppose I could have jumped out of the way. I don't really know why I didn't. Partly, I just couldn't *not* go for the tag. Part of it was pure stubbornness: I wasn't going to back down now. It's also true that fear kept me from thinking fast enough to move. Plus, I was naive enough to think he wouldn't really run me down.

Bay didn't slide. He ran right over me. My last thought before the collision was "Don't drop the ball."

We hit the ground about four feet behind second base. I lay motionless in the grass with my eyes closed, unable to breathe for a minute, and listened to the guys running toward us. I heard Kerry yelling, "You're out, Quinn." Then Tommy: "Yeah, and don't bother to come back." I squeezed my glove hand and, sure enough, the ball was there. My foot throbbed and I felt a sharp pain when I moved my toes. I sat up to see a red stain spreading around a jagged tear in the top of my canvas sneaker. Bay had not only knocked me down; he'd spiked me, too.

The rest of the day was a blur: a hasty bike ride home, Mom driving me to the emergency room, and five stitches in my foot. The doctor said that there was no permanent damage, but I couldn't play baseball for a few days.

I was back on the pitcher's mound in a week with a new pair of sneakers. The guys and I resumed our summer baseball rituals and continued them every year until so many of us entered junior high school that the games broke down for lack of players. Bay Quinn never did come back to play with us. I never saw him again, but the memory of that day has stayed with me. I learned about boys who think they're better than girls just because they're boys. I also learned that pride in my athletic talents makes beating guys like that especially satisfying. Most important, I became aware of something deep inside me that I did not then completely understand, an unexplored core that refused to let go of who I was in a world trying to force me to be something else. In the face of the Bay Quinns of the world, I learned that I loved me enough to take the hit, hold on to the ball, and come back for the next game.

women play **football**

THEODORA SOHST

Girls have at last entered the domain of football. That makes one more strictly masculine pastime to be subtracted from the rapidly diminishing list of exclusive sports. It has surely taken a long time for a pioneer to appear who had the courage to attempt to organize a girls' football team. But better late than never. Upsala College of East Orange, New Jersey, has been brave enough to put in the field the first football squad ever entirely composed of girls. The idea developed there last season.

One particularly brilliant basketball player had become bored with the game as played by girls' rules. The pace was too slow for her. Modifying the game sufficiently to make it less strenuous for the other players had so tamed it that she refused to play. Naturally, that started a new element working for a more spirited, a wilder game [like football] . . .

What a mighty squad they are! Strong, husky, good-looking Amazons in moleskins, tackling and mussing each other up just like regular fellows. Of course they do not cultivate the center rush to any great extent, but they do concentrate on end plays and forward passes.

. . .

A recent editorial in the [New York] *Herald Tribune* quotes Knute Rockne, the famous Notre Dame coach: "I regard the football field as an experimental laboratory where the young man finds himself. On the gridiron he experiments with himself mentally, physically and spiritually. He learns courage, sportsmanship and respect for an honored opponent and he develops a little backbone and the will to win." Do not these same theories and ideas apply to girls?

killer instinct

ANNE ALEXANDER

"Thank you," says the stranger, and I nod politely as I hold the door. "You're so nice," chide my friends, as I fail to battle for a coveted parking place in the urban landscape.

Fools, I think in response, you haven't seen me race my bike.

Cycling brings out my aggressive side—I love picking out the fastest cyclists in a race and drafting behind them, conserving my energy while they expend theirs. I thrill at "shooting the gap," squeezing between two riders with barely enough clearance for my handlebars. I enjoy the rush of adrenaline when I'm flying downhill at 46 m.p.h. in a pack of twenty, knowing there's a dangerous turn at the bottom.

Before cycling, I never knew the thrill of being brazenly selfish, of taking what I want and to hell with everyone else. This is because I spend my days being painstakingly polite: holding open elevator doors when I'd rather let them slam, giving away the last doughnut when I really want to sneak off and devour it myself.

A few years ago, I discovered that the road is a Darwinian jungle where these kinds of civilities don't apply. Riding a borrowed bike, the first thing I noticed was that there were cyclists ahead of me. My eyes narrowed. Instinctively I began calculating how to catch up and overtake them. When I got within earshot, some divine intuition told me to squelch my heavy breathing and make my triumph look effortless.

I liked passing people, and soon it got to be a habit. For this purpose alone, I needed my own set of wheels. I turned up my nose at low-end touring bikes; I wanted one with skinny tires and barely any frame. Eight hundred dollars later, sitting on top of a Bridgestone RB-1 Synergy Racer, I was happy. The habit continued.

Riding became my life. I even spent three months on a solo cycling trip through Europe, lugging two loaded panniers. When I returned to New York, my quadriceps were the size of Christmas hams, and I soon resumed my old tricks: eyeing cyclists ahead, pushing to catch up, and then just slipping by. *Swoosh.* My favorite victims were men struggling up hills. Not overweight or middle-aged men, but young, lithesome, athletic types. I liked saying something disarmingly sweet, like "Oh pardon me," as I pumped by. One guy asked what kind of batteries I had in my legs. I just smiled.

One morning, slightly embarrassed, I lined up with seventeen men for an 18-mile "open race" around Brooklyn's Prospect Park. I said, "Excuse me" and "Good morning," as I joined them on the starting line. Suddenly the gun went off and the disparate group formed a pear-shaped pack. I knew the technique: stay tight, draft, don't pull the pack. I stuck like glue to the guy's wheel ahead of me. On either side, men were trying to cut in and take the wheel I was "sucking." "Excuse me" became a dead language. My mind was barking "Damn you" at every offender.

I didn't win the race, but I never gave up the wheel. I'd fought off the challenges, had remained unperturbed when two cyclists collided and flew off their bikes, and had felt a rush of pure tenacity.

I began racing regularly. On weekends, a girlfriend and I would drive over two hundred miles to participate in especially grueling women's races. Once on a very hilly course in Schenectady, New York, I wondered why I was doing this. I'd been slow off the start and was trailing the pack. My wimpy thoughts pissed me off and, pedaling madly, I caught up with the other women just at the crest of a huge hill—in time to sail down the other side with the pack. The race organizers had warned us about this descent, particularly the sharp right at the bottom. Tempted to slow down, I checked my speedometer:

44, 45, 46 m.p.h. No one was braking, so I hung inside. En masse, we careened toward the bottom. Then, like a silent school of fish, we swerved in unison through the turn.

Suddenly one cyclist was bolting from the group, trying to make a breakaway. I furiously jammed to catch her. Just you try it, honey, I thought. No one's leaving me behind.

next game

NANCY R. NERENBERG

When I walk into the gym I look around and try to figure out who has "next game." There is a full court game taking place on my left, and I see three or four men sitting on the sidelines. I approach the one wearing the orange shorts and a very worn, very sweaty Air Jordan T-shirt.

I ask, "You have next?"

"Um-hm," he nods, avoiding eye contact.

"Can I run with you?" I continue. He hesitates. I know what he's thinking. A girl. White. Short. Three strikes already. I should tell him I'm Jewish, too. Everyone knows Jews are lousy athletes.

He shrugs his shoulders, like picking me up will doom his chance of winning but he doesn't much give a damn if he loses again.

"Okay," he says unenthusiastically.

It doesn't bother me much. Not anymore. I've been doing this for a long time now—about twenty years. I've never been in this particular gym, but it feels so familiar, anyway. This is where I am most myself, most at ease. This is home. My husband will never understand; he suspects there is basically something wrong with me. But gym rats understand. Here, time stands still, and for a few hours I am completely at peace.

It smells good here. I love that familiar, homey smell of sweat. Once my friend Dolly came by to meet me at the gym. "It stinks in here!" she said. "Does it?" I replied. "Seems okay to me. It's a gym."

I begin to carefully pull on my two pairs of socks, stretching them out just perfect, so that when my shoes are laced there will be no tiny little irritating creases bunching up under my feet. Then I slowly tighten the laces, pulling them snug at every rung. It's got to be done just right—not too tight, not too loose. You'd think I was preparing for a NASA liftoff.

As I go through this automatic routine, I am watching the court, trying to get a sense of the personality of this gym. Who is winning? How rough do they play? How much do they fight? To which men do the others consistently defer? Who cheats? Which males rely on the words "bitch" and "pussy" to insult other males? Usually within a few minutes, and certainly once I've been playing, the men seem to forget I'm there. Or maybe they forget I'm a woman. I'm not sure. I am let into this private male subculture, one to which most women are never privy. It fascinates me, so once my "invisibility" has been estab- lished, I play along.

I am continually amazed how men deal with men. I have this theory about sports: when we play we show how we truly are in life. On the court you are, in a sense, butt-naked. You can act arrogant, but in a clutch situation, when the game is on the line, we will notice when you choke. And when you hog the ball, it is obvious whether you do so because you are ignorant or inexperi- enced—which is unpleasant but acceptable—or whether you are simply selfish. When you call a foul, we know if it's a legitimate call or if you're just a crybaby. Do you make a bad pass and blame the person who couldn't catch it?

I've seen, too many times to count, a male outplay another male and rub it in with one of the most typical gym insults: "Take that, you girl!" I've seen men lose their tempers when they don't get their way and kick the ball so hard that it smashes up against the ceiling rafters. I've seen a man pout and actually hold the ball hostage until the nine other players give in to his will. Men have come to physical blows because they couldn't agree who had the right to the next game. I've seen dirty fouls and heard bold-faced lies, all in order to win a game and control the court. In the gym, I witness a less sanitized, more savage side of males. I'd like to invite some of these guys' girlfriends to watch through a one-way mirror sometime.

But there is a noble side as well. Most men play hard, giving themselves unselfishly to the game. Most play within their limits and make no apologies for it. There are the quiet players; they rarely speak and play so smoothly you don't notice their actions, but they are consistently the ones who get the job done. There are the diplomats, who keep the peace and the pace of the game moving. There are natural leaders; within moments they can create a cohesive unit out of five strangers. And last is my favorite breed: those rare players who realize the true value of team play and are willing to give the ball up to a weaker player in a critical situation, even though they know it may cost them the game.

Every gym has its own personality, its own rituals, etiquette, hierarchy, and rhythms. There are always two dances: that sometimes beautiful one on the court, and a bigger, more encompassing dance—the strange dance of the gym.

One shoe is laced, and I start adjusting the other. I'm beginning to feel another familiar sensation. Adrenaline races through my body. Usually I start getting this feeling long before I enter the gym. It's like a drug. Sometimes it starts first thing when I wake up in the morning, as soon as I realize that I get to play that day. In college, when I played guard for a Division I women's team, and later when I played pro ball in France and Germany, this feeling could even start a few days before game day. But in those days I was too invested in my performance. There was always an element of pressure and anxiety: Would I play poorly? Was I good enough? Now I just feel sheer pleasure. As I get older, I find myself wishing that I felt this passion for something else in my life: a job or career, for example. But it's never happened.

I've finished lacing my shoes. My heart starts speeding up. This electrical current is urging me to jump up and start running around like an overstimulated six-year-old. But I don't. Be cool, I tell myself. Take a deep breath. Follow your own rhythms. I'm just a short, thirty-nine-year-old female basketball junkie.

I shove my socks down around my ankles. I pretend to

ignore my teammates, the four men waiting on the sidelines. I know they're watching me, waiting to see what kind of a handicap they've picked up for their squad.

Here's how it works. Basically, with minor regional differences, you find this same system in any gym in the United States. It's a cultural phenomenon; I saw it nowhere in Europe. And I seek out gyms in foreign lands just like my father, an optometrist, seeks out low-vision clinics wherever he travels in the world.

There is an implicit set of rules. For full court—the elite game of pickup basketball—five play against five. If your squad wins, you win the right to hold the court. If you lose, you sit and wait your turn to play again. Someone on the sidelines or one of the "losers" announces (with witnesses), "I got next." (Not "I've got next." That would be grammatically incorrect in most gyms.) "Next" has the right to pick up his squad. For example, there could have been only that one guy with the orange shorts waiting, and he could've told me, "Sorry, I have five." It's his right; it's his "game." It happens all the time. If that happens, I follow down the line of "nexts" until I find the last one, and I tell him, "I have it after you." Then I have assured myself a game and the right to pick my own squad.

Sometimes it can be difficult to get picked up. One day, when I was first dating my future husband, Jens, I took him with me to the gym. Originally from East Germany, he had never even touched a basketball, let alone played the game. I wanted to share this part of myself with him; I wanted him to see me play. I was on the sidelines waiting for "next game" when one of the men on the court twisted his ankle and had to quit. The head of the squad came to the sidelines looking for a replacement.

"I'll play," I offered, springing up energetically.

"Naw, not you," he said, continuing to scan the sidelines. Then he spotted Jens. "You want to play, man?"

Men can be cruel. I've seen men not get picked up because they were wearing red socks. You've got to know better than that. You can't wear red socks and expect to get picked up. You might as well stamp NERD on your forehead.

There are just certain traditions. White socks and high-top basketball shoes are critical. The shoes should be black or white; any other color would be tacky. Recent trends indicate that it is a good idea to pull your shorts down onto your hips slightly, so the top of your boxer shorts show. And it is best to push your two pairs of socks down in a bunch near your ankles. I don't know why. There's some anthropological explanation, certainly.

Anyway, if the gym is crowded, it is very important to pick up a strong, winning squad. If you lose, you sit and wait. If you win, you play (hold power, reign). And one more important thing: if your team has been winning, you can't retire after a winning game. No, no, no. Even if you've played eight hours, have no fluid left in your body, just broke your ankle, and your wife is delivering your firstborn child at the hospital, you can't quit until your squad is finally dethroned. That would be bad etiquette, pure and simple.

One day one of the guys came in upset and told us that his new girlfriend refused to see him anymore because he had shown up an hour late for a date.

"But I couldn't leave the gym. My team was still winning," he protested.

We nodded sympathetically. We've all been there. I have lied to baby-sitters and told them I was stuck in traffic to avoid admitting I was "stuck" in the gym.

I've finished my shoe-and-sock routine, so I stretch a bit and pick up a ball to warm up. That's part of the ritual, too.

The game to my left has ended. One squad has won and looks smug. The losers limp off and the next team approaches. It reminds me of a stage crew changing the scenery between theater acts. I amble onto the court and choose the shortest man on the other squad to guard.

Someone says, "Shirts or skins? You're skins, ha ha ha." Manly chuckles. They always think they've said something so creative and original. I've heard it a million times. You see, one squad usually removes their shirts in order to keep straight who your teammates are. When I was younger I would give the man a look to let him know he was the biggest idiot ever to walk upright. Now I realize that probably most of the time they are actually just trying to be friendly and cut the ice. So I start pulling up my T-shirt, as if to strip. I catch them off guard, and they laugh. Somehow today (surprisingly) my team turns out to be shirts again. Well, I'll be.

We inbound the ball. "Next" is hesitant to pass to me. So is "Number 2." But "Number 3" and "Number 4" know the game: they use my screens, run the breaks, and hit me with the pass when I'm open. I'm a little nervous, but my first shot, a 12-foot banker, falls in. I relax and run back down court. A few trips downcourt later, I have the ball in the middle on the fast break. I fake right and pass left. "Next" doesn't expect it; he's taken his eyes off me. The textbook-perfect pass bounces off his nose and rolls forlornly out of bounds. Oh, well.

From the sidelines I hear, "Nice pass." And this ritual, too, has repeated itself. The barriers fall. Now we can just play.

never

MAXINE KUMIN

Good for you! he calls
beside me as I take
the chicken coop, the in-
and-out, the double oxer, all
without sucking back,
springing off my hocks
as if at Ledyard,
an Olympic champ.
Down the mud slide I whirl
clearing the drop jump,
the one my heart
lurches over, clinging
to my soft palate
where it thumps
like a snared rabbit.

O heart, we are
a pair of good girls
hurdling the ditch
at the bottom of the chute
and up the other side, *good
for you!* victorious
not over fear, my lifelong boarder,
morose skulker about the house,
but over time. The large
child inside leaps up
for daddy's loud kiss,
for daddy's lollipop.

Body on body riding hard
good for you! I play to spin
this game out to the end,
never coming to the part
where we stop,
where the jumps are set
too high, and darkness wins.

remembering stella **walsh**

GRACE BUTCHER

The book is small—maybe four by five and a half inches—
dark-green fake alligator leather with a green strap that fits into
a golden lock. *Five Year Diary*, it says faintly across the cover.
And inside, in my tight, small, teenage handwriting, a few sen-
tences shimmer on the page as if spotlighted as I read them for
the first time since I wrote them thirty years ago.

Mar. 9, 1949   I think we really are going to have that girls'
track team—oh dear God—please. I ran 25 laps of the
gym—good workout—legs and ankles and wind couldn't
be better.

Mar. 14   Was talking to Miss B. after gym—says the track
team for sure. Oh if only for sure.

Mar. 15   Got in a good ³/₄ mile.

Mar. 21   Miss B. said today that chances were quite poor for
girls' track. Somehow I'll get into it—I don't know
how—but I swear I will.

In March 1949 I was fifteen, a sophomore at Chardon High
School in Chardon, Ohio, and there was no such thing as track
for girls. There was hardly any such thing as track for boys, for
that matter, in our small rural high school (fifty-two in my
graduating class)—a motley crew of maybe a dozen boys, all
doubling and tripling and quadrupling in events. Girls didn't
even go to watch. Scarcely anyone did. Girls just barely played
six-man (yes, "man"—that's what we called it then) basketball:
three guards, three forwards, each group playing only offense

or only defense on only half the floor, allowed only two dribbles. These were the rules because everyone knew that girls couldn't run up and down the Whole Floor.

Why then this peculiar obsession of mine with running? I don't know. Was I born with it? As far back as I can remember, I ran. First I played horse: my toothpick legs were the horse, of course, and the rest of me was me. I galloped through my childhood into junior high. There I became vaguely aware that the boys had a sport called Track and that they did something called Running Laps. It seemed a Good and Right Thing to Do, so before and after gym class, my skinny body and I Ran Laps. The other girls would say, "What are you doing?"

"Running," I would say proudly, taking care to breathe easily.

"Can we run with you?" they would ask. "Sure," I would answer graciously, condescendingly. But they would run only a few laps and quit, much to my amazement and delight.

"Tired," they would pant.

"Hmm," I would say to myself, continuing to run, wondering why they got so tired so fast. Another girl or two would join me: they would get tired and drop out, and so on. I ran and ran, making myself look strong and smooth, making my breathing quiet as I passed them where they stood watching me. I could do something they couldn't. So I was skinny and got teased about it. So what! They couldn't do this beautiful thing that I could do.

I started talking to the coaches about track for girls.

"Who would be on the team?" they said at first.

"I'll get the girls," I said, and I signed up a bunch of my classmates who thought running and jumping and throwing things might be fun. I haunted the coaches' office. One day a girls' team seemed a possibility, the next day no one seemed interested.

Finally the coaches said, realistically enough, "You know, Grace, we can't really have girls' track here. To have a team here, you'd have to have one at other schools, too. Nobody has girls' track."

They were right, of course, in a kind of chicken/egg way. To have girls' track, you had to have girls' track, and no one had it.

I knew I could be the best runner in the whole country—I just knew it as surely as if God had told me so. But surely, somewhere, there were other girls like me! Wasn't there some place—some mystical kingdom where girls wore Warm-Up Suits and Ran Laps and Sweated and had Muscles?

Apr. 1, 1949   Ran $3/10$ of a mile and wrecked my leg. Oh it's agony.

Apr. 28   Well, I'll be darned—Keith asked me on a hayride this Sat. I'm going sure! He is swell—a miler on the track team!

May 3   Keith and I ran $1/2$ mile together. My legs are terribly sore—from now on I've got to drop down and keep off my toes—at this rate I'm killing my legs. That way will be better.

May 6   Keith brought me this book on *How To Be a Track Champion*—very good. Worked out and now my right leg is sore. Fine! From one leg to the other.

And all this time I was brooding, wondering, praying even, for something to happen. How did I go about doing something that girls simply didn't do but I did? In addition to all the usual teenage crises—boyfriends, girlfriends, school—my diary of those spring months in 1949 throbs with more than boy-girl catastrophes and delights. "A chance . . . a break!" How, where, for whom could I perform this miracle of Running Track?

How my mother knew about Stella Walsh, I don't know. I suppose any adults who followed sports at all, who read the papers, must have known about her. I suppose I must have told my mother about there being no chance of a girls' track team at school. (How many times had she told me about how she had beaten the boys in playground races when she was a kid!) I suppose she got tired of, or concerned about, or interested in, my melodramatic brooding (as only a fifteen-year-old girl can brood).

May 11, 1949   MOM CALLED STELLA WALSH AND THIS FRIDAY I AM GOING TO CUYAHOGA

HEIGHTS TO WORK OUT WITH HER TRACK TEAM! My break! It's unbelievable!

May 12   Boy, talk about being nervous—I'm scared. Will I make good tomorrow? If praying helps any, I should because I've been praying my heart out this past year. I've got my suitcase packed—T-shirt, brown sweat shirt, my slacks, and my shoes. Going to get to bed as early as possible—about 8 or so. I wonder, will I be able to think about school tomorrow? I doubt it. Just thinking about going makes my heart beat faster and my stomach thrill.

Suitcase? Well, I'd never owned a gym bag. Girls didn't usually have any reason to have one. The slacks were in place of warm-up pants. Girls just never wore warm-up pants, those glorious gray baggy things that meant you were a Track Star. My shoes were probably Keds or Red Ball Jets or some such. Or they may even have been high-topped basketball shoes, I don't remember. There was no such thing as girls' track shoes anyhow.

Bless my mother. Somehow she had concluded that the world-famous Stella Walsh, Olympic champion and world record holder who lived in Cleveland, might know whether such a thing as girls' track existed in the Cleveland area. And come to find out it did, in just about the only way it existed anywhere at that time: in small ethnic clubs here and there around the country. Stella Walsh—Stanislawa Walasiewicz—who had competed for her native Poland in the 1932 Olympics, now coached a small group of girls and boys representing the Polish Falcons. And it was to her stamping grounds on the southeast side of Cleveland that my mother drove me on that day—the Cuyahoga Heights High School track, forty miles from Chardon.

A real track: satiny black cinders around a gleaming green infield. I had hardly ever been on one. Chardon didn't have one. Head and stomach swirling with something I can only label as ecstatic anxiety, I got out of the car, walked down to the track, and over to where a woman who had to be Stella was standing with a couple of girls.

She had on navy-blue warm-up pants—real warm-up pants!—and a red, short-sleeved T-shirt, and she stood waiting quietly as I walked up to her. Spikes gleamed out from under her shoes like the claws of an animal. Real track shoes! We shook hands. (Lord, we shook hands!) Her curly black hair blew in the hot spring wind. I stared at her, awestruck. There was not much small talk.

"Well, Grace, what event would you like to run?" She looked at me intently. Were her eyes hazel?

"Oh, the mile," I said. The walls of my bedroom were papered with pictures of the world's great milers—Gil Dodds, Glenn Cunningham. The mile! The greatest glory! No other event had ever occurred to me.

"Girls don't run the mile," she said matter-of-factly. "You have good long legs, you can try the hurdles—the 220. Maybe high jump."

Girls don't run the mile? It scarcely crossed my mind to question that astounding piece of information, that sudden folding away of a dream. Hurdles? Why not? Hadn't Stella just said I had "good long legs"—I didn't remember anyone's ever referring to anything about my skinny body as "good" before. I would have gladly become a shot-putter if she had suggested it. The legendary Stella Walsh was now my first coach.

May 16, 1949   It didn't rain, thank goodness. What a workout—hurdles and broad jump, and it was worth every bit of sweat to get the praise I did from Stella.

May 18   Boy, some workout!—hurdles all the time except some relay practice at the end. I wore a pair of Stella's track shoes!

May 19   Mom says she won't take me in anymore after the meet this June 11. That can't be! I've got to keep at it somehow.

Back in those days parents didn't drive their kids on eighty-mile round-trips so they could run around some track or swim in some pool or skate on some rink. But I didn't know that. My mother had to take me. At fifteen I had no notion of what that must have been like for her—the time and effort involved even though I was an only child. I didn't care. I wanted what I wanted.

May 20, 1949 There weren't any hurdles out so I practiced the broad jump, relay, javelin. I can't throw a javelin worth a darn yet. Stella gave me that pair of track shoes to take home and use—her very own! I put them under my pillow the way Stella says she used to.

May 21 I made a javelin—cut down a little tree the right size and made a point out of a tin can—was throwing it all day. I worked out alongside Mayfield Rd. in Stella's shoes.

May 22 I built a hurdle—pretty good if I must say so myself. Also will set up a broad jump over on the side lawn if I can.

May 25 Am getting better at the broad jump—hit the board most every time right in the middle. Also practiced the high jump. Stella gave me a pair of her sweat pants. They are much better than my slacks by far.

June 1 Practice was wonderful! There were nine girls. I'm doing well. Broad jump and hurdles are good. I took my hurdle in and Stella said I'm a good carpenter and told me to make another one. She says I'm doing fine and not to worry about the meet. Ha! I've had butterflies for the last three weeks!

June 6 Went to bed with my shorts and sweat clothes on and my hair down. Too beat to change.

June 7 I worked out but my legs are awfully sore. At home my legs are dead when I try to practice but with Stella at the track even though they ache, I don't notice it so much.

At my first-ever meet on June 11, 1949, wearing the bright satin uniform of the Polish Falcons (I guess that really wasn't kosher, seeing as how I'm not Polish), I ran on the winning 440 relay team with Stella at anchor, but we were disqualified to second because one of our runners was out of her zone. I was third in the 220 behind Stella and a teammate and fourth in the hurdles. To run in the same race with Stella! To see her take off her warm-up suit struck me as rather like seeing a statue unveiled. I was almost glad I was so far behind in the race so I could watch her run. She almost never ran like that in training. Her acceleration seemed not of this world.

June 11, 1949 I'm going to work my head off on speed in hurdles and sprinting and broad jump and get better in my next meet. I sure am proud and happy and did better than I ever expected.

As it turned out, my mother continued to make that tedious drive—maybe not twice a week, but often enough. Two months after that first meet I was the Cleveland Junior Olympics 50-yard hurdles champion and paraded down Euclid Avenue in my white shorts and T-shirt with the rest of the WJW-Cleveland team. I couldn't have been prouder if it had been the real Olympics.

The following year Stella's team, always a pretty small, loosely knit group, gradually drifted apart. I read about her competing around the country in track and basketball and softball: she'd send me cards which I put at once into my track scrapbook. She coached track in California; I read about her in *Life* magazine and cut out the story for my scrapbook. I continued training on my own—sometimes with the track boys at Chardon. No, there was still no such thing as girls' track in the schools.

After a few years out for marriage and two children, I found myself back in competition again, and finally in the late '50s, after a long and bloody battle with the Amateur Athletic Union, women were allowed to run the quarter-mile and half-mile. (And eventually would come the mile, cross-country, the marathon.) Once the only non-Polish member of the Polish Falcons, I was now the only non-Hungarian member of the Cleveland Magyar Athletic Club, coached by Julius Penzes and Alex Ferenczy. Julius was mainly a runner, but Alex became one of the finest women's middle-distance coaches the United States ever had.

The first official running of the half-mile in national competition since the early '30s was in 1958 at the AAU Indoor Nationals at Goodyear Gym in Akron, Ohio. I was now twenty-four years old, and among the six or eight competitors lined up for this controversial and "grueling" event was—incredibly—Stella!

How old was she? Well, if she was twenty-one when she won the 100-meter in the '32 Olympics, she was now forty-seven. This was twenty years before masters competition became a reality— no one then dreamed of people from forty to ninety happily competing in their age groups against other "senior" athletes. For someone her age to go to the line against runners twenty years her junior was mind-boggling, but she must have felt ready or she wouldn't have been there. She looked exactly the same. "I can't picture myself beating the incomparable Stella Walsh," I wrote in my training diary on Thursday, March 20, 1958, two days before the race, "but I sure will do my darndest to stick with her!"

I had my own shoes now, to be sure, and my own warm-up suit, and another coach. But there was Stella, and we shook hands, and the gun went off.

Mar. 22, 1958   . . . and I found myself setting the pace, having started on the pole. So I settled into an easy tempo and held it, waiting for two things: first, when was I going to get tired? (and I never did!) and second, when was somebody going to challenge me? And there was nobody.

My coach told me later that a Canadian girl had almost caught me at the finish, but I hadn't known it. The headline the next day for this first national half-mile in several decades said nothing about my victory. It read, "WALSH FINISHES THIRD." That seemed only right somehow. I might not even have been on that starting line had it not been for Stella. Afterward we had shaken hands again. There was not much small talk.

"Nice going, Grace."

"Thanks." She put on her warm-up suit and walked off the track. I signed my first autograph.

Another entry from the old book:

June 13, 1949   Mom and I went to Cleveland to May's and I got my first pair of my very own TRACK SHOES!!!

Only $3.95—a great bargain—size 7—the last pair in stock.

But the first pair I ever wore belonged to Stella Walsh. She opened the trunk of her beat-up old car that day in May 1949 when I was fifteen years old and wanted to be a track star more than anything in the world—and from several pairs of spikes handed me a pair that fit. Did she know, I wonder, what that gesture meant to me? I think she made similar gestures many times to many people.

The very first piece of advice she ever gave me was to tie double knots in the laces of my running shoes so I'd never lose one during a race. That's the first thing I tell the runners I coach now. And even my street shoes sport double knots. You never know when you might have to run a fast half-mile for some unforeseen reason.

I watched, fascinated, as she took a trowel from her track bag and showed me how to dig starting holes in the track. Yes, dig holes. Rubberized asphalt all-weather tracks were unheard of then. A track was made of black cinders. If you were lucky, they were rolled firm and smooth; if not, you pretended they were and did the best you could. You dug the holes for your toes sideways to the track so you'd have a straight back wall to push against. Starting blocks? Never heard of 'em.

She never shouted; a gesture would bring us to her side for instructions. We watched her during practice as much as she did us, marveled at her techniques, knew when she wanted us, went eagerly over to hear what she would say.

Stella and my mother—in the cool dimness of the Polish Falcons hall, having a beer after training, talking quietly— grown-up talk—while I hovered in the background, tired, sand in my socks from the jump pits, glad for every extra minute together before the long drive home.

Stella in our car—my mother driving us to Hamilton, Ontario, for an indoor meet in March 1950, heater on full blast—Stella with a blanket around her legs to "keep loose." I suffered the heat gladly. At the meet in Hamilton we all ran the 50-yard dash down the middle of the infield surrounded by the steeply banked wooden track. The sprint ended abruptly just a few yards from a brick wall, and at the end of each lane stood a member of the 91st Highlanders, sponsors of the meet in full Scotch regalia, to catch the runners so they wouldn't crash into that wall. While the girls on the team and I argued happily about which of us would have the best-looking catcher, I looked down to the end of Stella's lane. Two Highlanders manned her lane, ready to brace themselves for the onslaught of her hurtling body.

July 14, 1949   The praise I got from Stella was worth every sore muscle I've had. She said she'd never seen me stronger than I was today—more speed and good form on hurdles—more endurance in the 220—ran my best in the relay and am high jumping well.

The truth is that I was never really very good in any of those events—the sprints, the jumps, the throws. I wasn't physically suited for them—never fast or big enough. But that's all there was for girls back then, and Stella always encouraged me to continue, nevertheless. Somehow I always knew that if I could run longer races, I'd be the best runner in the whole country. I never doubted it. And finally it all happened, beginning with that first half-mile in Akron. And Stella was there, just as she'd been at my very first meet. I wonder what her thoughts were as, from somewhere behind me in the race, she watched me winning, just as I had watched her nine years earlier. I've had many fine coaches since then, and I am even a coach myself at Kent State Geauga Campus, where I teach English, but it all started with Stella.

To have an Olympic champion and world record holder for my first coach at a time when girls running track was almost unheard of in this country—a woman whose silent and power-ful presence at trackside somehow made me feel like the star I'd always dreamed of being—was an experience beyond my wildest imagining as a fifteen-year-old. My track career has continued now for over thirty years, just as Stella's did, and I am extremely grateful. But it began that day in May 1949 on the track at Cuyahoga Heights as I felt my hand taken in her strong grip, those intense eyes studying me (" . . . good long legs, Grace"). She wore real track shoes and real warm-up pants and she was the greatest all-round woman athlete I have ever known.

awesome women **in** sports

RUTH CONNIFF

For the last few days I've been tearing pictures out of magazines—*Shape, Runner's World, Sports Illustrated*—collecting photographs of women athletes. I found a great shot of Gail Devers, Olympic gold medalist in the 100 meters, bounding out of the starting blocks, and I ripped out an ad for running shoes that shows two women striding side by side, silhouetted against an enormous blue sky.

I am pinning up these pictures on a bulletin board in the basement locker room of my old high school, Madison East, where I coach girls' track. East is one of those big, fortresslike public high schools you might mistake for a factory—or a prison. Concrete walls and floors and the bleak, locked-up look of the building contribute to a general feeling of gloom.

I decided to make the bulletin board at the beginning of this year's season, ostensibly to provide information—weekly announcements, workout schedules, team records, etc.—but also for sneakier reasons. One is to do a little public relations for track (gym classes pass through this locker room every day, and I'm hoping to win a few new recruits). Another reason is to boost the girls' morale. The bulletin board I captured runs the length of one wall of the locker room. Covered with purple and gold paper and glossy photos, it stands out. My hope is that it will reflect a picture to the girls who walk by it of energy and optimism and strength. Hence my hunt through magazines for inspiring images of women in sports.

They're not as easy to find as I thought.

I have mental images of women sports heroes from when I

ran track—Mary Decker Slaney kicking to the finish line with steely determination, Florence Griffith Joyner with her powerful legs and her outrageous long nails and lace tights. When I started my bulletin-board project, I thought of my contemporary, Suzy Favor Hamilton (I raced against her—behind her, I should say—as a student at East and again in college). Favor Hamilton was featured on the cover of *Runner's World* a couple of years ago. I thought it would be easy to find a more recent photo, and hundreds of other good shots of female runners.

But as it turns out, the great pictures I remember are mostly from stories that only appear every four years, during the buildup to the Olympic Games, and from a few memorable Nike ads. Beyond that, the pictures of women I want to find—strong, beautiful, *serious* athletes—are not so easy to come by.

As I began flipping through a stack of sports magazines I had around the house, I found that the images of women fall into two categories. There are the heroic portraits I've been tearing out. Then there are the more common pictures—sports cuties.

I am fascinated by the gap between these two types of images.

In *Shape* and other high-circulation "fitness" magazines, a plethora of ads for aerobics tapes and exercise equipment focus on female models with no faces, just body parts. A recurring theme is a leotard-clad rear end. NO BUTS ABOUT IT . . . , one of these ads quips. A similar ad shows a full-page set of buttocks and, below it, a much smaller picture of the owner, dwarfed by her own backside, and the slogan, A SMALL PRICE TO PAY FOR PERFECTION . . .

Shape is a typical women's magazine, with articles on diets, relationships, and thin thighs. The fitness hype blends right into the rest of the fashion-and-beauty market. It is tyrannically trivial: exalting physically "perfect" anatomical features over every other human attribute, quirk, and endeavor. Page after page features anonymous bottoms, bellies, and breasts—nary a whole woman to be seen. Spending a lot of time looking at these faceless fragments is a rather weird and alienating experience.

On the other hand, it is a relief to see, here and there among the health and beauty pages, entire women—faces and all—playing sports. Since I was a kid, more and more women have become involved in sports, and women athletes have become more visible.

Running magazines are clearly the best place to find the pictures I want. Running is a uniquely egalitarian sport. Female runners get coverage that is almost as good as men's, and there are women at every level of competition, including professional athletes. It is also a radically individual sport: people of all shapes, sizes, and ages get their pictures taken crossing finish lines—hometown heroes setting new records at local road races, old women and men winning masters competitions, adults and kids alike celebrating personal triumphs. But that's in the relatively small, hard-core running publications.

As running has gained popularity—pulled along by the yuppie fitness fad—Nike, Reebok, and other companies have been floating ads aimed at women, first for running shoes and now for all kinds of trendy athletic gear in the mainstream magazine world—that sea of body parts and marketing ploys.

In the beginning there were the words JUST DO IT, and Nike launched its ad campaign, creating its own images of women running, jumping, looking tough, cavorting in expensive shoes.

Market research must have shown that women like being treated as whole human beings, because the new ads have caught on, spun off, and developed into a whole new genre with a sophisticated "feminist" appeal. Aimed at affluent, athletic women, they combine hip, conversational ad copy with full frontal photographs of smiling, active women. They promise not just well-toned body parts but health, happiness, attitude, and "lifestyle." Small wonder they're a hit.

Of course, the companies themselves are not nearly so PC as the ads. Some—Nike in particular—are major exploiters of their (predominantly female) Third World workers. Their sole purpose in life is not to raise consciousness but to peddle their products, just as other companies peddle nylons, diet pills, and cigarettes.

But the new ads do reflect a significant demographic change in attitude and self-image among American women. It's a change that has everything to do with more women playing sports.

Women's Sports & Fitness [1]—a big, glossy magazine aimed specifically at women athletes—is another good indicator of this change. As the official publication of the Women's Sports Foundation (which, among other things, helps fund girls' sports teams and supports female athletes fighting sex discrimination in their schools), *Women's Sports & Fitness* is a kind of *Sports Illustrated* for women. It is full of stories about women excelling in sports, matter-of-fact profiles of Olympians and other world-class athletes, and advice for weekend jocks. I was practically bowled over the first time I saw it. Here is a slick magazine full of strong, beautiful women who look like people. No condescending beauty tips, no gratuitous cheesecake pictures. Reading it, you'd think women were a bunch of human beings—better yet, serious athletes. I love it. And so do a lot of other women, apparently. It has a paid circulation of 140,000.

Most of all, I see the change in women's images of themselves on a daily basis among the girls I coach.

The other day at practice, some girls on my team were talking about the hard-body heroine of the movie *Terminator 2*. One of the girls said she watched the movie with her boyfriend. "He said he wouldn't mind having a body like that, but he doesn't find her physically attractive," she said.

"Well, excuse me, but I find her physically *awesome*," one of the other girls remarked, to noises of assent from her teammates.

I like eavesdropping on these conversations.

Last year, at the beginning of the season, the girl who considers the *Terminator* woman awesome didn't want to lift weights, for fear she would get too "built."

That was before she became freshman city champion in the half-mile. Now she's hooked. She worked hard to earn her varsity letter in cross-country and showed up for preseason weight training for track. She and the other runners on the women's team have developed a touching camaraderie over the past couple of years, as well as a kind of jock swagger that has subsumed some of the cloying cuteness a lot of high school girls cultivate.

Still, the girls who come out for track and other sports at East are far outnumbered by those who do not. (The same is true for boys, but to a lesser degree.) This fact was driven home to me at the beginning of the season, when more than one hundred boys showed up for practice, as compared with about thirty girls.

My own experience as an athlete has been so rewarding, and so central to who I am now, that it pains me to think of all the girls in school who might never discover the pride and confidence that come from challenging themselves and excelling in a sport.

Shortly after I moved back to my hometown, I went to see a neighbor of mine compete in a high school gymnastics meet. I remembered her as a little girl, doing cartwheels and splits on the sidewalk outside her house. While I was away at college, she had grown up into a state-ranked gymnast. Watching her at the meet, surrounded by other girls in ponytails and sweats, warming up, getting nervous, and focusing fiercely as they got ready to compete, brought back a flood of memories. That's when I decided to coach.

It was all there, the way I remembered it, when I first returned to a high school cross-country meet. Tough girls with French braids from small Wisconsin towns (whose numbers used to include Suzy Favor) warming up together, striding side by side in intimidating packs, their nylon pants and jackets rasping as they moved in unison. The smell of Icy-Hot and nervousness. One new girl on my team wept in terror before her race, begged me not to make her do it. She did it. She threw up. She couldn't believe she made it. At the end of the season I gave her the Team Spirit Award because she improved so dramatically, became a cross-country zealot—full of pride in herself and joy—and was her teammates' biggest booster. That feeling of elation, of victory, comes over and over again from testing yourself and surviving the test—kids sprinting their hearts out and throwing themselves across the finish line.

For me it continued into college, where I made some of the best friends of my life among the other runners on the track team—men and women alike. We traveled together, shared hotel rooms, dragged term papers and books with us on the road, pushed each other, and partied afterward.

The guy who lived across the hall from me was also a distance runner. We used to come home and hit the showers on our floor at the same time, gossip, compare workouts, sing duets. One time after a meet he brought a wine cooler with him and we passed it back and forth over the top of the shower stalls. Whatever else anyone says about male bonding, women, and sports, I'm happy to know from being a runner that that kind of camaraderie exists.

The other day in the weight room, one of the shot-putters, who is also on the girls' basketball team, was doing squats. A member of the boys' team came over and demanded to know why girls' basketball hadn't made it to state. He'd been watching the weeklong tournament on TV, and he was disappointed when he didn't see East.

"We just didn't make it, okay?" the basketball player said.

It was a completely unsatisfactory response. "Why not?" the boy wanted to know.

"Hey, how come you're so concerned *now*?" one of the other girls on the team chimed in, helping her friend. "Where were you during the rest of the season?"

"I don't know. If you guys would've made it though, I would've liked to see it," the boy said.

Maybe next year he will. This was the first year that the girls' tournament got prime-time coverage, and there was an overwhelmingly positive response.

Slowly, over the past several years, *Sports Illustrated* has begun to recognize the appeal of women's sports, and to present women as sports heroes the way it has long presented men. In a recent issue of the magazine, there's a good story on a women's collegiate basketball game between rivals Vanderbilt and Tennessee. The game sold out weeks in advance, according to the article, and generated more attention than any game in the history of women's basketball. Even Vice President Al Gore felt compelled to comment.

On the other hand, the same issue contains a two-page photo spread of the Dallas Cowboys' cheerleaders, prone on a football field, white booties pointing skyward. On another page there's an ad featuring the Budweiser girls.

It's startling how slippery these images of women are. One minute you're a role model, the next you've been disassembled into body parts.

Last year, an old friend from high school came to the indoor city track meet, where I was watching my team. I was lost in the competition, getting nervous before the gun went off, taking times, chewing my nails. Then my friend started talking to me about the girls' bodies as they stood on the starting line. "Don't you think her arms are too big? . . . Her legs look fat . . . *Those* girls have *great* bodies, though. Maybe I should have run track."

It took the wind out of my sails to listen to her. It's easy to forget, and so annoying to remember, even if you're an athlete giving the performance of your life, some people will still look at you that way.

In March, *Playboy* magazine announced that it is recasting its centerfolds as athletes. Twenty-two Playmate sports teams will be competing in various exhibition events as part of a campaign to attract new advertisers. "Executives insist that athletic prowess will now be a real factor in selecting future centerfolds," according to an article in the *Toronto Star*.

"All of this comes at a time when the lines between the worlds of sports and racy entertainment are blurring," the article continues. "Some say the Dallas Cowboys' cheerleaders began the trend, and that the Laker Girls took it to a new level.

" 'It's simply a marketing project that happens to have the Playmates as the product,' said Michael O'Hara Lynch [*Playboy*'s vice-president of marketing]. It's really no different than marketing soap . . . "

So there you have it. No matter how much progress women make toward equal opportunities and accomplishments, someone can always make a buck selling us to men as sex toys.

That *Playboy* image of women as compliant sex kittens is such a far cry from the experience of being a real, active human being in the world. It's the difference between being a passive, pillowlike object and an engine, hurtling around the track.

You can see it in the way *Playboy* presents pictures of women in hardhats, military uniforms, or athletic gear, as if these occupations were a kind of titillating drag—buxom bunnies masquerading as real people. The sex appeal and the put-down are intertwined in these images. They are supposed to be funny—like cute pictures of children dressed up as adults, playing up the contrast between the hapless female and a serious, adult occupation.

I knew a woman at Yale who posed as one of *Playboy*'s "Women of the Ivy League." She also happened to be the girlfriend of a runner on the cross-country and track teams. I remember seeing her at a cross-country meet. A group of us were standing at the finish line, covered with mud from running, cheering as the men's team came in. She came tripping across the grass, looking radically out of place in a fur coat and high heels sinking into the soft ground, and waited on the sidelines for her boyfriend. I remember feeling sad when I saw her, outside the circle of happy track people hugging and laughing, filled with shared, postrace euphoria. She could hardly walk, much less run, and she seemed infinitely far away from taking part in that event.

I felt grateful for my muddy shoes and sweat clothes, grateful that I could be there fully and freely participating, not as a kind of crippled ornament standing on the sidelines.

So that's why I'm busy covering the wall with sports pictures and recruiting girls to run track. If I have anything to do with it, when I'm an old woman I'll be running road races with a crowd of other women, young and old, and every single one of us will be awesome.

1. Since Ruth Conniff wrote this article, *Women's Sports & Fitness* magazine has changed owners, and the Women's Sports Foundation is no longer affiliated with it. The foundation does continue to advocate for increased sports and fitness opportunities for girls and women. Eds.

o promised **land!**

ANONYMOUS

The official exercises for the day being over [horseback riding exhibitions at a fairground in Circleville, Ohio], just at sunset the ladies from Franklin County, with several others, went in to try their horses, and as there were no rules to be observed, they had a very refreshing time. The horses were willing and the ladies were willing, and the consequence was that some lively steps were taken. Mrs. Julia E. Harris, of Columbus, being upon a fine racer, distanced everything upon the ground, without disturbing her own or the horse's serenity in the least. Mrs. M. J. Stombaugh also executed some pretty spry riding. The party left the ground in high glee, Mrs. Dr. Davis, of Shadeville, singing, "O! talk of the promised land!"

smells like team spirit: portrait of a rank season

HOLLY MORRIS

Spring Training Bra

Each year, long before spring even occurred to Midwesterners, I was kicking up dust with the Chicago Cubs and being schooled in the rhythms and rituals of baseball. To our two-sportscaster family, February meant spring training and the annual pilgrimage to Scottsdale, Arizona. Free to scamper around the friendly confines of Ho Ho Kam Park, I learned the art of cheerful pessimism that flourishes with any losing team, and I developed ideas about sports celebrities. The Cubbie stars of the time, Ron Santo and Ernie "Let's Play Two" Banks, did nothing for me. I reserved my considerable pre-adolescent affections for barely known first baseman Pete LaCock. And through my devotion to Pete and his faltering career (not to mention the hapless Cubs), I developed a deep commitment to the underdog. I remember exactly three things about Pete: he had locks of gold, did yoga (ahead of Phil Jackson), and was the son of game-show guru Peter "Hollywood Squares" Marshall. To me, Pete was all-star material; to the Cubs' organization, he was not. After three valiant seasons, Pete was cut. I was crushed.

For some years after that, I indulged in an unhealthy diet of overwritten, underresearched baseball biographies—Hank Aaron, Babe Ruth, Mickey Mantle. My parents urged me to get out of the armchair and into Little League, which would have made me the first and only girl on the team. But I was suspended above that post-girl, pre-woman abyss where self-esteem and original nature are so often traded for new school clothes and a boy universe, *and* did not yet have Tatum O'Neal in *The Bad News Bears* as a point of reference, so I declined. As the seasons slid by, memories of Pete faded. I left baseball to pursue other boys and other sports.

So imagine my surprise when twenty springs later, while wallowing in a not-a-part-of-anything-larger-than-myself malaise, I conjured up an almost-forgotten, all-American antidote: baseball . . . well, softball. A quick call to the Seattle Parks and Recreation Department revealed an imminent deadline, and "Sorry, there's only one team slot open in the entire program—Division II." Division II *sounded* perfectly doable. Mining my Rolodex, I recruited every woman I knew. Experience not necessary. Attitude the key.

I called Claire, overworked proprietor of a classy women's sex-toy store. "Hey, let's play softball."

"Cool. My sorry social life could use a shot in the arm."

Claire was in.

Bookselling maven and renowned athlete Erin responded, "Forget it, the last team I was on got so competitive I had absolutely no fun. Good luck." (When she saw that we were anything *but* competitive, Erin "Home Run" Healy joined us midseason.)

Over the copy machine, I tossed the softball team idea to Nancy, marketing director and workplace sloganeer. She lit up like the perennially last-picked kid who'd finally escaped that fate. "Yeah . . . and let's call it Smells Like Team Spirit."

A few more calls, a bit more cajoling, and within forty-eight hours, Smells Like Team Spirit—an eclectic, happy, and profoundly inexperienced group of women—came together. We conducted our first and only preseason practice with strains of Nirvana blasting inspiration. Off the field, few of us actually listened to Nirvana, but in Seattle we were at grunge ground zero. We figured we were entitled.

Here We Are Now, Entertain Us

Game one loomed only six short days away. Had we been less worried about our T-shirt design and a bit more concerned with acquiring some skills and securing a coach, our opener might have taken a different turn. Rumors of an ace coach were flying around the team throughout our one-week gestation. Claire knew somebody who knew someone who dated someone who used to work with someone who knew a *fabulous* potential coach. But we were out of time, and with just that one disorganized practice under our belts, we showed up, all innocence and grins, for our first game. Our coach materialized only minutes before. She was tall and blond, and walked with a slight limp; she sauntered across the sunny haze of the outfield as in a scene from a Hollywood movie, and made her way to our huddle. She introduced herself: "T. J. Gregor. Go ahead and take your positions." T.J.'s gaze wandered over us. We were a herd of does in the headlights. We hadn't discussed positions. With a hint of understanding and perhaps a trace of regret, she mumbled, "Okay, well, go anywhere you want."

A vague memory of pitching in some junior high gym class passed through my consciousness. Suppressed yearnings rose up in me, yearnings of what should have been, what could have been, and what *still might be.* In a moment of misguided ambition, I volunteered for the mound.

From my elevated position, I surveyed the team as they spread out with the sort of random, intentless energy I'd witnessed in local mosh pits. I became concerned. The Smellies had such desire and enthusiasm. We had character *and* characters. We had guts and even raw talent. We had everything champions should have. We just didn't know how to play softball.

The score that day, a sobering 0–20. The umpire couldn't invoke the slaughter rule because we didn't make it through four innings (the slaughter reprieve requires twelve outs). But T.J. must have glimpsed some promise. Even after that humiliating opener, she stuck with us.

Coach T.J. proved to be our Prophet. This ex-ace was the classic broken player, the disillusioned, dropped-out former star who returned to her sport only when a morally pure, yet pathetically skill-less team *needed her desperately*. Brought down by a hip injury years before, T.J. thought she'd left softball forever. She provided leadership and a beacon of hope, and, in some small way, I'd like to think we gave her game back to her.

If T.J. was our Prophet, beautiful and lanky pitcher Barb, a new recruit quickly dubbed Barbarella, was surely our Savior. Offering us both a moral and a physical center, as any good pitcher does, she had a style that every Smelly secretly coveted: we all wished our clothes hung as they did on her, the well-tipped, exquisitely worn-out Union Local 203 hat, the loosely slung, holey Blackhawks jersey. Her clothes actually *fit* like the copy *reads* in one of those J. Crew catalogs. Shabby Chic incarnate. Plus, she could pitch poetry.

The rest of the lineup read like a list of *Star Search* callbacks. Bride-to-be and indomitable spirit Laura "Slev" Slevin had long blond hair perennially ponytailed, a prom queen smile as bright white as the Beemer convertible she drove, and an ever-present "dip" in her lip (Copenhagen, never Skoal). Slev refused to play any position other than part-time catcher, a role that allowed ample opportunity to refresh her chaw and chat up anyone within range (ump, batter, fans, pitcher). Catcher Claire "Claire-voyance" defied an old running injury, employing an entire hardware store on her knee. She proved to be a one-woman pep rally and a veritable font of information when it came to teaching us the all-important support chatter: "Just you and me, Barbarella, right in the bucket, one pitch at a time." Most of marketing director Nancy's movement was dictated by her utter fear of the ball. Yet in addition to giving us our ironic name, she designed our T-shirt logo: an infant girl with a ribbon stuck on her head, a ball in one tiny hand and a mitt on the other, floating guilelessly in a swimming pool. (The logo was *more* than just reminiscent of Nirvana's debut album. Sub Pop never sued.) As for yours truly, "HollyMo," I skated on my reputation as the team founder, brownnosed my way to second base, and obsessively dreamed of the day I'd be a part of a real double play (which wasn't to come for two more seasons). I never pitched again.

And there were many others in this colorful bunch, among them Harley-driving Nikki. Nobody really knew where she came from, but rumor had it she was some kind of private detective. Hairstylist and fielder Bettina, "Betty," had as many Mac lipstick colors as she did girlfriends. Shortstop Holly "Coop" Cooper studied calculus between innings. Flat-topped Holly "Bealster" Beal was planted at first base and kept us all in line politically with weekly updates on what products to boycott or rallies to attend. On-the-spot therapy was provided by shrink and fielder Laura "Funkster" Funk. She successfully derailed all post-strikeout stress syndrome and basked in the positive reinforcement of her own midget fan club, who chanted "Mom-Me, Mom-Me" every time she was at bat.

Grrrls of Summer

After witnessing our opening day performance, T.J. knew she had to start with the basics. As if we were a group of orphaned infants, she scooped us up and began with softball's equivalent of potty training:

> Don't be afraid of the ball.
> Head down for those grounders.
> No lattes on the field.
> *Please* don't put tampons in the ball bag.

That Sunday morning and every one thereafter, we donned our garb (usually our best Barbarella imitation) and practiced with the zeal of true converts, earnestly following Coach T.J.'s instructions. Her short list of priorities began with the Art of Backing Up and the Importance of Controlling the Ball. One ball through the legs, she explained carefully, does not *necessarily* have to lead to an interminably long play ending up in a score, or several scores, by the other team.

She put us through endless drills: pop flies, grounders, baserunning. Penance was paid if we failed to call a fly ball. We learned the Great Truth of Women's Softball: The players with bows in their hair are always the best hitters. But most important, she imprinted on our souls the three vital questions that became our mantra before each play:

1. How many outs are there? (umm)
2. What do I do if I get the ball? (pray)
3. What do I do if I don't get the ball? (thank god)

For inspiration, T.J. packed us off to study the Silver Bullets, the West's new women's professional baseball team, and off to the movie theater to see *A League of Their Own,* a cinematic romp about a little-known slice of baseball history. We watched P. K. Wrigley's All-American Girls Professional Baseball League of the 1940s and '50s slide, steal, subvert, and sass—proving once and for all that women *can* play hardball. The Smellies matched their camaraderie, yet coveted their competence.

Unfortunately, sports heroines like the All American Girls were not around during our girlhoods. We'd come of age during the doldrums in women's baseball history. The AAGPBL was long defunct, and the modern revolution started by the Joan of Arc of Little League, twelve-year-old Amy Dickinson, who fought the good fight for girls in that American institution, was only beginning to spread across the country as we hit adolescence. So as adults diving headlong into a new arena, we decided to lionize one another and celebrate our own brand of grit. We reveled in devoting ourselves to something as "trivial" as team sports, and we schooled each other in timeworn rituals. As we nursed sore muscles, there were late-night phone calls to toss around tips, including how to break in our new mitts:

"T.J. said to use mink oil."

"Put a ball in it, tie it up with string, and put it under the mattress."

"Get some Probe from Claire. I bet that slippery stuff will work."

At some practices, we'd sling bats over our shoulders, pile into a few cars, and head to the batting cages, where T.J. propped up our elbows, smooshed the wiggle out of our stances, unlocked our knees, and urged us to visualize actually *hitting* the ball. It was in the cages and in our Sunday morning batting drills that we first came to know the unparalleled satisfaction of a solid hit, the transformative powers of perfect connection, the poetry of motion that has inspired reams of baseball literature.

But those glimpses of baseball Zen didn't translate into victory. Come game time, we continued to lose. We got destroyed by the Desperadas, routed by the Radical Crew, swatted by the Mosquito Squad.

Our Kind of Athletic Supporters

Certainly we *wanted* to win, but our fun was not contingent on victory. We quickly developed our own brand of ambition, our own modest goals on the field. The score sheet may not have reflected our successes and strengths, but we definitely had them.

Our most obvious asset was the monumental support we lent one another. Coach T.J. set a shining example. After a dribbling grounder passed through two pairs of Smelly legs and then was overthrown to first base, she'd holler, "Nice idea, nice idea," as reward for throwing in the right general direction. If a Smelly base runner failed to run in a force play, T.J. would simply point out the problem and add, "But hey, it's okay, you confused the hell out of the other team." Each time a Smelly was up at bat, the entire dugout chirped encouragement: "Get a piece of it, Betty" or "Spank it, Claire." A whiff would elicit "Nice cut," a strikeout a chorus of "Don't worry about it."

Given our penchant for support, we were masters of the Backup by game four. Whatever that ball's trajectory, two or three of us would fall in line behind the poor soul who hope-fully had been pondering Question No. 2 (What do I do if I get the ball?). Since only a handful of us could throw the ball from the deep outfield all the way to the infield, we also became deft at the Relay. We'd line up like a dot-to-dot draw-ing in the kids' section of the Sunday paper and we'd throw, throw, throw until the ball landed safely with Barbarella. The discovery that the other team would stop running around the bases if it even *looked* like we had control of the ball signaled a major shift in our tenuous playfield paradigm.

Whether we were newcomers to the sport or jaded players on a quest of rediscovery, we were all extraordinarily *invested* in the team. That infectious Smelly spirit zinged through the fila-ments that connected the kitchen tables, office coffee breaks, and barroom stools across Seattle. Our fans turned out in force. Game after game, they came, they cheered, we lost.

The *Unnatural*

It would be reasonable to assume that a season's greatest moment would entail a daring headfirst slide into home or a game-winning grand slam in a clutch situation.

The Smellies' finest moment came with a midseason pop fly to center field.

To convey the grandeur of this play, it must be pointed out that we were a team that, despite innumerable practice drills, frequently dropped fly balls. (Caught fly balls were reason enough for whooping high fives in the outfield.) Nancy, whose terror of the ball was outweighed only by her dedication to the team, was stationed at "rover," a sort of extra center-fielder spot. She'd failed so far to catch a pop-up during the first five games of the season. It was now the bottom of the fourth, two outs (no small accomplishment), and our opponents were the division-leading Game Hens. We were hemorrhaging badly in the field, and this half inning had dragged on for a good thirty minutes. Our Savior was fading; we weren't backing her up. The Game Hens' pitcher, who looked and swung like a tall drink of water, popped a doozy to center field.

The moment hung as long as Long Dong himself.

It was Nancy's ball. We held our collective breath; not a sound was murmured. We shared the eerie feeling that even a slight move could change the course of what was about to unfold. After what seemed interminable hang time, amid several disconcerting shifts in Nancy's strategy for catching the ball, the wily orb plummeted from the sky.

Into her mitt.

The intensity of Nancy's smile alone could have lit Wrigley Field into the next millennium. The rest of us went *wild.* Fence climbing. Midfield pileups. Equipment flying. The works.

We lost the game, of course. But Nancy's catch was a victory for the entire team and inspired a dramatic postgame show. We hit the play button on the boom box, and Kurt Cobain's 1990s caterwaul crooning propelled us all from the bench onto the diamond, tossing mitts, bumping hips, and covering that grubby field with a showing of team spirit that flew in the face of our dismal record. It was as if we'd hidden a secret barrel of hooch in that league cellar.

We stayed in the basement, and had fun. As the summer lapped by, we continued to execute our modest goals on the field and to pursue our loftiest ideal—to attain the highest degree of pleasure at all times. But with a third of the season remaining, an odd transformation came over the team. We began to throw to the right bases without nine players having to yell direction. Not a single pop-up landed uncalled between two shamefaced players. And in the middle of a muggy Thursday evening doubleheader, I realized something amazing: I *wanted* the ball to come to me.

We had begun to operate on instinct.

And then it happened. We won a game.

Although they'd beaten us handily in the past, our opponent, Toho America, shared the league basement with us. We were hoping for a higher-scoring game (that is, *our* score would be higher), but the word *win* hadn't yet become part of the Smelly lexicon. All that changed in the bottom of the sixth. The score was 7–9; we were trailing, but Home Run Healy was at the plate, with runners on first and second. A rare silence settled over the assembled fans and players. Nostrils flared. Was that the scent of victory in the air? We sucked in the heady odor even though we knew it might not be good for us. But when Erin earned her nickname with a blast into the next county, we realized victory *tasted* even better than it smelled.

Hoo-Ha

That summer, Smells Like Team Spirit came to know the Thelma-and-Louise camaraderie of an all-girl venture, and we perfected the fine art of hoo-ha. Tossing aside daily responsibilities, anxiety, and *real* competition, we carved out a space—if only for a few hours a week—where the most important things were the three sacred questions, keeping our heads down, and having fun. We brought to the field few of the ingredients associated with competitive sports, yet we stumbled into an extraordinary kind of success and an unexpected summer of magic. As team mood ring Claire-voyance aptly summed up the season: "An amazing thing happened when fifteen people agreed to be bad at something. There was nothing at stake. In our case, winning would have gotten in the way of our being together."

We were a group of grown women with seemingly important, complicated lives—from lawyers, activists, and editors to mothers, sex-store owners, and coffee baristas—who traded the comforts of competence for the democratizing slouch and scrappy rewards of being part of a fledgling team. And it was *great.* We came to know the oddly appealing recipe of dirt, sweat, and repetition. We embraced the irony that a decidedly losing season created incredibly winning feelings. By season's end, our team gestalt was legend: we were the worst team with the best attitude and the most fans.

The Show

A series of rain-outs brought our season to an undramatic close. We decided to throw a banquet, harking back to school days past, that awkward time when teens with uneven bangs put on ill-fitting dresses to clamber up to the podium and accept a varsity letter. Slev hosted the banquet at her home, and Nancy's husband, an affable Brit named Richard, all dressed up in drag and looking like Dr. Ruth on steroids, made sure each grinning player got an award certificate and a Polaroid snapshot of herself receiving it. The night overflowed with beer, wine, girlfriends, boyfriends, husbands, and an unforgettable kitsch cabaret featuring dramatic renditions of cheesy scenes from B movies. An Oscar-caliber performance was delivered by two Friends of Smellies who, accompanied by the sounds of "Unchained Melody," reenacted the famously "erotic" pottery-wheel love scene in the movie *Ghost*. Out of dewy-eyed Demi Moore's magic fingers came a phallic symbol of a different ilk—not one that would ignite studly Patrick Swayze into amorous action but, rather, a baseball bat that *would* send the entire Smelly lineup into cheers and high-octave hoopla that lasted well into the wee hours. Even better than the variety show entertainment was Coach T.J.'s epic poem, "A Salute to the Smellies" ("So there you have it, / a season made of dreams. / And when we finally won a game, / we nearly busted at the seams"). We honored ourselves that night, securing our place, with our own Smelly flair, in the annals of the Great American Pastime.

The Inaugural Season Smelly Record

Lost	0–20
Lost	6–19
Lost	1–21
Lost	4–31
Lost	5–30
Lost	2–14
Lost	3–19
Won!	**10–9**

Lost   3–30
Lost   0–12

From the Outhouse to the Penthouse, or You've Come a Looong Way, Baby

It is an unusually chilly late July evening in the Northwest four years later. Along with a couple of Smellies from seasons past who have also hung up their sneakers, I am bundled up watching Smells Like Team Spirit play for the league championship. The packed stands are friendly with banter about the American women's softball team's gold medal, won only moments before at the Atlanta Olympics. It is a pleasure for us retirees to watch the cleat-clad, well-oiled sports machine that is the modern-day Smellies. I'm still in love with this team, but no longer with the kind of blind devotion reserved for an underdog. Now I feel distant admiration and a splash of pride mingled with nostalgia. Unlike the Smellies of yesteryear, this team throws with precision, runs with speed, and not only slides but slides with *style*. They actually get prone *intentionally*. The occasional error is not the result of fear or blunder but rather the result of flair and aggressive play, and is always followed by the trademark Smelly grin.

Only three names from our inaugural season roster appear in tonight's lineup: T.J., who remains the limping muse of leadership; Home Run Healy, now a league-famous hitter and pillar at third; and Betty, who has morphed from tentative fielder to tiger second basegrrrl, still flashing a rich shade of Mac. A fifth-inning rocket over the left-field fence by Home Run Healy has just given the Smellies the lead. Her trot around the bases is met by a phalanx of teammates, bowing in reverence on the third-base line.

The Smellies hang on to the lead. The bleachers rumble with our foot stomping, as the final out declares Smells Like Team Spirit to be the 1996 champions of Seattle City League Division II Women's Softball. Division II has proved to be perfectly doable indeed. This group of scrappers is still underdressed, but the team has created a slice of history to be forever enshrined in the hall of fame of our own minds. And, best of all, the Smelly team spirit still remains, undiminished by winning. I catch a familiar whiff as the champs swagger forth, in a frenzy of smiles and high fives, and gather on the pitcher's mound to hold aloft their five-foot trophy.

they're pooling **their** power

SHAWN HUBLER

It isn't an easy thing for a girl to grow up to be a woman, not nearly as easy as it is for her to grow up to remain a girl. You can spend a lifetime in this world acting winsome and blaming your troubles on PMS and men. But womanhood—that takes guts.

Women don't tend to walk around dwelling on such issues. (Or at least this woman doesn't, except for once in labor, right before her epidural kicked in.) But we are in the stands at the local high school, and our teenager and her school chums are down there whupping their crosstown rivals, and crosstown whuppings have a way of bringing life lessons to mind.

The whupping on this day happens to be in a game of girls' water polo, a quintessentially California kind of winter sport. Deceptively fun-looking, the game involves hurling a ball into the goal of your opponent while fending off attackers and treading water to the point of exhaustion in a pool. The bruising and dunking, the clawing and punching that go on under the churning surface are ruthless and perpetual. It is one of the roughest sports a kid can play, and in the past couple of years it has become one of the fastest growing sports among high school girls.

Two years ago, if you had asked us to name the activity in which our teenager was most likely to letter, this sport would have been last on the list. In fact, any sport would have surprised us. Her idea of a good workout was a little channel surfing, followed by a brisk trip to the mall. Then she started high school, and her father pushed her to get into sports and she found out that they were launching a girls' water polo team. To humor him, she put her name on a list. From that moment on, her whole life changed.

Women's sports have been in the spotlight this last couple of weeks, with names like Picabo Street and Cammi Granato providing inspiration in an otherwise ho-hum Olympic Games. But the dreams of Olympic gold that, in this country, have been fueled by legislation like Title IX are only half the story. The other half is in the smaller victories—such as the way the addition of just one more girls' team to a high school roster can bring a shy adolescent into her own.

In a single season, thanks to that addition, our teenager dropped twenty pounds, became a juggernaut of drive and organization, and learned how people act when they are part of a team. Learned how to compete, not with the manipulation and coyness that so many girls have been taught to fall back on but with hard work and focus. Learned that girls can have guts. And that girls can have dreams.

Yeahhh! Get wet!

Heads up!

Get on her! Drive it!

The bleachers are packed. The crowd is going wild. At the top of the stands, someone is calming the top scorer's dad, who has screamed so loudly at past games that the ref has had to tell him to pipe down. Down below, a beautiful freckle-faced girl whose team nickname is "Roach" is lunging for the ball in the face of an aggressive one-on-one defense. Underwater, the defender has pinched a particularly delicate hunk of Roach's flesh and given it a vicious twist. Roach has lashed back with a brutal shove. The girl backs off and Roach throws her head back, catches the ball with one hand—and laughs.

It is that laugh that will stick in everyone's minds the most, a laugh of invincible confidence. When the team recalls the face-off, no one will worry whether the pinch was fair or whether the big bruise will show. They understand: There is pain. It goes with the territory. They are big girls. They can handle it.

"She's, like, twisting it, and I'm, like, 'Duuude! Kick back!'" Roach will recount afterward. And everyone will double over in hilarity. And then they'll move on to the brilliant assist, the blocked goal, the Hail Mary score from half-tank. They understand this, too: There is glory. It, too, goes with the territory. And, as big girls, they can handle that as well.

There was a time when nothing in a teenage girl's life would have told her that she was capable, that she could just *handle it.* A quarter-century or so ago, when Title IX was signed into law, mandating equal opportunity for girls and boys in education—including sports—the only life lesson for female athletes was that if they excelled in sports, they could quickly learn the meaning of the word "homophobia."

Nice girls were supposed to be small and powerless or, at the very least, act that way. Pain and glory and all the rest of it—those things were supposed to be out of a teenage girl's league. You can't help but wonder how many women would be complaining today about sexual harassment and glass ceilings if they had been taught in girlhood to compete like grown-ups, to handle it. You can't help but ask—without making too much of it—whether the world's Monica Lewinskys would have been so unfortunately enamored of power if they'd known the personal power that comes with being a contributing member of a winning team.

And you can't help but marvel at the power of these girls as they splash to victory with their high fives and buff bodies and cheering sections of boyfriends in the stands. Here in the suburbs, or out there on the Olympic slopes of Nagano, there is something profoundly inspiring about a girl as it dawns on her that she isn't small and powerless, doesn't have to settle for shy. That she has guts. And womanhood. And dreams.

the value of girl's basket ball
A KOKOMO HIGH SCHOOL STUDENT

In this age of woman's movements, few people have realized yet that the movement which is doing most for womankind is centered in our High Schools. A new type of girl has sprung up in our country. A girl more perfect mentally, morally, and physically, than the girl of twenty years ago. This is the basket ball girl. Many are her detractors; numerous are her critics, but her champions and supporters see in her the future greatness of American womanhood.

. . . From the High School basket ball girl is being developed that strong, self-reliant woman, the woman who is cool and keen in her judgment, quick and sure in her action, calm and unselfish in her dealings. Altogether the perfectly developed woman.

a peaches **fan** for **life**

SUSAN E. JOHNSON

My most treasured possession is my Peaches scrapbook. I was ten years old in 1950 when I discovered the Rockford Peaches, one of the premier teams of the All-American Girls Professional Baseball League, the women who played professional baseball from 1943 to 1954 in "a league of their own."

The Peaches were the heroes of my adolescence. I went to as many games as I could, but—much as I might have liked to—I could not spend my whole young life in the stands. So each morning, to console myself, I cut from the paper the accounts of the previous evening's game, pasting them carefully in my scrapbook and poring over them on those lonely nights when the team was out of town.

I kept this scrapbook and my other Peaches memorabilia for nearly forty years. In 1990, when I turned fifty, I realized that my heroes were aging as well, and if I wanted to give some gift back, I had to do so now. The black-and-white-checked two-ring binder was tattered, and duct tape held the spine together, yet I was able to use my scrapbook to find twenty-six Rockford Peaches and Fort Wayne Daisies, whom I interviewed for *When Women Played Hardball*, my book about these All-Americans who were my heroes.

A portion of the first entry in my scrapbook reads:

Lois Florreich's string of shutouts was snapped at four Saturday night but she pitched her 16th win of the season when she defeated the Fort Wayne Daisies, league leaders, 4–2. Her victory put the Peaches within half a game of first place. One of

the largest Saturday night crowds of the season—2,658 fans—
saw the game.

—*Rockford Morning Star,*
August 1950

I like to think I cheered along with the other Rockfordians at
this crucial game, a turning point in the 1950 season. If so, I sat
next to my dad on the bleachers of "the Peach Orchard," a high
school football stadium adapted for baseball. The late summer
night was warm and humid, and my attention was riveted on the
field. Only when my Peaches drew safely ahead could I relax
enough to go get myself and my dad a bag of peanuts and a Coke.

I loved the Peaches from the moment I saw my first game.
My hero was Dorothy "Snookie" Doyle, the shortstop. I liked
her energy, her chatter to her teammates, her big grin, and
something else, some whiff I caught, even from afar, of ambition and competitiveness, some sense of this baseball thing
being a joy but not entirely a game.

The All-Americans were only girls themselves, of course, for
the average age of players in the league was just eighteen. But
to a ten-year-old, such girls are grown-ups. There were some
veterans, too. Snookie was twenty-six in 1950, and the next
oldest player in the league, Peaches pitcher Rose Gacioch, was
thirty-five. In 1934, before coming to the league, Rosie had
played with the All Star Ranger Girls, a "Bloomer Girls" team.
These highly successful women's teams barnstormed around
the country from the late 1890s until the mid-1930s, playing
men's semipro teams.

I knew nothing of all this women's baseball history and, like
the players themselves, had no idea I was helping to create a
significant moment in the history of women's sports in America. For—as it turned out—the twelve seasons of the All-
American Girls Professional Baseball League is the longest any
women's professional team sport has existed in this country.

I breathlessly attended fan picnics with my mom and dad,
brother Al and sister Becky. We ate hot dogs and potato salad,
and pointed out to each other the famous players who strolled

around the Sinnissippi Park picnic shelter, chatting with their fans. When I got up my nerve I bought glossy black-and-white photos of my favorite players. Then, with pen shaking in my small fist, I would approach each woman, thrust the picture and pen into her large rough hands, and wait with awe and trepidation for her to scrawl her autograph. The players were in no hurry, regarding the encouragement of small female fans as one of their reasons for being, but once I had a name captured, I dashed away. The up-close physical presence of my heroes radiated an intensity too powerful for me to share for more than a moment.

These working-class and farm girls hugely enjoying the chance to play a good game of baseball were living images of a womanhood that attracted me, that I could imagine myself into, a womanhood of throwing hard and running fast and wanting to win. Squirt Callow and Nickie Fox were close-to-sacred embodiments of what, prior to the Peaches, I had thought was a life reserved for men.

The firstborn in my family, I decided at about the age of six that boys did all the fun, exciting things in life. And so I became one. I loved being a boy. I dressed in jeans and T-shirts and sneakers, and my mother let me get a boy's haircut. I tried on boys' names, and would secretly think of myself for a while as Steve, then Chuck. I matured earlier than the real boys, of course, having the genetic advantage of being a girl, and was thus for many years stronger and faster than they were. I was fiercely competitive. I played baseball—hardball, not softball—and Capture the Flag and a weird and violent version of football, where you not only tackled the person with the ball but dragged her or him over your team's goal line. We built forts and in the winter played war with snowballs, in the spring with milkweed pods that had not yet burst, in the fall with dried-up crabapples.

Girls, I noted with disgust, were careful to play safe, clean games, like jacks and jump rope, and to squeal when a mouse ran across the front of the classroom. Girls sewed placemats for their mothers at a Brownie meeting while outside a huge snowstorm swirled around the school, burying cars that we boys could help out of ditches. I thought girls were really stupid. Clearly anyone with any pride would be a boy.

Until I found the Peaches. Here were girl people doing the things my 1950s Midwestern culture told me only boys did. I was transfixed by them. I knew in my heart of hearts I was a girl and would someday become a woman and . . . My imagination simply stopped there, the prospect too appalling to admit of further rumination. The Peaches gave my dreams somewhere to go, into a future where I might be content, even happy, with who I was.

The first thing I liked about the Peaches and their opponents—like the Fort Wayne Daisies, the Racine Belles, the Grand Rapids Chicks (!)—was that they played the game hard, with great skill and considerable ingenuity. The All-Americans played what baseball analysts term "little ball," relying on strategy, speed, and key hits to score runs, rather than "big ball," the power game where eight (male) players stand at the edge of the dugout, hoping the ninth will hit a home run. The women didn't even always need hits. Dottie Key, the Peaches' lead-off batter, would allow herself to be hit by a pitch, steal second, scamper to third on a sacrifice, and cross home on a long fly ball to right field.

Games were exciting. Baseball Hall of Famer Max Carey, a Pittsburgh Pirate for seventeen years and All-American League President from 1945 to 1949, said of the 1946 championship game between the Peaches and the Racine Belles, "Barring none, even in the majors, it's the best game I've ever seen."

In this contest Peach Carolyn Morris pitched nine no-hit innings. Joanne Winter, the Belles' pitcher, allowed thirteen hits but, incredibly, the Peaches couldn't combine them into a run. The game went into extra innings. Then, in the bottom of the fourteenth, Sophie "the Flint Flash" Kurys of Racine got a hit, stole second, and, in the midst of stealing third, saw teammate Betty Trezza slap the ball to right field. Kurys slid home to win the game.

Another of my heroes was Dottie "Kammie" Kamenshek,

the Peaches' first baseman, clearly a person of stature, all business and somewhat intimidating even from the safety of the stands. When she retired at the beginning of the 1952 season, she had led the league for one or more seasons in: at bats, runs scored, hits, singles, fewest strikeouts, and batting average (.316 in 1946, .306 in 1947). Wally Pip, himself a great fielding first baseman for the New York Yankees in the 1920s, called Dottie "the fanciest fielding first baseman I've ever seen—man or woman."

I liked the Peaches' team spirit. I have since reflected upon the fact that women's individual (and upper-class) sports—golf and tennis—have had more professional success by far than women's team sports. Apparently it is socially acceptable for one woman to compete against other lone women, but there is something about the idea of women cooperating that is radical and not quite right. And women getting dirty is equally suspect. Golf and tennis are clean. Baseball, soccer, and—heaven preserve us—football: such women's team sports are not only potentially dirty but demand physical contact and may even be a bit dangerous.

Years later, Ruth Richard, the Peaches' catcher and, many believe, the best catcher in the league, talked with me about the essence of team play. "Our infielders were so good. We played good together. You always knew what the next person was thinking, as far as what plays were coming up."

Even from the stands I could sense that the Peaches were, before all else, a team, women working and playing together to accomplish something difficult and worthwhile. Marilyn Jones, the Peaches' backup catcher, captured the mood exactly when she told me that "on a team you had everybody else helpin' you!" The Peaches' interdependence and loyalty to each other was contagious; we fans quickly learned that we could be a part of the team by showing up and cheering.

The Peaches, like all the teams in the league, played to win, something I, as a competitive little person and a rabid fan, approved of. This was a professional sport, after all, and professional sport is about two things, winning and entertaining the fans, in that order. As the Fort Wayne catcher, Mary Rountree, said, "It's like breathing, winnin' was."

The women of the league would do anything to win, including sacrificing their bodies. By league rules they were required to wear skirts, leaving their legs vulnerable to huge bruises when they slid into base. They also suffered the usual sports injuries and wear and tear. As older ladies, talking to me over a cup of coffee, they would complain about their aching knees and arthritic fingers. Catcher Marilyn Jones proudly showed me several oddly bent fingers broken forty-some years earlier. But under no circumstances would they have exchanged their ball-playing days for pain-free bodies now. As Peaches pitcher Louise "Lou" Erickson told me, "I could have gotten these sore joints knitting, too."

I loved watching my Peaches play to win and get rough if need be. They could argue with an umpire and kick dirt with the best of them. The Grand Rapids Chicks' Ruth "Tex" Lessing was once fined $100 for slugging an umpire. Fans collected $2,000 to pay her fine. But, though league owners wanted the girls to be competitive and to play good baseball, they also expected them to look—and act—"feminine." A picture much publicized at the time shows a player coloring her lips. The caption reads, "Applying Make-up Is Important to Ruth Lessing."

The explicit admonition was that the All-Americans should "look like girls and play like men." Players were subjected to something called "charm school," under the care of no less an expert than Chicago-based Helena Rubinstein, owner of a popular line of cosmetics. The erstwhile tomboys learned about makeup and carriage and deportment, how to apply lipstick and talk to strangers. There were league rules about hair length, and about wearing skirts in public and, of course, on the field of play. It was not all ridiculous, however. Some of the girls appreciated a little coaching in how to dress for, and relate to, the local Kiwanians, to whom the players were hometown heroes and frequent luncheon guests.

Newspapers like the one I read in Rockford covered the

games on the sports page with a great deal of space and seriousness, then tried to balance the message with features elsewhere in the paper portraying the players as just women at heart. A typical 1951 picture is captioned "Ball Playing Girls Are Domestic," and shows left-fielder Eleanor "Squirt" Callow sitting on the floor at the feet of pitcher Irene "Lefty" Applegren. (The nicknames are omitted from the picture caption.) Applegren is supposedly crocheting while Callow holds the ball of yarn. Both are dressed in heels, and readers are assured that the two "feel as much at home in domestic surroundings as on the playing field." But I notice a grin on Squirt's face. What can she be thinking?

The All-Americans knew that, with just a little posing, they would be allowed to play the game they loved, and to be paid for it. Some years later, when I asked Daisies pitcher Dottie Collins how she felt about playing in a skirt, she answered, "I would have played naked if necessary in order to play ball."

The emphasis on domesticity distressed my young tomboy self not at all. I must have taken it for what it was, the promotion of an image that delighted owners and perhaps reassured fans, but was far from the reality these women experienced or valued. And for me the tension between the image and the reality was itself important. It was the perfect mirror for my own confusion over sexual identity. Here I was, a tomboy approaching puberty, watching older tomboys dressed like girls playing a men's game. And seeing them being accepted. And cheered on.

The All-Americans accompanied me for five crucial years on my own frightening journey through adolescence. By their example of doing what they loved, even when it was not what nice ladies did, they helped this one tomboy turn into the kind of woman she needed to be. I had thought that in order to have any self-respect, I had to distance myself from other girls. Now life was not so lonely. The All-Americans did for me, and for other girls and women, just what role models should: they showed us that females can do anything. Fort Wayne slugger

Betty Foss told me, "The whole world thought we was nuts." That's the kind of role models we need, people nuts enough to do the things that can make them our heroes.

In the end, however, no amount of player craziness and fan dedication could save the All-Americans. After the 1954 season the league folded, the victim of declining attendance and administrative tangles, all occasioned by an increase in both fan mobility (we could travel more easily, both World War II and the Korean War being over) and immobility (the television had lured us into staying put in our own living rooms). Fans like me, and the players themselves, were desolate. I was left to negotiate my whole life, age fifteen and up, without the consoling and exciting presence of my Peaches.

I kept my Peaches scrapbooks and my glossy photos. Words and pictures gave tangible proof that women could play winning baseball. In my heart, the league was immortal, the games and especially the players—Kammie and Snookie and Squirt— forever alive in my memory.

Nearly forty years after the league disbanded and my Peaches racked up their bats for the last time, I committed myself to finding and talking with the women who had been my heroes. I contacted the secretary of the All-American Girls Professional Baseball League Players Association, which had been founded several years earlier to develop and maintain contacts among the players, and got permission to interview all the women still living who had played for the 1950 Rockford Peaches and Fort Wayne Daisies.

I traveled for three weeks throughout Illinois, Indiana, Michigan, and Wisconsin, talking with the women who had stayed in the Midwest, and attended a reunion in Fort Wayne to interview some players scattered farther afield. As I approached the registration desk at the Red Lion Inn and announced my name, an older, solidly built, and quite large woman grabbed my arm. "Are you Sue Johnson?" she nearly shouted, and introduced herself as Vivian "Kelly" Kellogg, the

Fort Wayne first baseman. "Come on over, here are some people you want to meet." She dragged me across the lobby to a group of older ladies laughing and talking together. "Here's Snookie Doyle," Kelly declared, laying her hand on the shoulder of a white-haired, grinning lady. "And of course," she continued, placing my hand in the large hand of another, more serious person, "you remember Kammie Kamenshek."

And indeed I did.

american past time

BARBARA CROOKER

1988

A June morning, the air hung with the scent of roses
as my mother irons, filling the kitchen with steam.
She sprinkles the laundry with water from a ketchup bottle,
showers the sheets, blesses the shirts.
Everything is pressed, even dishcloths.
Outside on the line, towels smell of wind.
The stack grows taller as the morning wanes.
Soon, there will be sandwiches,
tuna glistening with mayonnaise
on crushable white bread,
drinks made from syrup in lurid colors.
And then the long, long afternoons,
the sun, pitched and searing as a hardball
coming at you fast and clean.
Swinging hard, you connect,
hickory to rawhide,
a moment hanging in time,
stretching fresh and clean as the sheeted sky,
when days were caught, suspended,
when the dark meant only hide & seek
or time to come home.

in praise of bush leagues

MICHELLE BROCKWAY

In Houston's Spring Branch Memorial Sports Association in the 1970s, anybody with thirty-five dollars made a team. That was my luck: we had more money than I had natural talent. For the next five years my enthusiasms converged on the fields of fast-pitch softball—ponytails, pigtails, and pragmatic bowl cuts, mosquito spray and mown grass, hot coffee and Frito pie, finicky toilets, rattling bleachers, and nicknames: Shauna Bear, Witchipoo, Sue Babe.

Back then, street boundaries determined team assignments: I would join the Stingrays. Mom bought me a red, white, and blue glove and a pair of rubber cleats, and I attended my first practice without having played more than apartment complex games with a worn tennis ball and a wooden bat.

Our coach was Ken Hunter, the pitcher's father. One of the few flat-bellied men in the league, he worked for an electric company, outdoors, I guess, for he had a tan, lined face. His wry, slightly shy smile reminded me of my father's, sans the temper. After his workday he gave me a lift in his pickup to an elementary school backstop, where he threw batting practice to fourteen or fifteen players and then got behind the stick himself for fielding drills, somehow urging "Get two!" around the filterless Lucky between his lips.

I admired the older girls, who cracked wise jokes as they hummed and slapped that ball and on the bench swayed shoulder-to-shoulder singing, "Come on, baby, do the loco-motion." I couldn't compete with them—had the opportunity existed then, many would have played in more competitive leagues—but I was on their team. For two innings a game I crouched in right field under the lights misted by clouds of bugs, chattering at the batter, scratching my ankles, throwing a fist in the air at every out—accomplished, nearly always, by somebody else. I discovered good-fellowship, respect, the value of a lot of heart when innate excellence eludes you.

When Mr. Hunter's daughter outgrew the Stingrays, a new coach, L. C. Watts, took over. He was a Gulf Oil lifer, a landman who would soon confront early retirement. His daughter Cindy started first-string because, he said, she was "the purtiest girl on the team." She was also one of the few pitchers, so no one objected.

Mr. Watts was round and brought a hand to his belly when he laughed—to coach the Stingrays that year, one needed a sense of humor. Whenever we booted the ball, he hunched his shoulders as if hearing glass break. When a certain infielder threw a mid-play temper tantrum, he'd roll his eyes and labor to replace a grimace with a frustrated smile. Once, as he stood beside me at third base, I got it into my head to steal home. Two faces—the umpire's and my coach's—peered down at me through the dust cloud raised by the slide. "Safe!" they both cried above outstretched arms. Mr. Watts walked me back to the dugout. "Brockway," he said, "you're going to give me a heart attack." But years later, even as I passed into my third decade, he'd say of me to his old men-friends, in an appalling excess of generosity: "Best center fielder in the league."

In high school I moved up to the Vikings and my last coach, Ernie Lucas. Like the others, he puffed red-faced through batting practice—until he discovered the pitching machine. A lawyer, he handled difficult parents with the same bemused patience that he brought to couples' feuds over toaster custody. From his cheerfulness at afternoon practice one got the impression that the duffel bags of bats and balls under his truck camper brought him a lot more fun than a box of depositions.

When Ernie got excited, his voice pitch rose: "Come on, girls, come on, girls!" Pacing and bobbing along the third-base line, bent fifteen degrees, exhorting a languishing pitcher, urging us to keep our heads up, dive, hustle, hit the cutoff, hit it! During games his efficient wife sat in a lawn chair behind the plate and kept score; the rest of the time she trailed him, struggling to keep him all in one piece. "I know, Wanda, I know," he'd say, but Wanda was always right.

For many of the athletes, leaving home meant saying goodbye to the softball fields as much as anything else. Had I the glove or the bat, I'd have embraced the first college that asked, but for me serious sports ended at the age of eighteen. Some of my friends who did make college teams—Texas A&M, Sam Houston State—would today encounter more competitive options much sooner, long before high school graduation; quite likely we would never have shared the same bench. Perhaps they would have enrolled in the type of demanding camp pictured in last year's inaugural issue of *Sports Illustrated*'s *Women/Sport*. In the photos, physically brilliant teenage girls grind through training once reserved for boys. Their T-shirts read, "If it's too tough for you, it's just right for me."

Today's female superstars can revel in the full strength and talent of their bodies under the demanding tutelage of a professional—and for that I high-five the promoters of Title IX. But although intense competition ratchets up the payoff— glory, scholarships—it also increases the complexity of coach-player interactions. A broken foot no longer inspires such empathy, a slump shakes off not quite so easily. At thirty-six now, with more time to reflect than I ever had at bat, I guess I'm glad I was just a journeywoman, more gifted in passion and grit than in skill. My bush-league memories lack all ambivalence, and for their purity I credit three good men with the best of instincts and motives.

My coaches didn't need "policies" about how to treat girls. They weren't personal trainers or nutritionists or low-budget megalomaniacs—we weren't Eliza Doolittle jockettes to be whipped into athletic goddesses to their own glorification; no one ever got in our face. If we strove to win, we did not do so to compensate for grown-ups' own disappointments. They didn't earn a nickel for their time, they weren't social workers, they weren't sentimental about self-esteem—we had to get serious, we had to work hard. We weren't just a bunch of girls, we weren't cute—we were ball players. Just the title of the *WomenlSport* article—"The Coach as Sexual Predator: Are Young Girls Safe?"—would have made them blush; even in the late '70s, our affinities were not tainted by such concerns.

These men revealed to me the rewards of practice and persistence, the joy of camaraderie, the thrill of physical and mental mastery—and most certainly how to take a joke. But I cannot enumerate the values I carried into adulthood without listing the walking, talking blessings who still sustain and cheer me today—Cheryl, Cindy, Kelly, Shauna, Shirley—all of us pushing forty now, but who will always see in each other's aging bodies the scab-kneed teenager who overthrew backstops once, who clutched her nose after that wild pitch, who never missed a practice, moped if it rained on game day, and danced in the air with every victory.

I doubt one can set out to "build character" through sport; you have to love the game first, and more than anything, my coaches loved the game. In 1996, I visited Mr. Watts—L.C. to me by then—in intensive care. He'd suffered another of the strokes that would do him in that Christmas. I indicated the monitor above his head. "Who's winning?" I asked. He smiled, lopsidedly, and placed my hand over his heart.

At the funeral, you could have fielded a team—perhaps not a championship team, but a full team—with the women, my friends, who'd met him at the ballpark, twenty years earlier. Like all my coaches, he was just somebody's daddy—and always a little bit mine.

camper of the year

CAROL BERGMAN

Hot summer day. Mom says, Wear your halter top, carry water. I say, I'm taking my bike, I can't wear my halter top on the bike, Mom.

There it is in the garage waiting for me, black and shiny. I worked on it for hours last night with Dad. After we lowered the seat, waxed it up, and inflated the tires, I measured the wheels and recorded the diameter in my log book: 26 inches. First girl on the block with a 26-inch bike and I'm only twelve. The bike is a Raleigh from England, which impresses everyone I want to impress, Steve especially. Maybe now he'll let me into the softball game again, the one the boys play at the top of the hill every night before the sun goes down. I hit home runs when they let me, far and true.

Dad says I can borrow his rucksack if I promise not to lose it. In addition to water, I need to carry a compass, a wrench, a bathing suit, a towel, my lunch. He helps me pack it up the way he does when we go skiing together, the way he did when he was young and went on long hikes into the mountains in Austria. Roll the towel tight around the bathing suit, slip the water bottle into the outside strap, the wrench into a secret inside pocket, the compass into another pocket. Five leather straps to buckle down when I'm done.

While Mom's busy getting my sister, Joan, ready for Little Kids' Day Camp, I slip into the house and change my clothes. Instead of the halter and shorts I put on my jeans and a button-down shirt I starched so much it scratches my skin. It's 1956, my hair's in a ducktail, flipped up at the back, and my new white Keds sneakers—no scuffs, no bruises—squeeze my toes. By the end of the day they'll relax and I'll be able to see my toenails poking the canvas as they wrap around the pedals of my new bike.

Now I'm ready. I can hear the school bus lumbering up the hill and Mom rushing Joan. If you miss the bus again, I'm not taking you, she says. All the other little kids are at the designated stop in front of Steve's house. I pull the bike out of the garage and watch them for a while, hoping they've seen me. Rucksack, jeans and duck, my new Raleigh bike. A couple of them wave, I wave back. Then they're gone.

Dad's in the garage about to leave for work. I say, Thanks, Dad. And he says, You're welcome, kid. I say, Tell Mom I'll see her later. Don't tell her about the jeans. Just go, he says.

The first stretch of road is down the hill and the bike picks up speed fast. No gears, one hand brake for the back wheel. I know how it works, have been on many other bikes, but the weight of this one is different. I brake too much and slip on the gravel in front of the Segals' house. Sea Gulls, I call them. Old man Sea Gull looks like a bird. He's out there on his front lawn with his golf clubs, witnesses the fall. The bike skids and flies sideways, landing on top of me. Lucky I'm wearing jeans or my knees would be skinned.

I'm fine, I say, as he tries to help me up. Thanks, I'm fine.

Then I see Bryan standing behind him, laughing like a chipmunk, and Steve next to him, and Josh, their bikes, worn in, nearly beat-up, leaning against the fence. What are they doing here?

I'm glad you're okay, Sea Gull says. Your new bike is spiffy. From England, eh? I had a bike from England once. I bought it over there during the war, took it with me on the troopship coming home.

It's one of his stories. Bryan and Josh and Steve are still laughing. Now I'll be stuck here listening and they'll get to the field before me and tell everyone how stupid I looked when I fell. At Big Kids' Day Camp the boys are always laughing at the girls and the girls are always whispering about the boys.

I've got to go, Mr. Segal, I say. Thanks for helping me up.

I'm thinking more about the bike than about me. Maybe the fall dented the fender or threw the spokes out of alignment. No time to look. I want to get down to the field.

Now I'm riding fast again. Another five minutes and I'll be there. I don't see the boys, don't even think about them. It's just me, the seat of the bike under my bum, and fast thoughts, as I quickly turn onto a shortcut my dad takes when we've missed the bus and he drives me down. There it is in front of me, flat and hot. Nine a.m. and the steam is already rising off the gray-brown dirt. Or maybe it's the evaporating dew. Whatever it is, I'm reminded there's little shelter here, that we'll be out all day moving from one activity to the other, and that every other minute we'll be running to the water fountain or begging our counselors for free swim at the lake. The boys can hear us whining because whatever we do we're in proximity. They imitate us and then they giggle and poke each other in the ribs with their bony elbows. At the water fountain they poke some of the girls in the ribs and then there's more giggling. But they know better than to poke me. Last summer, I turned around and punched Josh in the stomach. Since then, they've let me alone. Now I'm older, I wouldn't mind a poke once in a while. Wouldn't mind the admiration the poke implies.

All day long I watch the boys in their own separate groups shouting, screaming, pushing, sweating, laughing. While the girls sit around making lanyards, they're out on the field busting balls out of their leather casings. I've got the schedule in my pocket, boys on one side, girls on the other. Arts, crafts, drama, free swim. Onto the field for the girls maybe once or twice a day. And, for the boys, just the opposite.

It makes me mad just thinking about this. The way boys get to play ball most of the time, the way the field is reserved for them. And, once we're out there, different rules.

Take basketball for instance. The boys have a full-press team, dribble dribble as they run down the court, then a toss to the basket. But the girls, you wouldn't believe it, no dribbling, walking, or running carrying the ball. Just catch, rotate, toss.

When I ask the counselor if we can play boys' rules, she says, Not in this lifetime, sister. She talks like a cowgirl on the westerns I watch on Saturday morning TV. Not in this lifetime, sister. Women in corsets talking out of the side of their mouths, shooting guns one minute and sidling up to the big boys in the bar the next.

Out on the softball field, I'm a slugger, but no one in my group can pitch or catch. I get up to bat and just stand there. It's an endless wait. Usually they ball me out and I walk around the bases. Today it's hot and I'm still not sweating, not as the boys sweat. I look over at my bike locked up on the rack and think, Hey, in a few hours I'll be out of here. Maybe earlier if I can slip away. My plan is to ride around the lake at full speed before I go home.

We eat our lunch at picnic tables under a shelter, the only shelter, on the far side of the field. Flies are buzzing around us like crazy. The boys are tossing garbage at each other and then at us, but after a while they settle down. More than the flies are buzzing today; there's a rumor the director of the camp is going to break color war, announce it as he usually does at the end of the day just before we lower the flag. Two and a half weeks to go to Labor Day, and if he doesn't do it this week, it won't happen. Everyone thinks today's the day, or, if not today, tomorrow.

So, big deal. Girls against girls and boys against boys in all the competitions, a mini-Olympics they usually tell us, just to get us hyped up. But for me it's the same old story. I want to smash the ball into the outfield, run against the boys in the leg races. When is someone going to understand that I can do this?

I'm not enjoying this day. In fact, all I'm getting out of it is the bike waiting for me at the rack. The girls are whining again about the heat and when they're not whining they're whispering in little clots—two, three, four of them. My peanut-butter-and-jelly sandwich is nearly melted onto the wax paper. The lemonade is sizzling. I want the boys to be my friends.

After rest time, sitting under a tree and working on the

green-and-blue box-stitch lanyard I'm making to carry my keys, we head to the lake for free swim. It's about a ten-minute walk from the field; no chance of taking my bike—I've asked. We're on a chain gang sucking up the air as we trudge the tarmac road.

Down at the lake, I get to be in a group with boys. It seems unprecedented, special. We're doing junior lifesaving, not that I get to save the boys or they get to save me or Shirley, the only other girl in the group. What would happen if Steve put his arm across my chest in a moment of life or death? Also during the artificial respiration, we're not allowed to touch. Instead, we get to work with the girl instructors. And occasionally one of the big-guy lifeguards lets me and Shirley pull him in. The rest of the time, we're sitting on the beach, listening to the instructor, studying first-aid manuals, serious business.

I don't know what the difference is between swimming and what happens on the field, why they let girls take junior lifesaving at all. It's a puzzle, I've decided. A brain bender. Maybe Dad made one of his phone calls, I'm thinking. Let my girl in. Let her in.

Midway through the afternoon, still down at the lake, I'm swimming freestyle races with Shirley in the lanes when I spot the copter in the distance. There's an army base near here so we see them pretty often, think nothing of it, then suddenly it's right over us churning up water, high-winding us onto the beach. We're huddled in our towels as the lifeguards and counselors start shrieking, COLOR WAR, COLOR WAR. The copter is so low now I can see a soldier dipping into a canvas bag and coming up with sheafs of paper, tossing them into the air right over our heads. In minutes, the paper is at our feet and the copter has banked away. They're headed for the field, one of the lifeguards says.

From now on, from this minute on, it's war.

We pick up the papers, scattered all around. It's a book, stapled top and bottom, more than ten mimeographed pages of instructions and schedules. The list of teams, one red, one white. Josh is on my team, Steve is on my team. And, by the look of it, boys and girls are going to compete against each other for the first time. I'm pumped.

That night at dinner, I tell Mom and Dad this news.

Why are you getting so worked up? my mother asks.

I get to play against the boys, I say. I get to hit. I get to run.

But there are thoughts I don't say out loud: Will Josh and Steve let me ride with them down to the field tomorrow morning? Or will they stick with Bryan even though he is on the white team?

Go, kid, my dad says. Go.

Next morning, I see Steve and Josh by the water tower with their bikes. We're all in red, the red team, Bryan nowhere in sight. This is the way it always is during color war; never associate with the enemy. I ride up to them, have one or two things to say, but before I can open my mouth, they take off.

I'm alone again riding down to the field, a red bandanna around my head, a red flag flying off my handlebars. I park the bike at the rack and head for opening ceremonies. The groups have been reorganized according to teams, red boys red girls, white boys white girls. Maybe I didn't read it right in the book. Maybe I'm excited for nothing. No, it's true. I'm going to get onto the field with the boys.

Suddenly I'm nervous. Suddenly I don't know if I belong here. But the excitement of the competition takes over. I want to win so bad I could spit. Now the girls are giggling, and the boys watching me warily.

I am all body and legs, motion and desire. Three days in and I'm winning everything. The 200-meter dash, the long jump, the backstroke, and the freestyle. Out on the softball field I smile so hard my cheeks hurt. Ten home runs. A double play from my favorite position in the outfield. On the fourth day, I'm appointed captain of the red team for twelve-year-olds.

Now I have to give instructions to everyone, keep the team spirit on the move. I don't want this role, but they've handed it to me. On the fifth day, I tell the counselors I can't do it. I'm not a coach, only a player. Give me a field, I'll run it. A ball, I'll hit it.

The red team's out ahead. The red team's going to win, they say. We're on the move, they say.

Closing ceremonies and Mom and Dad and my kid sister are in the audience. I'm called up to the podium to accept the trophy for my group, also a special award for me: CAMPER OF THE YEAR. I'm too young to make a speech and too innocent in my glory to grasp at this moment what has happened here.

recognition

KIM SCHAEFER

October
Colorado
The aspens are turning
A hue of yellow
I have never seen before
So golden
It is like riding my bicycle
Through waves of shimmering light
Adding to what is already
A truly dreamlike sequence

Rolling through the gates
Of the Olympic Training Center
Twelve women
Single-file
Single-minded
Heading toward Pike's Peak
To push, to climb
In rhythm
To take in gulps
Of the thin mountain air

We round the corner
An elementary school
A playground
Recess
Hundreds of children
It seems

As we roll by
The children recognize
Red
White
Blue
Suddenly there is silence
Movement stops

And in the next instant
The children
Begin to run
Yelling
Waving
Smiling
Toward the chain-link fence
Like a flock of seabirds
Descending on a beach

And I recognize
This as a moment
I shall remember
Forever
A moment
In which I am more
Than my mother taught me
I could be
More
Than my father expected
I would be
And I recognize
That this is what it is
To be exactly
What I am

from *a wheel **within** a wheel*

FRANCES E. WILLARD

> *. . . And so I called her Gladys, having in view . . .*
> *the gladdening effect of [my bicycle's] acquaintance*
> *and use on my health and disposition.*

From my earliest recollections, and up to the ripe age of fifty-three, I had been an active and diligent worker in the world. This sounds absurd; but having almost no toys except such as I could manufacture, my first plays were but the outdoor work of active men and women on a small scale. Born with an inveterate opposition to staying in the house, I very early learned to use a carpenter's kit and a gardener's tools, and followed in my mimic way the occupations of the poulterer and the farmer, working my little field with a wooden plow of my own making, and felling saplings with an ax rigged up from the old iron of the wagon-shop. Living in the country, far from the artificial restraints and conventions by which most girls are hedged from the activities that would develop a good physique, and endowed with the companionship of a mother who let me have my own sweet will, I "ran wild" until my sixteenth birthday, when the hampering long skirts were brought, with their accompanying corset and high heels; my hair was clubbed up with pins, and I remember writing in my journal, in the first heartbreak of a young human colt taken from its pleasant pasture, "Altogether, I recognize that my occupation is gone."

From that time on I always realized and was obedient to the limitations thus imposed, though in my heart of hearts I felt their unwisdom even more than their injustice. My work then changed from my beloved and breezy outdoor world to the indoor realm of study, teaching, writing, speaking, and went on almost without a break or pain until my fifty-third year . . . Sighing for new worlds to conquer, I determined that I would learn the bicycle.

. . . As a temperance reformer I always felt a strong attraction toward the bicycle, because it is the vehicle of so much harmless pleasure, and because the skill required in handling it obliges those who mount to keep clear heads and steady hands. Nor could I see a reason in the world why a woman should not ride the silent steed so swift and blithesome.

. . . At fifty-three I was at more disadvantage than most people, for not only had I the impedimenta that result from the unnatural style of dress, but I also suffered from the sedentary habits of a lifetime.

Gradually, item by item, I learned the location of every screw and spring, spoke and tire, and every beam and bearing that went to make up Gladys. This was not the lesson of a day, but of many days and weeks, and it had to be learned before we could get on well together. To my mind the infelicities of which we see so much in life grow out of lack of time and patience thus to study and adjust the natures that have agreed in the sight of God and man to stand by one another to the last. They will not take the pains, they have not enough specific gravity, to balance themselves in their new environment. Indeed, I found a whole philosophy of life in the wooing and the winning of my bicycle.

Just as a strong and skilful swimmer takes the waves, so the bicycler must learn to take such waves of mental impression as the passing of a gigantic hay-wagon, the sudden obtrusion of black cattle with wide-branching horns, the rattling pace of high-stepping steeds, or even the swift transit of a railway-train. At first she will be upset by the apparition of the smallest poodle, and not until she has attained a wide experience will she hold herself steady in presence of the critical eyes of a coach-and-four. But all this is a part of that equilibration of thought and action by which we conquer the universe in conquering ourselves.

I finally concluded that all failure was from a wobbling will rather than a wobbling wheel . . .

I began to feel that myself plus the bicycle equaled myself plus the world, upon whose spinning-wheel we must all learn to ride, or fall into the sluiceways of oblivion and despair. That which made me succeed with the bicycle was precisely what had gained me a measure of success in life—it was the hardihood of spirit that led me to begin, the persistence of will that held me to my task, and the patience that was willing to begin again when the last stroke had failed. And so I found high moral uses in the bicycle and can commend it as a teacher without pulpit or creed. He who succeeds, or, to be more exact in handing over my experience, she who succeeds in gaining the mastery of such an animal as Gladys, will gain the mastery of life, and by exactly the same methods and characteristics.

Once, when I grew somewhat discouraged and said that I had made no progress for a day or two, my teacher told me that it was just so when she learned: there were growing days and stationary days, and she had always noticed that just after one of these last dull, depressing, and dubious intervals she seemed to get an uplift and went ahead better than ever. It was like a spurt in rowing . . .

We saw that the physical development of humanity's motherhalf would be wonderfully advanced by that universal introduction of the bicycle sure to come about within the next few years, because it is for the interest of great commercial monopolies that this should be so, since if women patronize the wheel the number of buyers will be twice as large. If women ride they must, when riding, dress more rationally than they have been wont to do. If they do this many prejudices as to what they may be allowed to wear will melt away. Reason will gain upon precedent, and ere long the comfortable, sensible, and artistic wardrobe of the rider will make the conventional style of woman's dress absurd to the eye and unendurable to the understanding. A reform often advances most rapidly by indirection. An ounce of practice is worth a ton of theory; and the graceful and becoming costume of woman on the bicycle will convince the world that has brushed aside the theories, no matter how well constructed, and the arguments, no matter how logical, of dress-reformers . . .

We saw with satisfaction the great advantage in good fellowship and mutual understanding between men and women who take the road together, sharing its hardships and rejoicing in the poetry of motion through landscapes breathing nature's inexhaustible charm and skyscapes lifting the heart from what is to what shall be hereafter. We discoursed on the advantage to masculine character of comradeship with women who were as skilled and ingenious in the manipulation of the swift steed as they themselves. We contended that whatever diminishes the sense of superiority in men makes them more manly, brotherly, and pleasant to have about; we felt sure that the bluff, the swagger, the bravado of young England in his teens would not outlive the complete mastery of the outdoor arts in which his sister is now successfully engaged. The old fables, myths, and follies associated with the idea of woman's incompetence to handle bat and oar, bridle and rein, and at last the cross-bar of the bicycle, are passing into contempt in presence of the nimbleness, agility, and skill of "that boy's sister"; indeed, we felt that if she continued to improve after the fashion of the last decade her physical achievements will be such that it will become the pride of many a ruddy youth to be known as "that girl's brother."

If I am asked to explain why I learned the bicycle I should say I did it as an act of grace, if not of actual religion. The cardinal doctrine laid down by my physician was, "Live out of doors and take congenial exercise." But from the day when, at sixteen years of age, I was enwrapped in the long skirts that impeded every footstep, I have detested walking and felt with a certain noble disdain that the conventions of life had cut me off from what in the freedom of my prairie home had been one of life's sweetest joys. Driving is not real exercise; it does not renovate the river of blood that flows so sluggishly in the veins of those who from any cause have lost the natural adjustment of brain to brawn. Horseback-riding, which does promise vigorous exercise, is expensive. The bicycle meets all the conditions and will ere long come within the reach of all. Therefore, in obedience to the laws of health, I learned to ride. I also wanted to help women to a wider world . . .

It is needless to say that a bicycling costume was a prerequisite. This consisted of a skirt and blouse of tweed, with belt, rolling collar, and loose cravat, the skirt three inches from the ground; a round straw hat, and walking-shoes with gaiters. It was a simple, modest suit, to which no person of common sense could take exception.

As nearly as I can make out, reducing the problem to actual figures, it took me about three months, with an average of fifteen minutes' practice daily, to learn, first, to pedal; second, to turn; third, to dismount; and fourth, to mount independently this most mysterious animal. January 20th will always be a red-letter bicycle day, because although I had already mounted several times with no hand on the rudder, some good friend had always stood by to lend moral support; but summoning all my force, and, most forcible of all, what Sir Benjamin Ward Richardson declares to be the two essential elements—decision and precision—I mounted and started off alone. From that hour the spell was broken; Gladys was no more a mystery: I had learned all her kinks, had put a bridle in her teeth, and touched her smartly with the whip of victory. Consider, ye who are of a considerable chronology: in about thirteen hundred minutes, or, to put it more mildly, in twenty-two hours, or, to put it most mildly of all, in less than a single day as the almanac reckons time—but practically in two days of actual practice—amid the delightful surroundings of the great out-doors, and inspired by the bird-songs, the color and fragrance of an English posy-garden, in the company of devoted and pleasant comrades, I had made myself master of the most remarkable, ingenious, and inspiring motor ever yet devised upon this planet.

Moral: *Go thou and do likewise!*

grandmothers nowadays **play**

THEODORA SOHST

Visions of jet and real lace, thin, snowy-white hair, a little frilled cap and knitting! That delightful picture of the old-fashioned grandmother is rapidly fading from our memories . . .

Grandmothers nowadays play the game with us . . . In a letter to the [New York] *Herald Tribune* a few days ago a grandmother fifty-three years old relates how she won a swimming race against her daughter . . . The writer of the letter ends it with the question, "Will the grandmothers twenty years from to-day excel this?"

This is not only difficult to answer, but a dangerous speculation. If the seniors continue to improve at the same rate of speed as in the last generation the juniors will be obliged to do double quick time and then to "go some" to hold their own in the race. Judging from a few personal experiences and several observations, the modern girl looks like a losing bet.

Formerly no such thing as rivalry existed between mothers and daughters. Mothers quietly stepped aside and vacated cheerfully. Now they are in the ring on all occasions, not giving way an inch without a terrific battle . . .

my mother, **my** rival
MARIAH BURTON NELSON

The first time my mother and I competed against each other she was thirty-seven and I was five. We swam one lap of our neighbor's pool. She won.

As a five-year-old I didn't realize—and I don't think my mother realized—that she was teaching me about love. We thought we were just fooling around.

Later we had diving competitions, which she also won, though I would argue, and she would concede, that I deserved higher marks for versatility. For my jackknife, I would boing into the air, desperately grab my toes, then splash down on all fours. For my back dive, I would reach my hands meekly overhead, then fall into the water as if I'd been shot. Mom had only one dive—the swan dive—but if you do only one dive you can learn to do it very well. She'd fly skyward, arch like a ship's proud figurehead, then streamline toward the water and quietly, tapered toes last, disappear.

Eventually I gave up diving—pointing my toes always seemed so unnatural—but I joined a swim team, and by the time I was ten, I could outswim Mom. ("Oh, I don't know about that," responds my mother now. "I think you were eleven.")

Mom was my fan, too, when I would race against Jean and Joan Spinelli, the indomitable twins at Cedarbrook Country Club in our mini-town of Blue Bell, Pennsylvania. Jean had skinny arms as sharp and swift as Osterizer blades; Joan had furious legs that started kicking in mid-racing dive, like a windup bathtub toy. I didn't stand a chance.

But Mom would root for me anyway, yelling from the sidelines as if I could hear her underwater. She'd transport my friends and me to swimming meets all over the county (she liked to drive fast over the hilly, back-country roads so we'd fly up out of our seats and scream), and she even arranged practice time for me during family vacations to the New Jersey shore. It made me feel important to skip deep-sea fishing trips with my dad and siblings to work out at a pool.

Mom was also my teammate; the two of us ganged up on the Spinelli twins in the mother-daughter relay races at Cedarbrook's year-end championships. Mrs. Spinelli, a lounge lizard of sorts, had a great tan but no speed, so Mom and I were undefeated for six years until adolescence caught up with me and I left swimming for more important things, like basketball.

So when I think about competition I also remember the Spinelli twins, who would join me in the showers after the meets, the three of us giggling and whispering until all the hot water ran out. I think about Gordon, whom I later met on the basketball court; he would guard me by pushing on my waist with one hand and I still remember that push, and how much more honest it felt than my boyfriend's gropings. I remember six-foot-three-inch Heidi, my teammate, who would rebound the ball viciously, sharp elbows out; I hated her elbows but loved her audacity and her long strong hands, mirrors of my own. When I think about competition I realize that beginning with my fiercely, playfully competitive mother—who at fifty-five took up tennis and at sixty tried downhill skiing—athletes have taught me most of what I know about love.

Competition is about passion for perfection, and passion for other people who join in this impossible quest. What better way to get to know someone than to test your abilities together, to be daring and sweaty and exhausted together.

"If you compare yourself with others," a line in the inspirational prose poem "Desiderata" warns, "you may become vain and bitter, for always there will be greater and lesser persons than yourself." Yet I find that by comparing myself with other athletes, I become both self-confident and humble. Through competition, I have learned to acknowledge my failures and make allowances for the failures of others. Isn't that what intimacy is about?

But competition is not all fun and games. Like families, competitors can bring out the worst as well as the best in each other. Like romance, competition has many faces, some of them ugly. In addition to showing me my grace and graciousness, the mirror of sports has reflected back to me my jealousy, pettiness, and arrogance.

For instance: I have taken a friend to a tennis court and said, "Let's just hit a few," then fired the ball down her throat. I have, during a recreational, two-on-two volleyball game, refused to pass to my partner so we could win.

Believing that "competitive" was a dirty word, I used to say, "I'm not competitive, I just happen to be the best." My teammate Heidi and I had a tearful yelling match one night after a basketball game, and I accused her of not passing me the ball. "How am I supposed to score more than 19 points if you won't even look in my direction?" I screamed. "Why are you so competitive with me?"

"Look who's being competitive!" she countered. "Since when is 19 points something to be ashamed of? Only when it's compared to my 29, right?"

Later I told friends, "I've realized that I am in fact very competitive."

"No!" they said sarcastically. "You?"

I guess I was the last to notice.

But despite such humiliations, Heidi and I are good friends, and because we have played basketball together, she knows me better than friends who only chat with me over lunch. I am never more naked than in the heat of competition. I never feel more vulnerable than after flubbing a catch in the ninth inning, or rolling a bowling ball into the gutter.

In sports, as in love, one can never pretend.

For this reason some women avoid sports altogether; they choose not to unveil themselves in that way. In a society in which women's attractiveness is of utmost importance, why get muddy and sweaty and exhausted? Why risk anger, frustration, aggression, and other unseemly emotions? It is far safer to stay seated demurely in a café.

"I hate competition!" some friends have said to me. These are the women who were never taught how to throw or catch a ball, and I don't blame them. As an untrained musician, I know that if my childhood had been filled with music competitions, and I were chosen last for music teams and humiliated in front of other great musicians, I would resent both music and competition. Who enjoys doing things poorly?

A third reason many women have an ambivalent, if not downright hostile attitude toward sports—and why others embrace sports—is that team sports are an intense, physical activity. To play sports with women is to love women, to be passionate about women, to be intimate with women. How scary. Or, depending on your point of view, how thrilling.

So competition is about love, I noticed early, and, I noticed later, about fear. That's why I like to remember my childhood, when the love part was relatively pure, untainted by fear of failure, fear of looking like a fool, or fear of loving women. I feel blessed to have had a big brother who taught me how to throw, and a mother who never let me win. Even today, when I compete at water polo, bad-knee tennis, Nerf basketball, Ping-Pong, billiards—whatever I can persuade someone else to play with me—my favorite competitor is my mom. She is sixty-nine now, I am thirty-seven, and when I visit her in Phoenix, we still race. "Give me a head start," she'll suggest, "or better yet, I'll do freestyle and you swim backstroke, just kicking, okay?" If she wins, she smacks her hand against the wall, jerks her head up, and yells, "Ha! Beat you!"

I complain that she must have cheated. She splashes me. I dunk her. We laugh a lot. And I think, Yes, this must be love.

# of high-tops and home plates
DEBORAH ABBOTT

I am sitting by the river, by a wide lazy stretch of the American River. I feel lazy, too. A friend lies beside me on her belly, offering trail mix to some visiting ducks. Yesterday, our first on the water this season, was a long one. Up early, with just enough time to gulp coffee, we began hauling rafts to the eddy; pumping them up until they sounded as ripe as melons; rigging them with ice chests, medical supplies, emergency ropes, and bailing buckets.

We then greeted our passengers—a friendly group of men with AIDS—and assembled them in the boats. After final adjustments of the ten-foot ash oars, we were pushing off into the current. I gave a loud whoop of joy: back on the river again; the sun on my face; the muscles in my arms, back, and belly falling into that familiar rhythm. The water level was dropping, exposing more rocks than usual. So it was a "technical" day, requiring a sharp eye and more intricate rowing to avoid snagging obstacles. But all went well. The men got wet and silly, got tossed around the rafts through the rapids, with just enough mishaps to chalk it up to an adventure.

Today I'm feeling a little sore, somewhat weary and full of the contentment that rafting always brings. I cannot imagine my life without this distinct pleasure, without the challenges, that good fatigue. And yet, five years ago, I had never rafted, had never even sat beside a river for any time at all. Aside from an occasional swim, brief walks with friends, and some wild nights of lovemaking, the adventures I had had for much of my life had been in my imagination.

I was born with an insatiable curiosity, though, a lively spirit, and a strong body. My mother didn't believe in children sitting in darkened rooms watching TV on sunny days and so fed me breakfast and shooed me outside. There was a pine woods close by and half a dozen girlfriends with whom to explore. We built forts together, climbed trees, dug holes, buried and unburied treasures, played ball, swiped food from our mothers' kitchens, and generally ran amok. Nobody seemed to notice or care that I had one leg in a metal brace and wore only ugly brown high-top shoes. My friends walked a little slower for me, and Missy, who was the fastest sprinter and most ruthless slider, was my pinch runner. I felt good about my body. I had two sturdy arms, one extra-strong leg, and an endless supply of energy. Because I got included in everything, I barely noticed that I couldn't run bases, could only bicycle downhill.

In junior high, my adventures abruptly stopped. I spent most of seventh grade in an enormous cast in a narrow steel bed at Shriners Hospital in San Francisco. Orthopedists took turns slicing me open, rearranging my bones, sewing me up, and promising me a brace-free future. I would walk "normally," they assured me, without a limp. My body, which had taken so much delight in climbing, skipping, and moving freely through the woods, now required a nurse to turn from back to belly. My leg, which had never suffered more than the usual bruises and scrapes, was now ribboned with incisions, penetrated by metal pins, and consumed with pain that even Demerol couldn't relieve.

I returned to school in eighth grade and got put into Adaptive PE. While my friends were across the field playing baseball, a game I loved, I spent week after week playing four-square with girls who had cerebral palsy and could not catch the ball. I was humiliated; they were humiliated. My well-coordinated, agile body was bored, unchallenged. I skipped class as often as I could, feigning cramps and headaches. I began to hate my "bad" leg.

I became an intellectual; I disdained "dumb" jocks. Being a

clarinetist in the high school band, I had to go to football games. Between tunes I read Faulkner, Sartre, and O'Connor, rolling my eyes at the cheerleaders, the hulky players. I felt safer among the writers and artists. My leg was hidden beneath the café tables. I avoided beach parties, swim parties, and dances—any situation where my disability would be revealed. I had a witty mind, a quick tongue. I did a good job of distracting people from my difference. When friends walked ahead of me, I remained quiet, hoped they wouldn't notice, and concentrated on catching up.

I played this game, my only game, very well for twenty years. During this time I read many books, wrote a handful of stories, went to readings and concerts, and had countless animated conversations with friends. I kept busy with work, my education, and raising two sons.

Yet there was a growing restlessness in me. My lovers were mostly musicians who worked late into the night and slept until noon. I woke beside them as the sun rose, my insides screaming with impatience and the desire to move.

Somehow, despite my self-consciousness, I began to swim. I had learned to swim when I was two and recovering from polio. It was the only physical therapy I ever liked. I had fond memories of my big bear of a father carrying me on his back into the deep end of the pool, calling over his shoulder, "Kick, Debbie, kick!" It felt good, after all those years, to be back in the water. Once in the pool, my leg was mostly inconspicuous. I quickly developed speed and endurance and secretly challenged the swimmers in the lanes beside me. My friends began commenting on my broadening shoulders, my more confident stride.

One day, sometime later, I was standing with a friend, admiring a tall, muscled woman passing by. I sighed and said aloud, "If it weren't for my leg, I'd surely be a jock." My friend looked at me, puzzled, and commented matter-of-factly, emphatically, "But Deb, you *are* a jock."

I was startled. I shook my head. There was no such thing, I

knew, as a disabled jock. The terms were incompatible, as immiscible as water and oil. I had never seen a disabled athlete, though I had heard of one "courageous" man who had raced the Wharf to Wharf in a wheelchair.

Then I met a woman, an able-bodied woman, who was strikingly strong and physically capable. I was surprised to be approached by her, astonished to be seduced by her. Since childhood I had witnessed able-bodied people's discomfort with me, had grown accustomed to averted eyes and nervous smiles. I had experienced this avoidance particularly with athletic types. Disability is, after all, a jock's worst fear. Many jocks eventually become disabled from the accumulated stresses of the game, retiring from their sport to become coaches, sportswriters, and fans.

But this woman, who became my lover, seemed unfazed by my leg. Her wounds were on the inside, she said simply, mine on the outside. She pulled my brace out from under the bed where I always hid it and appreciated it for the interesting and valuable device it is. She was tender with both of my legs, with all of my body, and I believe that she found it more attractive and loved it better than I did. She came to know it well and to understand its possibilities, its limitations.

One morning, very early, she brought me to Seabright Beach. I peeled off my clothes, pulled on my swimsuit, took off my shoes and my brace. We walked arm in arm to the water, and for the first time in twenty-five years, I felt the surf swoosh over my bare feet. She held me as I walked into the waves, laughing and sobbing. The water was numbingly cold. I gasped as I plunged in and began to swim past the breakers. I was elated and terrified. I kept stroking. I looked back at the shore and said to myself, "There's no turning back now."

There has been no turning back. Over time, my lover taught me to row, to Boogie-board. She literally dragged me up mountainsides, pushed me over boulders, carried me down riverbanks. Years later, I can say, with only slight hesitation, that I am a jock. I spend a good deal of time on my tandem, in the ocean, on the river, in the pool. I work springs and summers as a sea-kayak and whitewater-raft guide with a company that specializes in making trips accessible for people with special needs.

In all this time, I have met only one other disabled athlete, a woman in a chair who plays basketball. She invited me to watch a game, to join the team. I have not yet had the courage to go, or join. While I long to be part of a team, I am a klutz in a wheelchair, and honestly, I have a great fear of the thing. One day I may need one, not just for playing in. My brace slows me down and constrains me in some ways, but I do not experience the profound barriers or the stigma that wheelchair users do. Not yet. As I imagine myself watching a game from the sidelines, a huge grief wells up in me. Even watching my children play soccer, or my able-bodied friends play softball, can be hard. I get sad. I get mad. I feel excluded. I *am* excluded.

Being disabled and athletic isn't easy. I am constantly reminded of my limitations, confronted with my pain. Sometimes I want to go back to the world of concerts and poetry readings, to take refuge in that place.

But most often, I want to go back, way back. I want to be ten again, at bat, with Missy poised to charge to first base for me. I remember what a powerful hitter I was, how my friends had to scramble to the far reaches of the field for the ball. I want to be ten again, in my clunky little brace and my dusty old high-tops, squinting at home plate from the pitcher's mound. I want to be regular, just one of the girls.

swimming and writing

MAXINE KUMIN

I can't remember when I learned to swim. I know that as a small child of four or five I was terrified of the waves at Atlantic City, where we spent a few weeks each summer in my grandmother's Victorian apartment overlooking the beach. Waves that seemed reasonable to adults toppled me even though I was held firmly by the hand, perhaps even swung between two grown-ups who endeavored to lift me over the largest combers. That was when I learned the little ditty: "I hate to swallow ocean and it's all God's fault. / He could have put in sugar but He went and put in salt."

The combers were so menacing some days that lifeguards strung ropes out to their rowboats and bathers were forbidden to go beyond the prescribed limit. Bathing in saltwater was thought to ensure good health. Weekend afternoons in July there would be hundreds of people of all ages and stages crowded into the roped-off areas, nervously policed by life-guards continually manning their oars to hold their positions. Sometimes they put on exhibitions to demonstrate their skills to the general public. They swam short, choppy crawl strokes with their heads held high, breasting out over the waves the way I imagined seals might do. I was in awe of these burly, magnificent showmen and their noble calling.

Swallowing ocean makes you wary. This awareness of the nervous balance between staying alive and drowning taught me to respect the power and majesty of nature. However much I might have longed to be one, I learned early that I was not an amphibian.

And then one magical day, I floated with my face in the water. My feet rose to the surface of their own accord. I blew bubbles, exulting in my buoyancy. At a rather casually run day camp in Ambler, Pennsylvania, the summer I was eight, I turned into a swimmer. Released from the Tadpole Group into deep water, I learned how to execute the sidestroke. That same memorable summer I learned how to jump into deep water and graduated to performing a rudimentary dive.

Breaststroke, elementary backstroke, Australian crawl, and back crawl came later, at sleep-away camp in the Berkshires. Back crawl was done in the Eleanor Holm tradition, a sort of straight-armed windmill style. The butterfly stroke was harder to master. In those days, before the dolphin undulations were developed, it was accompanied by a whip kick. And the inverted breaststroke, my favorite resting stroke, taught me to accept wavelets washing over my face as I glided on my back.

Summer camp was my salvation. I returned year after year, first as camper, then junior counselor, then assistant to the head of the waterfront. I finally succeeded to the top post the summer after my sophomore year in college. That same year I studied English poetry from Chaucer to Robert Bridges and began to appreciate the rules of prosody, but there was no conscious overlap between my twin responsibilities. While poetry absorbed me in the winter, there was no question of my loyalties from June to Labor Day. Only marriage removed me—rescued me, my husband likes to say—from those hectic and happy Berkshire summers.

The waterfront counselor, my first three summers as an overnight camper, was a member of the Dartmouth swimming team and he possessed a real stopwatch. And he didn't discriminate between the genders; girls were encouraged to race against each other and against the boys from the other side of the campus as well. At ages eleven or twelve, we girls took great pleasure in besting the skinny, shivering preadolescent boys we were ranged against.

In addition to his stopwatch, Johnny the Dartmouth Man had an eight-millimeter movie camera. He took pictures of our crawl strokes, then played the film back for us slow motion, critiquing our faults. It was wonderful to be taken seriously. What I learned about the freestyle, or Australian, crawl was how to achieve maximum thrust with minimum exertion. Many years later, I learned to apply the same criterion to the poem, seeking a seemingly artless effect with the maximum thrust—pages and pages of worksheets subjected to formal compression.

I remember practicing my racing dive those summer afternoons until my entire torso ached from the repetitive harsh contact with the lake's surface. I remember practicing the cross-chest carry, the surface dive to retrieve a ten-pound weight in ten feet of water. I remember wrinkled fingers and toes from long immersion and deep suntans, then the swimmer's badge of honor.

My idyllic summers at camp also included distance swimming, and I think it was there, crossing the mile-wide lake solo (accompanied by a counselor in a rowboat), that I first began to match the rhythm of memorized poems to the stroke-breath-stroke of the trudgen crawl. Sometime around my sixteenth birthday I had been given a copy of A. E. Housman's "A Shropshire Lad" and, without making any conscious effort to do so, had committed a good portion of the book to memory. I swam to Housman's cadences, his classic romantic elegiac voice suffusing my long-distance swims with gentle melancholy. "With rue my heart was laden," I droned, swiveling my head for the next intake of air. "For golden friends I had," I bubbled, breathing out into the water.

Summer camp was the setting for my poem "Morning Swim," which speaks to those early-morning solitary swims half a mile down the lake, half a mile back. It was my dearest dream at that time to become a member of the women's Olympic swim team, and in pursuit of it—I hesitate to put the connection into words—I merged with the water, moving in and through this medium that recalled unconsciously the amniotic fluid where I had begun. "Morning Swim" concludes: "My bones drank water, water fell / through all my doors. I was the well / that fed my lake, that met my sea / in which I sang 'Abide with Me.'" I hesitate to undercut these lines with creeping exegesis, but obviously they convey that sense of merging with what Conrad called "the destructive element."

By now I had acquired my American Red Cross junior and senior lifesaving certificates as well as the advanced swimmer's logo, proudly if somewhat crookedly sewn to my best bathing suit, the one I wore for showing off at swim meets. Now I was swimming winters as well at the Broadmoor pool in downtown Philadelphia, where I had the good fortune to encounter an exacting instructor. I wish I could remember Alex's last name, but I can never forget his earnest manner, his insistence on exactitude. He inspired me to be even more economical of breath and stroke. Nothing was to be squandered, everything was to be streamlined to achieve perfect harmony with the water. "Now, class," Alex would intone, "I want you simultaneously, at the same time, together . . . " to perform whatever the next maneuver was to be. The parallel with poetry is obvious—economy of expression, nothing squandered—but even more delicious was his entirely innocent redundancy. *Simultaneously at the same time together* became a kind of mantra for me, something I muttered grittily to myself in the last turn of the 400-meter freestyle.

Just before my eighteenth birthday, the directors of the summer camp I had attended faithfully from age eleven paid my tuition to attend a two-week-long crash course in Annapolis, Maryland. The goal was to acquire my Water Safety Instructor's certificate. Once I passed this course, they intended to hire me back as a senior waterfront counselor. It was a watershed moment (no pun intended) for me; it provided entry into a possible career teaching swimming and lifesaving, and training other swim instructors.

Teaching Junior Lifesaving to a group of shivering twelve-year-olds gave rise to one of my early poems, "Junior Lifesaving," which again addresses the paradox of immersion in and giving in to the water:

Class, I say, this is
the front head release.
And Adam's boy, whose ribs
dance to be numbered aloud,
I choose to strangle me.
Jaw down in his embrace
I tell the breakaway.
Now swimming in the air
we drown, wrenching the chin,
clawing the arm around.
   . . .
Class, I say (and want
to say, children, my dears,
I too know how to be afraid),
I tell you what I know:
go down to save.

That same year I was approached by a representative of Billy Rose's Aquacade, an outfit that performed synchronized swimming routines in public pools and hotels around the country. Synchronized swimming was touted as poetry in motion. A perfect fit. The pay seemed munificent, one hundred dollars a week plus all expenses. A chaperon was provided; travel was by streamlined bus—in the 1940s, travel by air was uncommon and expensive. An adventure! My father was horrified and forbade me even to consider such an offer. He had never particularly approved of my swimming addiction in high school and found it offensive that I came to supper with my long hair only hastily toweled, still dripping chlorinated droplets onto the dinnerware. Even when I made the swim team at college he felt I was wasting time better spent in intellectual pursuits.

For the poet, nothing is ever all for nothing. This incident worked its way into a poem, "Life's Work," ostensibly about my mother, whose desire to be a concert pianist was thwarted by her stern Germanic father. The poem describes my eighteen-year-old self at the dinner table, inwardly rebelling, outwardly conforming:

My mouth chewed but I was doing laps.
I entered the water like a knife.
I was all muscle and seven doors.
A frog on the turning board.
King of the Eels and the Eel's wife.

In each of these figures of speech, I am something other than human: first, as narrow, as precise (and perhaps dangerous) as a knife; then, a creature made all of muscle, with seven orifices; next, the magical amphibious frog, at home in and out of water; and, finally, the royal and androgynous Eel and Wife of Eel, wily, swift, and incredibly graceful in its element.

I longed to go to Wellesley College because it had a regulation-sized swimming pool surrounded by high windows and an underwater observation room that permitted close analysis of the swimmer's movements. The admissions committee rejected me. Radcliffe was my second choice. Radcliffe, however, had only a dingy little swimming pool, five yards shy of standard length and housed in a basement room without windows.

Team sports got only a cursory nod from the administration; back then, Cliffies were notorious for their indifference to athletic pursuits. Thus it was no great feat to make the team. Our only competitions were with nearby schools. Tufts's Jackson and Brown's Pembroke are two I remember. Of course neither Tufts nor Brown was coeducational in the 1940s. Women's teams were condescended to, underfunded, and unpublicized. Still, we took ourselves very seriously; we trained, we strategized, and frequently we lost. But the camaraderie of belonging to a team, the participatory democracy of choosing who was to swim what stroke in the medley, the cheerful determination to do the best we could with the personnel we had made my four undergraduate years in that dank basement a rich experience.

My poem "400-Meter Freestyle," the only "shaped" poem I have ever written (the beginnings and endings of each line reproduce the flip turn at the end of each lap), arose from my memory of those glory days of college competition, the somersaulting turns, the punishing pace. The poem is written in the male persona only because at the time of its composition—the late '50s—I did not think the average reader would be willing to invest much emotion in a female competitive swimmer. The language of the poem attempts to describe the event from two points of view, that of the swimmer:

> THE GUN full swing the swimmer catapults and cracks
>
> s
> i
> x
>
> feet away onto that perfect glass he catches at . . .

and that of the observer:

> . . . We watch him for signs. His arms are steady at
>
> t
> h
> e
>
>   catch, his cadent feet tick in the stretch, they know
> t
> h
> e
>   lesson well. Lungs know, too, he does not list for
>
> a
> i
> r . . .

When our children were young, I renewed my Water Safety Instructor's certificate and became head counselor of the waterfront at a Girl Scout Day Camp not far from our home in suburban Boston. It was a hectic schedule, getting three kids ready to catch the morning bus that transported us to the camp, monitoring more than a hundred youngsters all day in and out of the water, and experiencing a rising sense of helplessness as I was unable to teach our youngest child and only son, then going on six, how to swim. This was a child who almost died at birth and subsequently spent his first weeks on oxygen in an incubator.

"Poem for My Son" came out of that difficult beginning, heightened for me by our son's inability to take to the water with the other kids of staff members at camp. I set it at the ocean, no doubt harking back to my own early years at Atlantic City when the ocean seemed menacing as well as exciting. Once again, it examines the dangerous balance between breathing air and inhaling water. It's metrically a very taut piece written in iambic trimeter, rhyming *abab cdcd* and ending on a rhymed couplet, an exacting discipline that paradoxically makes it easier for me to confront charged issues—in this instance, maternal love. Here is the first stanza:

Where water laps my hips
it licks your chin. You stand
on tiptoe looking up
and swivel on my hands.
We play at this and laugh,
but understand you weigh
now almost less than life
and little more than sea.
So fine a line exists
between buoyance and stone
that, catching at my wrists,
I feel love notch the bone
to think you might have gone.

I could point to at least half a dozen other early poems of mine that attend to the art of learning how to swim, learning to perform the simple sidestroke, as in "The Lesson": "and let us change sides, remembering / it is the top leg goes forward / forming the blade of the scissors." At the close of the lesson,

> I lie flat
> on the rib cage of a canoe
> assaulting the thin edge of water,
> holding the noon on my eyelids.
> Now there is only the water
> and the sound of water forming
> under the slope of my spine.

It seems I am once again attempting to pinpoint the relationship of human to water, water as friend but also as foe. The sensuous experience, the closeness of body to pond as the speaker of the poem lies sunbathing in a canoe, ends with three lines repeated from the body of the poem, followed by an ominous fourth:

> wherefore the season reverses,
> the dragonfly clicks and is gone,
> the cattails resist in the marshes,
> drowned men thrust under my bone.

I still swim regularly, from mid-June to mid-September in our own pond on the farm, and catch-as-catch-can the rest of the year, when I'm on the road doing readings and residencies. Swimming competitively taught me the value of daily discipline, for muscles unused soon atrophy. Lines of poems unattended disappear. Rilke said it best when he counseled the young poet to "keep holy all that befalls." For me, swimming is another way of keeping holy.

green afternoons

BARBARA DAVENPORT

The photograph is a three-by-three-inch black-and-white square, bordered in white, with a scalloped edge. Inside its frame Nancy Schmidt and I squint into the September sun that glares in our eyes, bleaches the detail out of our faces, turns the red-gold maples behind us to a dark blur. Nancy's arm rests on my shoulders, a reach for her, because the top of her head comes even with my cheekbones. She is compact and solid; even in this casual pose her body looks strong, conveys her sense of determined purpose. Her hair, white in the photograph, is blond, thick, poofed on top, and combed into thin bangs across her forehead. My arm, which might have draped across her back, hangs stiff at my side between us.

We're wearing our field hockey uniforms, white broadcloth blouses, short-sleeved, with round collars, and Bermuda shorts that the photograph makes black but I know to be our school color, navy blue. We wear white Keds and white ankle socks.

Fifty of us show up for practice in the hot September afternoon. In two weeks we'll be cut to thirty, fifteen for varsity, fifteen for JV. After school, carrying our sticks and shin guards and water jugs and the heavy canvas duffels that hold the nets, we walk in a long, unhurried, and talkative procession the three blocks from school to the Bell Tower field. The field is limed for hockey and surrounded on three sides by woods that are green at the start of the season. The trees' earthy, leafy smell mingles with the grass scent that rises as we run our warm-up laps.

After our laps we sit panting on the grass and buckle on our shin guards. They are gray leather, with rows of vertical stitching that hold in place strips of bamboo that stiffen them. They look martial, reminiscent of medieval Japanese armor. Two leather straps stretch across the backs of our calves, slip into chromed buckles. We find our sticks, which look like J's with their curls cut a little short. The shaft, taped and sweat-stained at the grip, tapers to flat on one side and slightly rounded on the other; at the bottom is the curve, where we hit the ball with the flat side. Armored and armed, we troop onto the field, array ourselves for scrimmage.

My afternoons fill with running, against a backdrop of greens. The grass is bright and lush under my feet, prickly against my cheek when a defender's stick sends me sprawling face first into it, and the trees' darker shade flashes at the edge of my vision. My ears ring with the hard clatter of sticks against each other, the muffled thunk of stick against shin guard, and the solid smack against the ball. The taste of metal hangs in the back of my throat, sweat drenches my shirt, and I learn the sweet, hard pleasure of my body at work.

I don't say anything about the grass smell or my animal pleasure in running. No one else talks about what they smell or see. I wonder whether Nancy likes the grass smell. I read a story by Hemingway, about a man and his friend in Austria, jumping from a train into a snowdrift, walking herringbone on their skis up the side of a mountain, skiing down together. Their day is rich with sensations and pleasures, and all they say to each other is "It's good." We are as contained as Hemingway's men.

The girls who come out for field hockey are a surprise. Rosemary Crain is small-boned, delicate, her outfits perfectly matched, her hair unmussed; I cannot imagine that she sweats. But there she crouches, blocking my path to the goal. She maneuvers her stick behind mine, flicking away the ball I thought I had, smacking it down the field. Sue Pollard, a senior, unapproachable and aloof at school, here runs and shrieks with the rest of us. Lisa Reiner's arms jiggle when she trots; her huge thighs bulge out of her shorts, and her ankles buckle permanently outward. How can she be here? What can she do? I find out: her passes always go where she aims them, and of all of us, only Lisa can drive the ball the full length of the field. Field hockey teaches me to suspend my assumptions about bodies and about what people can do.

Nancy just started at Mariemont this fall. She's in a couple of my classes, but she's so quiet I hardly notice her. At practice she's just as quiet, but I can't miss her. She goes at everything we do with a focused, stubborn intensity. She runs every warm-up lap, pays attention in all the drills, really works at them. She learns every pass and stick maneuver and shot, practices them even after the drill's over with anyone who'll do it with her. When we scrimmage she plays every shot as though it will decide the game.

Mrs. Hobbs watches us scrimmage, makes notes on her clipboard. Her thighs are wide and muscular, and she is very tan. Her hair is cut short, her face is square, and her voice is low and husky. She wears warm-up suits to school, even to teach her health classes, the first time I've seen anyone other than a basketball player wear them. I'm curious about her, and I want her to like me, but I don't want her to think I'm interested in anything about her. I don't want to be a gym teacher.

"Center halfback runs the team on the field," Mrs. Hobbs tells us. "Center half follows the flow of play, directs the other players."

Nancy knows that's her position.

I play center forward. I'm not an especially skillful ball handler, and I'm not as fast as the wings or as good a shot as the inners. What I am is willing to charge upfield into a mess of defenders, work the ball through the welter of legs and flashing sticks out to the rest of my line, who can sweep it down the sidelines, back in toward the goal, and shoot. Nancy plays behind me. When I lose the ball, Nancy chases down the defender, battles her for it. She shoots it back to me, tells me when to pass, shouts at me when defenders are bearing down from behind.

On the day the teams are posted, I stroll with forced casualness to the bulletin board outside Mrs. Hobbs's office. Nancy's already there, her usually stiff face relaxed into a broad grin. She clamps the back of my neck and squeezes.

"We made JV!"

"Hey, great." I turn from the list and look at her. "You made it work."

"What do you mean?"

"You feed me the ball."

"You're doing your own job."

"I wouldn't be there if you weren't behind me."

Her blue eyes light up. She looks at me so hard I know I'm right, that she set out to get us on the team together, me playing in front of her.

I'm amazed. The only place in my whole life I know how to make anything work, or even feel I could, is schoolwork. I can read fast, figure stuff out, know the answers. Everywhere else I'm a field hockey ball, caroming off other people's sticks.

Nancy's getting a B minus in English, and she knows how to do this.

Lisa Reiner brings her Brownie camera to our first game, and Mrs. Hobbs takes a picture of the whole team. Then girls come up to Lisa in twos and threes, and she poses them in front of a big maple. Nancy grabs my arm, pulls me over to the tree, and when it's our turn we grip our sticks and squint into the sun.

On a day in mid-October the trees around the field are burning orange and yellow. We play Hillsdale, the girls' school that Ann Early and Ellen Brooks went to when the rest of us moved to junior high. We always want to beat Hillsdale.

Their sticks are brand-new and unscarred. They wear green kneesocks over their shin guards, and they have real uniforms, short jumpers with a block H on the front. They have lots more players, so they can sub in and out and the players on the field are always fresh. Their forwards play better than we do. They move the ball better, pass around our fullbacks and score. Their fullbacks are a stone wall. I charge and pass, our wings shoot when they can, but nothing gets through. Their players are polite, almost detached; we aren't worth their getting excited. They beat us 6–0.

As we walk back to school afterward the carillon chimes five o'clock. The sky is losing its light and the trees are silhouetted black. Now that we've stopped running, the air is chill against our damp backs. I forgot my sweatshirt, and I'm starting to shiver. Nancy is walking beside me, still breathing hard. I feel the heat rising from her body; I want to stay close to her.

"Jeez it gets cold."

"You want my sweatshirt?" she offers.

"Then you'll be cold."

"Take it." She's already pulled it off, and she holds it close to my face. "Take it. I don't want you cold."

I pull it over my head. It's still warm from her body. I want to throw my arm across her shoulder. I don't know what she'd think. I mutter, "Thanks."

We walk, and the silence between us is cozy, like being inside her sweatshirt. I don't want it to stop.

"You played great today," I say. "I wish I could have done better with what you gave me."

"They were tough."

I take a deep breath. "Even when it's 6–0, I really like playing with you."

We're looking down at the sidewalk as we walk. Nancy slows, and turns toward me with the gaze I've come to know. She studies my face, looking for something. She smiles a cautious half smile. "I like it, too."

The silence blooms between us, too big, too important. I have to break it.

"Hey, Lisa," I yell. "Let's catch up with Lisa." I grab Nancy's arm, break into a trot, pull her along until we've caught up with Lisa. "Hey, Lisa, you sure made 'em work for everything they got."

Lisa and I talk the rest of the way back to school. Nancy walks beside me, and she doesn't speak.

. . .

If I knew Nancy only in class, I'd never know what she was like. I wouldn't even know she was there. She never offers anything. Speaking up is dangerous for her, as though her thoughts could get her in trouble. She looks at me in class, walks with me over to the field, never lets on what she's thinking. I pretend I don't notice, but I'm pleased she wants to be around me.

When we are sophomores Nancy and I make the varsity squad. Nancy makes it because she can think on the run, call the moves. I make it because I'm not afraid of running into people. My teammates admire me for this; they think I'm brave. It doesn't have anything to do with bravery. I like running into people. There's something about taking the slam that makes me feel powerful, more alive. I don't tell anyone this. It feels weird and wrong. Girls aren't supposed to hit people, and they sure aren't supposed to like it.

By our junior year, Nancy and I and Lisa and Rosemary and Ginny Catlett and Meg Safer have played together enough that we know each other's moves. We can pass on the run with the certainty that the other will know where to go, will be where the ball is going. The moments when it works like that give me a deep pleasure.

In the fall of our senior year we walk the familiar three blocks to the field, run our warm-up laps without being told. This is our last season to play together. That knowledge hangs in the air from the first lap we run.

"Last year's varsity players over here," Mrs. Hobbs calls. We gather around her in clumps, breathing hard. "Indian Hill's coming next Monday."

We look at each other. We've only practiced a week, and she hasn't even made cuts.

"Just a scrimmage. A chance for their coach to get a look at her players, and for me to see what you can do."

Indian Hill's team was good last year. On Monday it looks even better. They have two new defenders who are taller than any of us and very fast. In the first half we're scrambling. At halftime it's 0–0. Just before the whistle blows to start the second half, we huddle at midfield.

Nancy looks around the huddle. "Let's break this open. This is our year."

Their center forward snakes her stick around mine and steals the ball. She chips it to her left wing, and their whole team surges down into our half of the field. Their forwards and halfbacks swarm our goal, a blur of red pinnies. Their wing shoots; it's deflected, but a red inner gets it from our fullback and shoots again, for the far corner of the net. Meg, our goalie, wheels, barely gets her stick on it. She recovers, dribbles a few feet to her left, then shoots it out to Lisa, who dodges through the pack of players until she's in the clear, and then lofts it fifty yards upfield.

When I see Meg send the ball to Lisa I dash upfield; I know what's coming. An Indian Hill halfback sees it, too, runs hard, tight on my right shoulder. Lisa's ball soars over our heads, and now it's coming down ten yards across the field to our right. The red halfback veers in toward it.

From the corner of my eye I see Nancy get there first. She looks across the field at me, and our eyes lock. Hers are intensely blue, hungry and sure. She waits until the halfback is nearly on top of the ball, fully committed in her swing. Then she flicks the ball neatly over the halfback's stick, to about ten yards ahead of me, so as I run down the field, slanting in toward the goal, it's there waiting for me. I gather it with my stick, and turn forty-five degrees, toward the goal. The goalie charges out to meet me. I run straight at her, and when she shoots out her stick to block my shot, I drop a half step right and drive it hard behind her heels, deep into the back of the net.

I'm still running, following my shot. Nancy's running in from her side of the field, in case she needs to assist. Our angles converge in front of the goal, and we fall into each other's arms, holding each other for a long moment. Our forwards and halfbacks swarm down the field and surround us. I hear their voices, feel their hands thumping my back, but they are very far away. I've buried my face in Nancy's shoulder so I can't see her. If I looked at her now the way she looked at me across the field, I wouldn't ever let go.

After the game Mrs. Hobbs talks to us. "You've got the skills, and you've got the chemistry. Keep playing like you did today, and we can take the league."

The scene runs over and over in my mind: Lisa's soaring pass, Nancy's sure pounce on the ball, her look across the field to me, then flicking it past the halfback to where she knew I'd be. The chemistry, Mrs. Hobbs called it. Then she's holding me, and I don't want to let go. If we keep playing like this, there'll be more looks between us, more goals, more holding.

With every practice Nancy and I know each other's moves more surely. The better we play, the more nervous I feel around her. The better our game gets, the more I need it to stop.

Nancy's arms are hard against me, and her back is solid and hot. Her neck where my face lay was soft and smelled of grass and sweat and perfume. My hands press her muscular arms again, my fingers rub the hollow between her shoulder blades, caress the small of her back. I press my body against hers, push all of her into me. Then my hands find the buttons of her shirt, I unbutton them, and I look at her. I sit up in bed, shaking with desire and terror.

I can't want that. I do. I can't.

The next day I walk out of Government, my last class, and instead of heading down the stairs to the girls' locker room, I walk to the door and start out for home. All that week I don't go to practice.

Friday, game day, Nancy finds me in the auditorium, where the seniors have homeroom. She walks up to me, her jaw set, her eyes full. She speaks without preface.

"Where've you been all week?"

"I had stuff to do."

"You've had practice."

"I always have practice. I've had practice for four years. Sometimes I feel like doing other stuff."

She looks at me uncomprehending.

"I'm really getting tired of field hockey. I'm thinking I might not play this year."

I might as well have slapped her. Shades come down in her eyes, her face empties to its classroom blankness.

"Well, I'm thinking about it," I plead.

The snapshot of Nancy and me has sat at the bottom corner of my mirror, edge slid under the frame, for two years. I can't look at it anymore. I pull it out from the frame and shove it into my top drawer, under a pile of hair ribbons, old programs, notes and pictures and scarves.

I know what I have to do.

Before class on Monday I find Mrs. Hobbs in her office. I talk fast. "I don't think I can play this year. I've got college applications and Advanced Comp— that's a theme every week you know—and I'm co-editor of the paper, and I'm just too busy."

She lifts her eyes from her papers, leans back in her chair, and looks at me, a long, open look. She exhales slowly. "We'll miss you. Turn in your equipment to my office."

What does she know? Can she tell?

Away from Nancy, away from the grass and the running and the long passes across the field, it's easier not to think about her. I need to stay away from that. The afternoons are delicious, the first fall afternoons since eighth grade I haven't spent on a hockey field. I walk home with Margaret, scuffing through piles of leaves as we talk. Some days we do homework together. I read A. E. Housman; once in a while I take a nap.

That stuff I was thinking about was just a mistake. Sports are so sweaty, and Mrs. Hobbs and some of those girls get so worked up over the game it's ridiculous. Anyway I care more about literature. I work hard writing my themes for Advanced Comp, I keep myself busy on the paper, and I do my best not to think about Nancy. Sometimes at night, when the house is quiet and I'm the only one still awake and I'm too tired to think about my work, I see her face when I told her I was quitting, and I know how much I've hurt us both.

I couldn't help it. There wasn't anything else I could do. I can't be one of those girls. I can't turn into someone like Mrs. Hobbs. I can't want to kiss a girl.

There are days that October, and there are days still, when the air snaps with cold and the sky is bright and cloudless, and I wonder what I could have had if I'd stayed. In my mind I run down the wide green field toward the ball, and from across the field Nancy runs toward me, her eyes shining and her arms reaching for me. I drop my stick and turn across the field and run to her, my arms open wide.

from *swimming* the *channel*

SALLY FRIEDMAN

I have swum for almost as long as I have walked, at first because I had an aptitude, later because it soothed my soul, kept me sane. Swimming lessons began the summer I was three years old. I think I remember learning how to swim, but it is possible that my memories have become entangled in years of seeing others taught, slippery little children slithering through water, holding the hands of their teachers as they try to master the art of blowing bubbles, or turning their heads to the side to breathe. Those first few years, before I started competing, I swam only in the summer. Afraid that I would forget how to swim over the winter, I tried to practice in the bathtub.

My earliest trophy is dated 1960. I was four years old, almost five, and wore an inner tube because that was the rule. The race was half the length of the pool, from the rope across the middle to the wall at the shallow end. Each child was held by a parent, who pushed as hard as he or she could, to give their own the best start. I had already passed the deep-water test, as my mother has told friends and strangers so often that I almost remember it. I was allowed anywhere in the large pool, unsupervised. As the years passed, I felt more and more out of place at my parents' country club, but I still coveted that swimming trophy, there to be won at the end of every summer. I might not have been very popular but I could swim faster than anyone my age, boy or girl.

By the age of seven, I was swimming on a team. Workouts took place after school in the days before goggles. Most nights I lay on my bed with a cool, wet washcloth resting heavily on my face, soaking my burning, red-rimmed eyes. Maybe this is why I have always cried too easily, a tearing reflex meant to soothe the pain. Lights were nestled in multicolored halos, my bad eyesight blurry even with glasses. The advent of goggles sent swimming times plummeting. Athletes could suddenly train for thousands of yards without hurting their eyes. But they arrived too late for me. I had already given up. Most world-class athletes thrive on the adrenaline rush that races produce; the tension had the opposite effect on me. The starter's gun was fired and time stopped. I flew through the air, plunged into the water, arms outstretched, streamlined, and all that was familiar became strange. My rhythm was out of sync, the water slipped away from my reaching hands, my shoulders tightened like rubber bands ready to snap. I was one of the fastest swimmers on our local team but was put to shame whenever we had a national meet. The Olympics were never in my future. I retired from competitive swimming my senior year of high school, tired of losing to girls who had grown so much bigger and faster than I, tired of spending the better part of meets in the bathroom with a queasy stomach. But I never stopped swimming. I have the sense to know that it is what keeps me from going off the deep end.

My marathon-swimming career was born in 1983 out of disappointment, out of a need to prove something. For the second time I had failed the United Scenic Artists exam (the test to get my union card), without which it was extremely difficult to make a living in my chosen field, painting scenery. A friend called and said she was thinking about swimming around Manhattan in the annual race, was I interested in joining her? What the hell, I thought. I may not be able to get into the union but I'll show them, I'll swim around Manhattan.

There are two schools of marathon swimming. The first consists of those who want to swim from here to there, no matter how long it takes. The distance covered is all that counts. The second school includes those who try to swim the distance in the least amount of time possible. That is what I aspired to, no doubt due to my past as a competitive swimmer, and my nature. A respectable time was as important to me as finishing.

It annoys me that I'm not the fastest swimmer in the world, but I've grown accustomed to it. During Olympic years, I comb the early heat results to figure out what small, undeveloped country my times would qualify me to represent.

I don't remember when swimming the English Channel entered my consciousness. It's as if it has always been there, part of who I am, like a family story told so often that it is absorbed into one's personality long after the memory of the event is lost. It's the one swim that everyone knows, that has the weight of history behind it, across a stretch of sea that has brought ruin to countless ships and has changed the shape of nations. The shortest distance across the Channel is 20.6 nautical miles, or 22 land miles, from Dover, England, to Cap Gris-Nez, France.

I would imagine there are a fair number of people who wonder, Why would any sane person put herself through such an ordeal? Maybe the crux of the matter is sanity, but I prefer to think not. I could try to explain why I do these things until I am blue in the face, and my dear father, who never learned to swim, would still never understand, thinking that I swim halfway around the world only to annoy him, to rebel, to negate his values. And perhaps in a sense he is right. It is foolish to deny that there is a desire to say, "I have accomplished this. I have swum around Manhattan. I have done something beyond the realm of normal middle-class life, out of the ordinary, unexpected." It becomes a secret source of confidence, a private wellspring of originality. Mostly I think I just wanted to swim the English Channel because it appealed to me, and all the explanations put forth, all the talk about goals and ideals, is just a rationalization for what was, in effect, a whim. It was a dream that caught my fancy as a young child, from which I hadn't awakened. There are those who will never understand why anyone would want to climb Mount Everest or travel to the North Pole if not for fame and fortune, and then there are the rest of us for whom such endeavors seem admirable and courageous only if done for more singular reasons. It's mostly a matter of personality, of quirks and idiosyncrasies, and for these there are no rational explanations, only excuses.

Schroon Lake, June 2, 1990

When we arrived that morning the lake was as still as death, shrouded in the slightest promise of fog. The water had the dark opacity of disaster, of depths not meant to be tested. Floating apprehensively through a hazy dream, I left Paul to take care of the basics, such as putting the canoe in the water. Silence prevailed, so that when the boat slid along the floor of the truck bed the noise jarred. I stepped out of my sandals, hitched my sweatpants above my ankles, and walked reluctantly down the boat launch, gasping as the water pierced my feet. It was as if it were solid and sharp, as if it were still the ice it had been but a few short weeks before. I stared into the pale mist ahead of me, glanced down the ramp toward the deeper water, turned around, and walked away. "Forget about it. Put the canoe back in the truck. I can't even get in that stuff above my ankles." The water thermometer read 58 degrees F, 40 degrees below my body temperature, 26 degrees above freezing.

Paul ignored me. I knew he was thinking that if I couldn't do this I wouldn't be able to make it across the Channel, and all my life, or at least for as long as I could remember, I had wanted to swim the English Channel. Because it was what I wanted, it had become what he wanted for me. Our neighbors, who had driven us here in their truck, were watching from a bench, warm and snug in flannel shirts, jackets, jeans, shoes, and socks. I had only taken off my flip-flops, barely wet my feet, and felt ready to quit. They assured me they wouldn't think less of me if I changed my mind. Paul made no such assurance as he continued to load thermoses and towels into the canoe, using that reproachful silence to coax me into trying again.

I slowly, lingeringly made my way back down the boat launch. Somehow, this time, it didn't hurt as much. I should have known that would happen. It was a lesson learned again and again; one can get used to the cold gradually, slowly enough to deaden the pain. Once again I turned around, this time with determination in my step. I found my cap and goggles and pulled them on. That was the easy part. I took off my sweats in the 50-degree air and tossed them into the canoe, knowing that it would be a lifetime before I felt warm again. Shivering, covered with gooseflesh, my arms held tightly across my chest, I walked the ramp one last time. Paul sat floating in the canoe, tantalizingly out of reach. He encouraged me, praising my progress, cheering every inch, until I was in up to my neck with nowhere to go but toward him, and so I pushed off and started to swim. The shock was too great. An iron band instantly clamped itself around my forehead. I turned back, seeking the safety of solid ground, gasping for air as yet another tight band encircled my chest. Ten strokes and I was on dry land without making a dent in the nine miles ahead of me.

Experience had taught me that the water felt marginally warmer on the second try. Clinging to this memory, I steeled myself for another attempt. Paul was waiting and the neighbors were watching, and the quicker I started and the faster I swam, the sooner it would be over. So I slipped back into that liquid ice and started swimming for real. Paul was there instantly, my guardian angel gliding along at my side. The cold tightened my joints, making it difficult to lift leaden arms out of water that was surely heavier, darker than any I had ever encountered. I seemed clumsy, disjointed, not at all the way I usually felt while swimming. Tingling pinpricks turned my skin into something strange, a foreign substance separate from my body. "Numbness" is generally defined as the absence of feeling, but the process by which one achieves it is invariably painful. And once achieved, numbness is nothing more than agony in a different form.

Seeing the mud and weeds beneath me, I tried to convince myself that shallow water is always warmest, forgetting that the temperature difference is only noticeable at the end, when swimming into shore, into the warmth. It is then that the lake feels so comfortable that one wonders how it ever seemed cold. Instead of making my peace with the shallow water, I only increased my dread of the deep. I turned inside to my imagination for help, telling myself that I was an island of heat, pulling my way through a chill that couldn't touch me, but the ice cut straight through the lie. Even my teeth ached, as if I had bitten into ice cream. The sloshing of water in my ears, the rhythmic splashes of my arms and the oars were all I heard. In my head I tried to get a sound track going or a daydream or anything to keep my mind off the bitter frost. But even my mind was frozen; no thoughts lasted longer than an instant, the time it took for the cold to overcome any attempts to escape it.

We had agreed that Paul would stop me every hour for food—for this swim, mostly hot chocolate and chicken soup. When it seemed that an hour would never pass, I asked him to stop me every half hour, assuming that it had been at least that long since the start. Not only hadn't it been, but an eternity remained until that half-hour mark. When I finally paused, my hands shook uncontrollably as I gulped the hot liquid, feeling the warmth travel through my body as if tracing an anatomical road map. Treading water generated even less heat than swimming, so I didn't linger over those longed-for respites. At each stop, Paul reassured me: I was doing great, I looked wonderful, I was almost there; and I accepted what he told me, wanting desperately to believe what I, had I been rational, would have known could not be true.

At no time during that swim did I ever feel right, never swift and strong, never sure of reaching the end. While swimming usually brings out all that is graceful in me, that day I fought to free my arms from the water lest they be frozen in place. Each stroke shattered the brittle surface, every breath was a frantic gasp. I thought, Okay, I'll make it to the next half hour and then I'll get out. But then the hot chocolate would fool me with the illusion of warmth, and Paul would encourage me, and I'd think, Okay, that's better, maybe I'll go just a little farther. But then I couldn't stop until the next half hour was up, at which time the vicious cycle would repeat itself, until four hours and eighteen minutes later I walked out of the water, up the town beach, into the haven of Paul's waiting arms.

mvhs x-country **team**
DEBRA PENNINGTON DAVIS

Mountain Village, Alaska

No asphalt for these
Delta feet—just
sponge moss, bog
grass, plucked
stalks of Eskimo
tea, a sneaker
stuck in the peat since
yesterday's run,
fox bones,
moose shit,
and blueberries
ripe for the tongue.

privilege
LEILA GREEN

We who are college girls in 1900 will watch and wait, and, I hope, aid and further with particular eagerness the progress of every department of our college work, especially in the branch in which we take so much keen interest and delight,—gymnastics. We, who are women, will always be earnest champions of that which has done so much for us, and raised us from the pale, weak, fragile, delicate, drooping invalidism that was one of the prevailing types [of the 1800s] to the healthy, strong, and glorious womanhood which will be the heritage and right of every twentieth-century girl. Woman was once man's burden; now she is his helper, his equal; and the gratitude which fills every true woman's heart at this changed state must be given to gymnastics, for it is this which has accomplished so much.

It was so interesting, you know, so really aristocratic, to be an invalid; and dear me, it was once actually quite vulgar to be well and robust and altogether healthy. But now, thanks to gymnastics, all this is quite changed. The girl of to-day would not give up the dearly earned and dearly prized fights for the world; and woman having once known liberty will never be forced back to her old position. She has taken her place beside her brother in the tennis-court, in the golf links, on the wheel; and in athletic sports of all kinds she feels an interest second to none . . .

. . .

The most important privilege woman has won is her place in the gymnasium. There it is that she develops and strengthens the muscles which she puts into practical use elsewhere. It is there that she receives her life training, which is to fit her for the struggle, the trials, the strains, and the hardships that fall to the share of all. There she receives the exercise and training which is to make her strong, capable, and prepared to fight life's battles.

dawn staley (from *venus to the hoop*)

SARA CORBETT

She had always been a squirt, small for a girl, even, and given that playground basketball was ruled by a strict meritocracy—play until you lose, lose and go home—Dawn had been forced to learn a creative game of basketball in order to earn her time on the court. Playing had become an addictive thrill. "Being so short, I wasn't able to get my shot off all the time, so I had to perfect different parts of my game. I had to learn how to dribble, I had to learn how to pass, and I had to learn how to be just tough," she said, looking back. "I mean, the guys have molded me into the player that I am today. Some players are sort of finesse-type players, but growing up in the inner city, that's nonexistent. We all go out and we play as aggressive as they come."

She played with a style designed to unsettle her larger opponents. She dribbled with dizzying speed, pattering around her back, through her legs, and so low to the ground that stealing from her was nearly impossible. Passing the ball was something she did slyly, an abrupt no-look or her trademark over-the-shoulder all delivered with astonishing certitude. When she slipped past the boys and scored on them, they told her to go back to the kitchen, to go jump rope with the other girls. But that was the thing about Dawn Staley, even at the age of twelve: telling her to go was the best way to make her stay.

"You had to be good to play," she said, recalling the hot summer nights when crowds of thirty and forty people would gather in the small Moylan gym. "I mean, of course there were times when they didn't let me on the court. I had to wait and wait until I had winners and I could pick my team . . . To be one of the first ten picked is a privilege, and I don't think I could say I was one of the first ten for maybe a couple of years."

When the Moylan was locked for the night, sometime around eleven, someone would hunt down a milk crate, pop out the bottom, and mount it on a telephone pole so that the game could go on. Dawn was always there for it. "She came home only to eat and sleep," remembered her mother, Estelle. "We couldn't get her home for anything."

Estelle Staley had moved to Philadelphia from South Carolina in 1957 and had lived in the Ray Rosen projects since 1965 with her husband, who was on disability. She had two daughters and three sons, and though she worried equally about her children, Dawn, the youngest, was at times the hardest for her to understand, disappearing for hours on end with the neighborhood boys, coming home at three in the morning on summer nights.

When Estelle asked where she'd been, her answer was the same every time: "Just playin' hoops, Ma."

Late one night, motivated as much by curiosity as by suspicion, Estelle Staley went out looking for her baby girl on the streets. She found her just where she'd said she'd be, under the streetlights, the lone girl among a bunch of sweaty boys, just playing her game. Whatever skepticism she'd felt previously about Dawn's obsessive ballplaying evaporated after that. Basketball, Estelle came to understand, was a blessing for a daughter. When years later an offer came from the University of Virginia for a four-year athletic scholarship for Dawn, Estelle bowed her head and thanked God for taking her youngest girl's restless soul out of the inner city. One blessing would come from another. Dawn would graduate from college, have opportunities to travel, meet a nice boyfriend, a Temple football player named Lance, and always care enough to come home every chance she got. When Estelle separated from her husband in 1993, she moved out of Ray Rosen to North Philadelphia's Logan section.

Though she had followed her daughter's career closely over the years, Estelle Staley could have no way of knowing the extent of her fame until the day in April when she boarded the No. 33 bus going east on Market Street, headed toward the heart of the city, where people were gathering to celebrate Dawn's homecoming with the national team. Nike, Dawn had told her, had commissioned some sort of mural that would be dedicated in a ceremony. It was noontime on a Friday, the streets rivered with businesspeople in suits on their way to lunch. They were in the heart of the city now, on a bustling downtown block of department stores and sandwich shops and beauty salons, nothing like the broken-down streets of North Philly, where every other building was boarded up, everything looking frayed and ready to crumble. Estelle wore a black sweater and skirt, her hair was brushed back smoothly from her face. Dawn had said there might be television cameras, though she knew her daughter well enough to predict that she'd surface in a sweat suit herself. Just then the bus lurched around a corner at Philadelphia City Hall, and Estelle happened to glance out the window. Normally she was soft-spoken in public, but what she saw caused her to shout before she could think about it. "Oh, my God!" Then came the tears, pearling down her face, while a sob seized up her throat.

The woman in the seat in front of her turned around, looking surprised but kindly. "What's wrong?" she said.

Estelle Staley drew herself up slightly and pointed a finger out the window. There on the corner of Eighth and Market, so high she had to crane her neck to look up at it, so big and lifelike she could hardly believe it, was a painting of Dawn dribbling the ball, her jersey billowing, her mouth open, eyebrows arched, just playing her game. Estelle's lips trembled as she answered the woman, "That's my baby up there."

The mural, seven stories high and sixty-seven feet wide, had shocked Dawn when she'd come down to look at it the night before. "I thought this was going to be *little*," she said, shaking her head at her own image looming above. "Seeing myself up there, it seems like it's not even me. It's someone else." Nike had eight other murals of its athletes around the country.

Charles Oakley hung over a New York block. Michael Jordan and Scottie Pippen soared over Chicago, Barry Sanders was in Detroit, Jerry Rice in San Francisco, Cal Ripken in Baltimore, Mike Piazza in Los Angeles, and Mookie Blaylock in Atlanta. And now, the girl among the boys, Dawn Staley in her great city of Philly.

"I'd like to thank [Philadelphia '76ers rookie sensation] Jerry Stackhouse for signing with Fila," she quipped for the hundred or so people who'd gathered in an unpaved parking lot across the street from the mural for the dedication. Her teammates, along with Carol Callan, Tara VanDerveer, and her assistants, had gathered in the sun, next to a collection of Dawn's aunts and buddies from Moylan. Later, they would all head to an aunt's house and eat home-cooked soul food to celebrate. The event was, as Nike events often were, Swoosh-happy. Nike had put up a hoop with a Swoosh on the backboard, representatives were passing out Nike posters and Swoosh paraphernalia, but in the end these were just window dressing on a moment that belonged purely to Dawn Staley, her family and friends, and her supporters in Philly. For the women on the team, during the half hour or so they stood beneath Dawn's likeness in the city that meant the world to her, everything that could ever divide them was banished. It didn't matter who wore Nikes and who wore Reeboks. It didn't matter who played the game and who sat on the bench, who showed up in the magazines or for whom the fans screamed the loudest. For a minute, even the gold medal didn't matter. This was about Dawn and her people.

Lisa Leslie stood alongside Estelle Staley and wept proudly. From there, she and Dawn's family would go back to Moylan, which was now called the Hank Gathers Recreation Center, to give a clinic for the neighborhood kids. The Ray Rosen towers had been razed a year earlier, but the rest of it—the gangs and violence, the tight-knit community and the basketball—still thrived. To the children in the neighborhood, Dawn Staley was a hero, and, more important, a hero who always came back to the neighborhood to play ball with them.

Standing behind a podium, Dawn told the assembled

crowd what she would later tell the kids. "When I see the mural, I see positivity and hope," she said, squinting out at the crowd. Despite her showiness on the court, she was not a public speaker at heart, but today the words seemed to come easily. As she spoke, she tried not to look at her mother's new flood of tears. Her teammates had never seen her cry, and she wanted to keep it that way. She continued, "I see hope for people like me who grew up in the inner city and thought that was all there was. Life is out there for you. You have to take it."

Every[one] must have something [s]he follows—
something that serves . . . as a lodestar.

The Discus Thrower

Even as her right hand cupped itself
to a lover's,
its palm, the bend of its fingers
belonged to another seduction.

Fate had taken a shape
she could hold.
She loved its weight,
its smooth rim,
how it tapered from the center.

Rehearsal for years of the same motion
'til every sinew knew
its release:

a crouch   a pivot
the torquing of her body
a circle within a circle,
desire's   cyclone,
destiny's   spiral
of focused devotion;

the discus quick
in her hand.

dreams on ice

APRIL MARTIN

I turn off my alarm at 4:15 a.m. every day and stumble to the bathroom planning the two-hour workout to come: I will work on spins and correct that tendency to lean forward on my jump landings. At 5:20 I am on the ice, in a world that gives political correctness a slight shudder, but without which I would be bereft.

I did not grow up on the ice, devoting my childhood to early morning practice with Olympic aspirations. I was never built like Kristi Yamaguchi and I will certainly never skate like her. I am a slightly chubby forty-five-year-old psychologist and mother of two with at best only a modest talent. I took my first skating lesson at the age of forty because I was looking for a little exercise, but it changed my life forever. Within a couple of weeks I was skating daily. Soon group lessons gave way to individual coaching. Every new step—the first back crossover, the first little waltz jump—was an occasion for such excitement that I didn't sleep for days. Public skating sessions were replaced by serious freestyle sessions. Music was chosen, programs were choreographed, costumes designed and competitions entered.

I am part of a group known in skating parlance as "adult skaters"—a term used somewhat derisively by many. It is less a reference to our current ages than to the fact that we began skating as adults. (Adults who skated as children are simply "skaters.") You can pick us out on the ice without too much trouble. We move more slowly, our jumps are lower, our limbs less extended, and there is often a touch of fear on our faces. It is unusual for an adult skater to ever achieve double-rotation jumps. Triples are unthinkable. When we compete, it is against other adults. The U.S. Figure Skating Association has just begun to tolerate our presence in the skating world, but it can't be said to take us seriously as competitors. Still, we are athletes. We devote an astonishing amount of time, energy, and money to pursuing personal excellence, whatever that may look like to an observer.

It still sends a shiver through me to describe myself as an athlete. When I grew up, athletes were boys. I could never run fast and never learned how to throw a ball. All I knew about sports was that men watched other men play them on TV. Athletes had nothing to do with me.

That doesn't mean I didn't like to move. My most joyful childhood memories are all about movement. Because I was badly pigeon-toed as a young child, my parents put me in a ballet program in my preschool, hoping it would help me overcome my clumsiness. It did more than they expected; it sparked a passion.

Whether ballet's appeal came from something in my genetic makeup—some tendency toward musicality and expressiveness, perhaps—or whether it was just the only avenue for physical activity ever shown to me, I don't know. Long after the ballet lessons had stopped I was pirouetting around the living room, walking *en pointe* in bare feet, dreaming ballerina dreams. Over the years there was little family money for nonessentials, and my interest in dance was discouraged. By seventh grade my life contained no physical activity at all to speak of. The worst part was that I never even noticed what was missing.

Other girls might have protested against being robbed of the chance to strive for strength, skills, and physical goals, but I accepted it without question. The only goal I recognized for my adolescent female body was to look like a fashion model. It was a game with two measures of success: the mirror, and the boys who asked you out. My utter and complete failure in the mirror made for relentless anguish. I was short, chunky, had acne and the vaguely ethnic features of my Italian and Jewish heritages. That Twiggy and I were of the same species was a taxonomic anomaly.

Boys were interested in me, but the sexuality of it was confusing: the same attention that meant success could also get me branded as disreputable. Nevertheless, I relied on attracting male interest to get some affirmation of my worth. It never worked, and I remained convinced that the body I had just didn't measure up.

In the 1960s my crowd didn't even dance. It was a distraction from grooving on the music. We were cerebral—political, literary, philosophical—and we were above petty vanities. The proof, of course, was that we didn't wear makeup or cut our hair.

This business of vanity is dicey. Figure skating is a celebration of beauty. It is also about exhibitionism—sequins and crystal, velvet and chiffon. It is about pointed toes and graceful arms. And about a feminine mandate: Take fiercely honed skills, raw power, and courage and mask them with an illusion of fragility and vulnerability. As I glide past the mirrored end of the ice rink in a spiral position, I study the line my body creates, pleased to see a hint of elegance. I, who spent the '70s discovering the oppression of women, trying to recover from the notion that my worth rested in my physical appearance. I, who at twenty-nine fell in love with my life partner, a woman, and discovered a depth to passion and devotion that transcended social images. Here I am, in a teensy skating dress, wishing someone would notice how terrific my spiral is looking today.

Many of the people in my psychotherapy practice are living with H.I.V. infection or AIDS. Most of my clients, as well as my friends and I, are coping with the devastation of loss after loss. One woman spends her life in a wheelchair after a catastrophic illness. They are reminders of how quickly the joys of owning a body can be snatched from us. Other clients are recovering from childhood abuse, the ravages of racism, the sufferings inflicted by homophobia. All are seeing me because of pain in their lives. And though my work is deeply satisfying, it is intense. I am often immersed in heartbreak.

By contrast, what I do on the ice feels self-centered, superficial, and of little social relevance. I care desperately about whether I will ever land a clean Axel. I make guilty jokes about spending my children's college education money on skating. The critical questions are whether my leg is sufficiently turned out, or if the new costume should be red. I have had to own up to a vanity and an exhibitionism that would have shamed me once.

And yet within that glitzy, frilly realm, I have discovered something very close to love: the ballerina of my childhood. Skating has helped me to reclaim the body with which I spent too many years at war. I stop briefly to reflect on the apparent contradictions: I have deepened and matured as a woman in a sport geared to little girls. And I am now nourished and replenished by a sport whose standards of femininity were once a form of bondage. Though I bring to the ice the painful bunions and chronically stiff muscles of middle age, I also bring one of its benefits: the increased capacity for living comfortably with contradictions.

My coach bellows across the ice, "You call that *speed*? My dead grandmother can move faster than that!" I bend deeper, push harder, feel the sweat start to run. There is deep pleasure in being pushed to my limits with the same gruff encouragement used for the serious competitors. I'm just another jock.

a swimming **lesson**

JEWELLE GOMEZ

At nine years old I didn't realize that my grandmother, Lydia, and I were doing an extraordinary thing by packing a picnic and riding the elevated train from Roxbury to Revere Beach. It seemed part of the natural rhythm of summer to me. I didn't notice until much later how the subway cars slowly emptied most of their Black passengers as the train left Boston's urban center and made its way into the Italian and Irish suburban neighborhoods to the north. It didn't seem odd that all of the Black families sorted themselves out in one section of the beach and never ventured onto the boardwalk to the concession stands or the rides, except in groups.

I do remember Black women perched cautiously on their blankets, tugging desperately at bathing suits rising too high in the rear and complaining about their hair "going back." Not my grandmother, though. She glowed with unembarrassed athleticism as she waded out, just inside the reach of the waves, and moved along the riptide parallel to the shore. Once submerged, she would load me onto her back and begin her tireless, long strokes. With the waves partially covering us, I followed her rhythm, my short, chubby arms taking their cue from the power in her back muscles. We did this over and over until I'd fall off, then she'd catch me and set me upright in the strong New England surf. I was thrilled by the wildness of the sea and my grandmother's fearless relationship to it. I loved that she didn't continually consult her mirror but looked as if she had been born to the shore, a kind of aquatic heiress.

None of the larger social issues had a chance of catching my attention in 1957. All that existed was my grandmother rising from the surf like a Dahomean queen, shaking her head free of the torturous, useless rubber cap, beaming down on me when I, at long last, took the first swim strokes on my own. She towered over me in the sun with a confidence that made simply dwelling in her presence a reward in itself. Under her gaze I felt like part of a long line of royalty. I was certain that everyone around us—Black and white—felt and respected her magnificence.

Although I intuited her power, I didn't know the real significance of our summer together as Black females in a white part of town. Unlike winter, when we're protected by the concealment of coats, boots, and hats, the summer is a vulnerable time. I am left exposed, at odds with all the expectations handed down from the mainstream culture and its media: narrow hips, straight hair, flat stomach, small feet. But Lydia never seemed to notice. Her long, chorus-girl legs ended in size-nine shoes. She seemed unafraid to make herself even bigger, stretching the broad back of a woman with a purpose: teaching her granddaughter how to swim against the tide of prevailing opinion and propriety. It may have looked like a superfluous skill to those watching our lessons. After all, it was obvious I wouldn't be doing the backstroke on the Riviera or in the pool of a penthouse spa. Certainly nothing in the popular media had made the great outdoors seem a hospitable place for Blacks or women. It was a place in which, at best, we were meant to feel uncomfortable, and at worst—hunted. But the potential prospects for actually utilizing the skill were irrelevant to me; it was simply the skill itself that mattered. When I finally got it right I felt I held an invaluable life secret.

It wasn't until college that the specifics of slavery and the Middle Passage were made available to me. The magnitude of that "peculiar institution" was almost beyond my comprehension. It wasn't like anything else I'd learned in school about Black people in this country. It was impossibly contradictory trying to make my own connection to the descendants of slaves—myself, others I knew—and at the same time see slaves not exactly as Americans I might know but as Africans set adrift from their own, very different land. My initial reaction was, *Why didn't the slaves simply jump from the ships while still close to shore and swim home?* The child in me who'd been taught how to survive in water was crushed to learn my ancestors had not necessarily shared this skill. Years later, when I visited West Africa and found out about the poisonous, spiny fish inhabiting much of the inhospitable coastline, rocky and turbulent, I understood why swimming was not a local sport there as it is in New England. I often remember that innocent inquiry, and now every time I visit a beach I think of those ancestors and of Lydia.

The sea has been a fearful place for us. It swallowed us whole when there was no other escape from the holds of slave ships, and did so again more recently with the flimsy refugee flotillas from Haiti. To me, for whom the dark recesses of a tenement hallway were the most unknowable thing encountered in my first nine years, the ocean was a mystery of terrifying proportions. In teaching me to swim Lydia took away that fear. I understood something outside myself—the sea—and consequently something about myself as well. I was no longer simply a fat little girl. My body became a sea vessel—sturdy, enduring, graceful.

Before she died in the summer of 1988 I discovered that she herself didn't really swim that well. All that time I was splashing desperately, trying to learn the right rhythm—*face down, eyes closed, air out, face up, eyes open, air in, reach*—Lydia would be brushing the sandy bottom under the water to keep us both afloat. As she told me this it didn't seem such a big deal to her, but I was shocked. I reached back in my memory trying to put this new information together with the Olympic vision of her I'd always kept inside my head. At first I felt disappointed, tricked. Like I used to feel when I learned that my favorite movie stars were only five feet tall. But I later realized that it was an incredible act of bravery and intelligence for her to pass on to me a skill she herself had not quite mastered—a skill she knew would always bring me a sense of pride in accomplishment.

And it's not just the swimming, or the ability to stand on any beach anywhere and be proud of my large body, my African hair. It's being unafraid of the strong muscles in my own back, accepting control over my own life. Now when the weather turns cold and I don the layers of wool and down that protect me from the Eastern winter, from those who think a Black woman can't do her job, from those who think I'm simply sexual prey, I remember the power of my grandmother's broad back and I imagine I'm wearing my swimsuit.

Face up, eyes open, air in, reach.

the athletic girl

ANNE O'HAGAN

With the single exception of the improvement of the legal status of women, their entrance into the realm of sports is the most cheering thing that has happened to them in the century just past.

The general adoption of athletic sports by women meant the gradual disappearance of the swooning damsel of old romance, and of that very real creature, the lady who delighted, a decade or so ago, to describe herself as "high strung," which, being properly interpreted, meant uncontrolled and difficult to live with. Women who didn't like athletics were forced to take them up in self defense; and exercise meant firmer muscles, better circulation, a more equable temper, and the dethronement of the "nervous headache" from its high place in feminine regard.

. . .

In dress, since the day when the Greek girdle became the Teutonic corset, no boon has been granted to woman so great as the privilege of wearing shirt waists and short skirts. When the tennis players of ten or fifteen years ago first popularized that boneless, free chested, loose armed bodice they struck a blow for feminine freedom . . .

To have improved half the race in health, disposition, and dress would seem almost enough for one movement to have accomplished. But athletics have done more than this. They have robbed old age of some of its terrors for women, and they promise to rob it of more. The golfing grandmother is a subject upon which the humorist occasionally whets his wits; but those in whom the sense of humor is not so strong can only rejoice in everything that adds to the pleasure, the interest, and the health of the good lady . . . It is a magnificent institution which has exchanged her felt slippers for the calfskin boots of the athlete, and has delayed for fifteen or twenty years the purchase of the lace cap of her decrepitude.

. . .

Today no college for women would think of sending out a catalogue without its alluring half tone cuts of the interior or exterior of its gymnasium, its duly set forth attractions in lake or river, tennis and hand ball courts, golf grounds, and the like.

. . .

From being the chief factor in the athletic life of the women's colleges, the gymnasiums have grown to be distinctly subsidiary. They supplement the outdoor exercises which the location of most of the institutions for higher education makes so natural and attractive. Each has its specialty in the line of sport, and the young woman who wins a championship in rowing, swimming, track events, basket ball, bicycling, or whatever it may be, is a lionized creature who tastes for once the sweets of the cup of utter adulation.

. . .

An old graduate of Vassar tells somewhere a delightful tale of the faculty's blinking at small accidents in the days before gymnasiums, when the world of outdoor sports was undreamed of so far as women were concerned.

In those dark times, the irrepressible energy of the young women found its outlet in a form of baseball played with some skill, great vigor, and the utmost secrecy. The faculty knew, of course, that the young women were emulating the idols of the bleachers, but they sanctioned the game to the extent of not prohibiting it. One day a young woman broke her leg in a game. Dread sat heavily upon the other enthusiasts. They had no hope that the faculty would allow them to continue their pastime; but the authorities proved unexpectedly reasonable, admitting that accidents were liable to occur in the best regulated sports, and agreeing that baseball was no more to be condemned for the young woman's broken leg than dancing would be if she had slipped upon the floor in a waltz. Whereupon, to bear out this benign judgment, a girl fell a few months later while she was dancing, obligingly broke her leg, and thereby saved baseball from exclusive aspersions.

. . .

. . . To whomsoever the athletic woman owes her existence, to him or her the whole world of women owes a debt incomparably great. Absolutely no other social achievement in the behalf of women is so important and so far reaching in its results.

precious medals
ANNA SEATON HUNTINGTON

While I trained for the Olympics, I lived for the moment when I might step up onto the medal platform. I imagined crossing a threshold to an exalted, sacred place where only a handful of the world's elite are allowed to tread. Who could ever forget the 1968 photograph of Tommie Smith, gold medal around his neck, boldly raising his fist in a black-power salute in Mexico City? Or, twenty years later, the sight of dynamo Janet Evans beaming as she stood shoulder to shoulder with the silver and bronze medalists, despite her station on the gold-medal block six inches higher? I wondered, *What will my moment up there be like?*

I missed out on a medal in Seoul and rowed two or three times a day for four more years, a gold medal in Barcelona my single purpose. At any point during my training, the mention of one—by my coach, a coxswain, or my pair partner, Stephanie Maxwell-Pierson—filled me with want, sent my heart racing, my legs driving harder.

When the day of our final race arrived in 1992, Stephanie and I sat together at the starting line. We were in lane three, the fast lane; we'd posted the best time in the semifinals and placed second at the world championships the year before. I turned around on my little wooden seat and searched the horizon for the finish line, barely visible 2,000 meters, or about a mile and a quarter, away. When we got there, in seven minutes or so, my decadelong life as a rower would be over, its measure taken. We'd practiced and visualized this precious peak race thousands of times. I believed I knew how every moment would unfold. Winning was the only acceptable outcome.

Images of that race under the relentless Barcelona sun will be burned into my mind forever. Stephanie's sweaty, muscular back attacking every stroke. The simple test of will three-quarters of the way through, when pain sank its savage teeth into my legs, blew flames down my throat, and dared me to pull harder. And, with twenty-five strokes to go, the digital 42 on the small electronic strokes-per-minute meter at my feet, telling me we were sprinting harder than ever.

When our slender thirty-foot boat crossed the finish line, Canada's pairs team was several feet ahead. The difference between second and third came down to a photo finish between us and the German team. Gasping for air and squirming from lactic acid, we floated around just past the line and waited for the scoreboard to display the results. I leaned over the gunwale and threw up. Finally the board lit. We were third. Bronze.

Failure.

Speechless with fatigue and disappointment, we paddled over to the medals platform in front of the stands filled with our families and friends and with people from all over the world. On the dock, we hugged each other, then shook hands with the Germans and Canadians. Noticing that our time on the board was 7.08, faster than we'd ever gone before, Stephanie and I shared a moment of satisfaction. But as we stood together, medals around our necks, arms full of flowers, and listened to the Canadian national anthem, I felt numb.

wheelchair flying

CARRIE DEARBORN

After seeing me do stand-up comedy from my wheelchair, people ask if I get nervous. I laugh at that one. Nervous is standing at the top of a slalom course at an international race, thirteen years old and the only girl on the team, knowing that how you ski will decide the team's fate.

When I turned fourteen, I went down a racecourse composed mostly of rutted ice, skied over to my parents, and told them I'd never race again. I had always dreamt of being a national team member. (A friend of mine had been on the 1962 Swiss team, and she'd shown me her medal and pictures. I wanted that.) But what started out fun turned into a nightmare. I kept losing by tenths of a second. My competitive nature and good skiing form just weren't quite enough.

Finally, I decided to become a ski instructor like my mother and father. Teaching turned out to be a wonderful choice. I had the aggressiveness and strength to survive in an all-male professional environment, I loved entertaining people, and teaching let me be around children, whom I really enjoyed. In time I graduated from college and started working with computers. I drifted away from teaching after ten seasons, partly because I'd come out as a lesbian. Anita Bryant told Americans that gay and lesbian people recruited children, and I thought it best not to argue.

Two years later, I had a stroke.

Now I indulge in a sport few people have tried—flooring my electric wheelchair. I call it wheelchair flying.

Wheelchair flying takes place on an asphalt path around a

pond. I quite startle people as I zoom by them at a full-out 7 m.p.h. Part of the high of this sport is that people get a new slant on wheelchairs and wheelchair users. One time, a little kid pointed at my chair and said, "Look, Mom, can you get me one?"

Wheelchair flying gives me the freedom to, well, stretch my "legs." While negotiating the able-bodied world, I must constantly stretch or squeeze myself. I strain to hear and see, speak slowly so I'm understood, force myself to be polite to people with patronizing attitudes (they don't know better, although I try to educate them). I'm carried in and out of some places, and in others maneuver the chair very, very carefully to avoid hitting cars, furniture, or the many people who think they have the right to walk directly in my path.

When I'm wheelchair flying I don't need to deal with any of that.

The pond is known for fast runners and bicyclists. Parents hold their children's hands. Runners keep their dogs on leashes. And I leave room on both sides of me so bikes can get by. Wheelchair flying there is like driving a motorcycle down a winding back road in a country where they drive on the "wrong" side. Now *that's* a challenge.

I wouldn't do this if I had no reflexes, or couldn't see or hear well with correction. And I make certain my seat belt is fastened. Although I just laugh when I'm told adaptive athletics are dangerous. Give me a break. I'm *already* in a wheelchair. And flying fine.

baseball is **about** playing

WENDY PATRICE WILLIAMS

Each spring season Marty and I made our way to the Spring-
dale Little League Baseball Field on Gary Street—to the loud-
speakered voice announcing the players, to the refreshment
stand selling blue ice pops, to the rows of shiny, forest-green
bleachers, to the big black scoreboard with removable numbers
and letters.

I wanted to be the one who ran the scoreboard, hung the big
black square plates of metal with thick white numbers. Numbers disappearing and reappearing—presto!—as on the game-
board of my favorite TV quiz show, *Concentration.* There was a
platform running along the bottom for the scorekeeper, who
was always a boy. Later it was automated and tiny bulbs of yellow light replaced the thick white numbers. I heard that the
announcer changed the scores from up in the field house and I
imagined him clutching a control stick, pressing a plastic button with his thumb like pilots when they drop bombs.

The announcer sat behind a row of windows above the
refreshment stand, removed from the crowd with an exclusive
view of the entire field. I never saw him sitting up there, but I
always imagined him looking like Howard Cosell with a large,
wide, sloping nose and plump bags under squinty eyes, eyes
with the knowing look of an insider, wise to all the behind-the-
scenes secrets, like the criminals on the Dick Tracy Lie Detec-
tor Game.

One winter, Marty and I climbed up onto the first-story
roof of the field house to see into the announcer's box. A
skinny silver microphone tilted on its stand, poised as if the

announcer were due any moment and the game about to begin, as if the microphone were frozen awaiting the spring thaw. I heard the crack of a bat and the booming voice, "GOING, GOING, GONE!"

Marty and I were at all the Little League games, school night or not, even when it was drizzling. One evening, just after a shower, we rode up expectantly on our bikes surveying Gary Street for fellow fans. But our hopes crumbled as we gained full view of the empty parking lot. We parked our bikes anyway and stomped around in the puddles on the black asphalt, kicking water out in all directions, complaining about how it was just a little sprinkle and they could've played anyway.

When it was nice out, I sailed down Gary Street hill on my blue English Racer bike, the multicolored streamers flying out from the handlebars, my baseball cards flapping in the spokes *thwack-thwack-thwack.* Speeding into the Little League driveway, my mitt and ball stuffed into my saddlebag, I scanned the scene for Marty. She was usually there first, waiting by the bike stand or up on the top bleacher overlooking the parking lot. "Got the ball?" she'd ask, punching her fist into her glove. During the games, we always played catch near the third base bleachers.

Once we had both forgotten to bring a ball and stood staring at each other in disbelief. Angrily, Marty threw her mitt down. I loved to see her like that. She got that way in kickball games, too, when the umpire made a bad call. She'd yell, "Oh, c'mon, man!" and thrust her chin and chest forward, her hands on her hips. One time I lied and told her I forgot the ball just to see her throw her glove down. When I told her I was only kidding, she growled, "Okay, Miss Williams," and chased me all around the parking lot, slicing at me with her huge mitt, like a crab attacking with her claw.

Marty was in my fifth-grade class with Mr. Cohen. Her real name was Margaret, Margaret Krilovich, but everyone called her Marty. Her skin was very fair and her upper body solid and taut like a bulldog's. Her hair was brown and, in the lower grades, she had worn it shoulder length and curled under, pushed behind her ears with different-colored hair bands. Now she had a short cut like a boy, so when she put on her baseball style preparing for the pitch in school softball games, she looked like a real player, one that you had to take seriously.

When Marty was up at bat in gym class, she acted just like Elston Howard, the New York Yankees' catcher. First she banged the bat in a deliberate way against the insole of one sneaker, then the other. I never understood why big leaguers did that until I saw the bottoms of my brother's Little League shoes, dirt clinging to the tiny pieces of metal sticking out all over like fungus on a tree stump. He told me cleats were for gripping the field so you could run faster, but it seemed to me they would hold you back.

Then Marty held the bat between her thighs while she spit into her hands and rubbed them together. She squinted darkly at the pitcher and made slow, deliberate practice swings, each time tapping the same spot in front of her, as if pressing some small invisible button on a wall of air. I tried to do stuff like Marty, bang my sneaks with the bat or tap a hovering button, but it felt fake.

Marty and I were a team. We took games seriously and didn't throw like girls. We picked each other first for ball games at school and were dedicated to our catch dates. Her eyes twinkled when she'd see me at the Little League field, her thin lips giving way to a smile. Her teeth were straight and very white, and each tooth had a slight roundness to its surface that made me want to hug her. I'd toss the ball to her as a way of greeting. She'd flip the ball back, saying, "Hiya, kid," as I'd fold the web of my glove over it saying, "Hey, Mart," and that's how we always began.

Then we headed over to what we called our pitcher's mound, a place near third base outside the ball-field fence. It was our pretend bull pen, and while the Little League pitchers warmed up along the sidelines for the game, so did Marty and I. When I was catcher, I'd woo her: "C'mon, Marty, thata girl. Marty, pitch-it-in-there, right in the center, thata girl, Marty, way-to-go," a hypnotic, repetitive chant like a tom-tom beat. I'd punch the pocket of my glove, focusing her in on the target.

"Steeee-rike!" I'd yell, when she'd pitch it over the plate. When it was my turn to pitch, her voice was steady and low.

"C'mon, Wendy, put it right here," she'd insist, holding out her mitt as if it were a basket demanding to be filled. Before each pitch, she'd send me secret signals from between her legs with her fingers as she crouched. We never decided ahead of time what one finger pointed toward the earth meant, or two fingers spread apart, but I always nodded my head knowingly, as if an important secret had just been whispered into my ear.

At the crack of a bat and lots of cheering, we ran to the fence. If it was a hit, we watched for a couple of plays until the game slowed down or the inning changed. But most times, except when my brother, Will, played, the world of Marty and Wendy engrossed us, the ball whizzing back and forth.

Will was the catcher for Rotary, a team that had green caps, green-and-white-striped socks, and green numbers on the backs of their shirts. Will's number was eight, my favorite, but it was also the number on the eight ball and that wasn't so good. Torrell was Rotary's home-run hitter, a giant boy with massive shoulders, and cute like that TV detective on *Hawaiian Eye*, the one whose hair was pomped up high like the wave they showed with surfers on it at the beginning of the show.

When Torrell was up, the crowd was silent and expectant. Always out for the big one, he swung fully, tipping it, line driving it foul, or simply swiping at air. Then the loud crack and the ball sent flying. I followed its arc climbing, climbing, the wide, full trajectory, the ball slowing, stopping midair as it reached its apex: then the ball dropping without spin, a slow-motion M-80 bomb plummeting to earth. A comet burning out. As it fell, I fixed my eyes to the top of the outfield fence as I would the horizon at summer sunsets over the ocean, waiting for that moment when the edge of the ball sliced past the horizontal limit. Bread disappearing plunk into the toaster. Another KIZZYMA'S!

A KIZZYMA'S was a home run that fell behind the Kizzyma's sign. A wooden fence behind the outfield displayed advertisements on each section for the different businesses in town. One was for Kizzyma's Hardware Store. It bordered center field and stood the farthest from home plate. I loved the word KIZZYMA'S. It was something about two Z's together— Marty and Wendy at the third base baseline.

Sometimes, though, we had to let Jill Krowley's cousin, Buddy, play. Jill was our friend and we didn't want her to get mad at us. Buddy lived next to the Little League and would come over and beg to play. When he played, we spread out into a triangle and just played plain old catch. Marty and I threw the ball extra hard to him or way over his head into the blackberry bushes. We smiled at each other as we watched him stamp around in the brambles searching for the small patch of white. "Ouch!" he yelled, the blackberry stickers pricking his fingers as he reached for the ball. Then he threw it wildly and we had to run far to get it. Buddy was younger, and we were always glad when we heard his mother calling him in.

One evening when Buddy was retrieving one of Marty's killer throws, he scratched his face on the blackberry bushes. Red marks streaked his cheeks, and the lines blew up swollen. He threw the ball at me so hard it whizzed past my outstretched glove and onto the Little League ball field. Horrified, I watched it bounce along the green of the infield, roll across the brown packed earth of the baseline, and dribble out onto the grass in right field.

"TIME OUT," the announcer called. "WOULD THE TWO GIRLS AT THE THIRD BASE BLEACHERS PLEASE REFRAIN FROM PLAYING BALL! I REPEAT: THE TWO GIRLS AT THE EDGE OF THIRD BASE, STOP PLAYING." Buddy had bolted, and it was just Marty and I looking shamefacedly at each other.

We slunk into the bleachers and the frowning third base coach reluctantly tossed us our ball. In silence we sat stiffly staring out at the field. Good thing Rotary wasn't playing, I thought; my brother would have killed me. After sitting out an inning, we began to squirm. Our legs got the jitters and we shifted in our seats. Marty threw the ball into my lap. We began tossing the ball back and forth and soon we were back at our old spot, pitching and posing and high-popping. After all, baseball is about playing.

Then boomed the dreaded pronouncement: "WOULD THE GIRLS OUTSIDE THIRD BASE PLEASE LEAVE THE GAME. I REPEAT: LEAVE THE GAME." Marty and I looked at each other in disbelief. He couldn't be talking to us. But it was us, we at the sideline who thought ourselves invisible. Outsiders without the stamp of legitimacy. Girls, damn it, girls. We walked away on weak legs, bowing our heads as we marched single file along the black asphalt walkways. Past the field house under the dreaded announcer and past the lady behind the refreshment window who knew Marty's mother. Past all the anonymous fans in the bleachers who might be our neighbors. Past Vinny Balducci, the class clown, on the highest bleacher above the parking lot yelling, "Ooooh, you did it now." Past the parked cars, row after row, our bikes forever unreachable. The announcer's words, "AND NOW BACK TO THE GAME," stabbing at our backs. The game continuing without us—devoted players, star pitchers, dogged fans. Without us—Elston Howard and Tom Tresh. Without us—the girls who had been to every game, the girls who were part of it all, but not really part of anything.

The innings came and went, batter by batter, pitch by pitch. Marty and I heard the cheers and the announcer from down the street at the Super Diner parking lot as we rode around and around in circles, hard pedaling, slicing in and out of each other's loops, my baseball cards thwacking loudly in the spokes as each one smacked the prong of the front wheel fork. The sound lulled me into a daydream.

I hop over the fence at third base. The grass is luminous and the green of the field fans expansively toward the horizon. The dirt of the baseline is surprisingly hard and the cleats awkward under my feet, like I have to balance to walk or I'll fall. I am Rotary, green in my cap, socks, and number 8. The drawstring of my uniform pulls tightly around my waist and elastic hugs my calves. I am third in the lineup, the batter before Torrell, and my teammates are counting on me with two on base and two outs. "WILLIAMS . . . NOW IT'S WILLIAMS AT BAT," the announcer proclaims.

I straddle the plate, pulling the cap brim down over my sweaty forehead. The bat is heavy in my hands as I let the tip fall over my back and then practice swinging it forward again and again, tapping an invisible button on the wall of the air. I bang the dirt off my cleats, first the left, then the right. All await my readiness for the pitch. I spit, shake out my shoulders, and extend the bat slowly. I am Torrell preparing for a KIZZYMA'S, and Marty will deliver the perfect pitch.

I steady my bat over my right shoulder and squint darkly out at the pitcher. The windup, the pitch. "IT'S OUTSIDE," the announcer bellows as I lower the bat. Pitch two. I lean into it but snap back when I know it's low and will go for a grounder. But the third. The third is pitcher-perfect. Straight down the middle and barely spinning, the world in slow motion dropping in for the strike. *Whack!*

I'm off! It's high and long, Torrell-style, but it's the running I'm concentrating on. So this is how it feels, the cleats launching you forward, the cleats casting you through the air. First base. Will my cleats rip the bag? I step on and off quickly, the way you throw in Hot Potato. Tapping second, I hear the announcer: "IT LOOKS LIKE A KIZZYMA'S, FOLKS . . . GOING, GOING . . ." Second base to third is glorious. I feel the strength in my pumping arms and the proudness in my out-thrust chest. The fans are standing in the bleachers, waving at me, cheering. The announcer's box is dark but I hear his amplified voice: "AND THAT PUTS ROTARY THREE AHEAD." Marty gives me the thumbs-up as I round third, but it's there I get into trouble.

My cleats grab. The earth is quicksand sucking me down. Down, down into the baseline I'm sinking, more with each step, home plate in close view, but I can't reach it. The more I pull up with one leg, the more the other sinks. I am sweating, as in those dreams when someone chases me and I'm running but staying in the same spot no matter how fast I pump! I'm

baseball is **about** playing

sunk up to my waist now, and the plate looms large, floating above the dirt, an island I'll never reach.

I broke out of the daydream as lines of cars idled at the stoplight on Lloyd Street, waiting for green. The announcer's voice had finally gone dead. Marty and I headed our bikes home, she crossing at Liberty, me cutting through the gas station and down Potter to avoid the Little League field. We never did find out who won the game.

It took us a week to go back to the Little League. We were not the first to arrive. In fact, the first batter had already struck out as we stood in line for refreshments, my blue ice pop and Marty's Raisinets. Most of the seats were already filled as we made our way to the top of the parking-lot bleachers. Thank God Vinny Balducci was not there.

No beloved pitcher's mound for us. We were far from the third base baseline and had left our mitts and balls in our bike bags. We would play together in the parking lot after the game. The field seemed smaller now, pressed in tightly by the enclosing fences. Quietly, we watched as each batter came and went and the scoreboard numbers changed. Even when the announcer boomed "GOING, GOING, GONE!" we were mute. We stood with the crowd but let them scream for us. It's not good to be visible, we understood.

But we had a plan, a strategy of subtlety and stealth. We were to inch our way back to the third base baseline, to our pitching, popping, and posing, but it would take weeks. Next game, we'd sit lower in the parking-lot bleachers, then, halfway through the game, move close to home plate. Skip a game, returning to plant ourselves at the very top of the third base bleachers, then mid-game move to the lowest seats. Before the next game, toss a few at the third base line, and again, after the game. And then we'd be back at it, pitcher to catcher, catcher to pitcher, the back-and-forth of the bull pen. The Little League world of Marty and Wendy, our voices sweetening the air like overripe blackberries.

from *an american **childhood***

ANNIE DILLARD

On the yellow back wall of our Richland Lane garage, I drew a target in red crayon. The target was a batter's strike zone. The old garage was dark inside; I turned on the bare bulb. Then I walked that famously lonely walk out to the mound, our graveled driveway, and pitched.

I squinted at the strike zone, ignoring the jeers of the batter—oddly, Ralph Kiner. I received no impressions save those inside the long aerial corridor that led to the target. I threw a red-and-blue rubber ball, one of those with a central yellow band. I wound up; I drew back. The target held my eyes. The target set me spinning as the sun from a distance winds the helpless spheres. Entranced and drawn, I swung through the moves and woke up with the ball gone. It felt as if I'd gathered my own body, pointed it carefully, and thrown it down a tunnel bored by my eyes.

I pitched in a blind fever of concentration. I pitched, as I did most things, in order to concentrate. Why do elephants drink? To forget. I loved living at my own edge, as an explorer on a ship presses to the ocean's rim; mind and skin were one joined force curved out and alert, prow and telescope. I pitched, as I did most things, in a rapture.

Now here's the pitch. I followed the ball as if it had been my own head, and watched it hit the painted plastered wall. High and outside; ball one. While I stood still stupefied by the effort of the pitch, while I stood agog, unbreathing, mystical, and unaware, here came the daggone rubber ball again, bouncing out of the garage. And I had to hustle up some snappy fielding, or lose the ball in a downhill thicket next door.

The red, blue, and yellow ball came spinning out to the driveway, and sprang awry on the gravel; if I nabbed it, it was apt to bounce out of my mitt. Sometimes I threw the fielded grounder to first—sidearm—back to the crayon target, which had become the first baseman. Fine, but the moronic first baseman spat it back out again at once, out of the dark garage and bouncing crazed on the gravel; I bolted after it, panting. The pace of this game was always out of control.

So I held the ball now, and waited, and breathed, and fixed on the target till it mesmerized me into motion. In there, strike one. Low, ball two.

Four balls, and they had a man on. Three strikeouts, and you had retired the side. Happily, the opposing batters, apparently paralyzed by admiration, never swung at a good pitch. Unfortunately, though, you had to keep facing them; the retired side resurrected immediately from its ashes, fresh and vigorous, while you grew delirious—nutsy, that is, from fielding a bouncing ball every other second and then stilling your heart and blinking the blood from your eyes so you could concentrate on the pitch.

sikes room, **princeton** boathouse

SANDRA J. CHU

I go to the trophy room first. I make sure
that in the years following my graduation
no one has lost or stolen the plaque where my name
is the only record that I spent any significant
time here. My urge to return is always strong—
I am looking for my name among the elite.
It is there. I read the list of the women in my boat,
and I am back in our last race, panicking, frantic
that we might come in third; and then after,
rowing the last thirty strokes to the algae-slicked
dock to get the silver medals nobody wanted.
Back at home, we shroud the boat,
shelve it over our heads for the summer.
Somehow, despite our defeat, we will earn our places
here, acclaimed as the *Outstanding Princeton Crew of 1991*.
My small athletic accomplishment—
how does my grandfather, who is ninety-six
remember National Team Basketball? At 5'5" he defeated
the shorter Japanese; lost to the Filipinos
who used American GIs as ringers; won
a silver medal in the Pan Asian Games.
No one knows this except us. Anything
that might have recorded them was bombed
in the Japanese invasion of Shanghai
or confiscated with everything
he didn't bring to California on the steamer.
He hadn't given me other details. I don't think he hoarded

them. I think he chose not to know how many penalties
he got that day, whether he had assists or was assisted,
whether he was a forward or a guard.

Instead he pushed me to a chair, *tell me about this*, picking up
my racing notebook, *what is it like to row in a snowstorm?*
And I, to feel the edges of each etched letter, run my finger
over my name.

coming home
JOLI SANDOZ

Homecoming Weekend 1987. On the long drive south, I search for calm. I own a successful business now; it's ridiculous to relive battles a decade old. Still, my palms slip slightly on the wheel. If coaching is a home, it's one to which I dread returning.

First, the requisite football game. Just like old times. I park and walk across campus in the general direction of the Redwood Bowl. Yellow and orange flowers in neat beds nod among the spiky green leaves which decorate California. The university apparently still holds its ground. Making my way between aging buildings, I wonder—cynically—if the new paint is standard alumni whitewash. But there's also that faint, undeniable stirring . . . The grandstand roof rises ahead, and I think with some surprise, *We were heroes here.*

Sportswomen in my part of the world had to approach the heroic to survive the 1950s and '60s. Although my mother remembers seeing big-city national-class female softball players snap the ball around a pristine infield years before I was born, my own early athletic opportunities consisted of low-key local contests. We girls wore mismatched T-shirts and shorts, slid on school-yard base paths slippery with gravel, and felt lucky if someone's father showed up to umpire. Summers I watched my younger brothers don uniforms complete with caps and stirrup socks, to play in a park with three diamonds, announcers, scorekeepers, and an honest-to-goodness concession stand.

Everyone I knew considered watching boys and men proper

activity for white middle-class girls and women. We females who stuck to playing sport through adolescence had to be willing to put up with public humiliations like the one the (male) sports staff ran in our high school paper, when they named my best friend and school record-holder in three girls' swimming events "Athlete of the Weak."

My sports heroes, of course, were male: Mickey Mantle, Roger Maris, Yogi Berra. Adult sportswomen only rarely surfaced—in occasional newspaper articles and for a few minutes once every four years during TV's Olympic coverage. Sports*men* we could follow on a daily basis. They hit home runs, spit, acted taciturn or famously goofy as their personalities took them, but always, always exhibited on the field a tough, no-nonsense attitude I'd been taught to call "masculine." They got the job done.

And that—getting the job done—was maybe the thing I liked best about sport. That sweet, sweet *kiss* when bat met ball. The solid *smack* of a sneakered foot stepped hard on home plate. Things looked clearer on the field than off; I knew where I stood when I guarded first base. Outside the foul lines, life got fuzzy. My own no-nonsense approach, clothed in the cotton blouses and pleated skirts we wore to school, seemed to confuse and offend people who expected something more feminine. It confused me, too. But no matter. I could hit a ball with the best.

Above all, sport served as my stage, a place to act out—if only for myself—heroic virtues. Where else could a timber manager's daughter, one of the relatively privileged in a predominantly blue-collar mill town, show grit and gumption and have it *matter*? The stories I knew about famous sports figures like miler Glenn Cunningham and decathlete Rafer Johnson taught me what took the prize. If I practiced discipline, set high goals, performed with grace under pressure, and, above all, displayed enough desire, then I—like any athlete—could earn my way onto the team. And from there, I could perform that most transcendent of all feats: the well-deserved win. This sports creed, I thought, made me the equal of any male; like sportsmen, I could earn the right to do rather than be, act instead of watch, and hit home runs over flashy ads painted on a genuine outfield fence while someone cooked hot dogs and kept score for *me*.

The Redwood Bowl, when I finally reach it, resounds with Homecoming cheer. Helmeted players whose pads exaggerate their masculine outlines—broad shoulders, big chests, powerful thighs—stretch and sprint before us. The feel is so different from the lonely quiet the women's track team encountered here that it takes me awhile to settle in. Gradually, my memories sharpen to match the faces of people I taught beside a decade ago. Several of us stand on the 50-yard line to be introduced as part of the Sports Hall of Fame ceremonies. Later, at dinner, I will present a nominee.

I coached at Humboldt State University for two years in the late 1970s, at age twenty-four the youngest faculty member in my department but already a veteran of three seasons of intercollegiate coaching. My own average performance on teams in college convinced me that coaching would take me further than playing; I didn't think much about what coaching might do *to* (as apart from *for*) me. Besides teaching courses in recreation administration, I came to this far northern outpost of the California state university system to rebuild a sagging women's track and field program.

Down on the field in front of us the football moves back and forth. This is sport as drama of beef and bluff; my attention soon wanders. At halftime I slip out the stadium gates, around the back of the practice field, and down a shaded forest trail. On the dark earth of this very path, I conducted my first workouts as head coach. My shrill new whistle echoed from these massive redwood trunks. For two years here, teaching young women to pursue their own excellence—fiercely—formed the axis of my life.

In my journal I wrote:

1978 and 1979

Coaching. I feel myself coming alive on the deepest levels. Coaching challenges me to the core, forcing me to use all of my capacities and abilities, demanding everything I can give. I love the exhilarating feel of being used fully, of concentrating everything I have been and am in the hope that what is possible will be. The spiral of hope lifts—striving, discipline, patience, beauty— and I am everywhere forced to evaluate, to stretch out, in, up. [I feel] the immense satisfaction of stretching others, of knowing how to teach and inspire people to do difficult things well, of molding community from the crossings of diverse lives. The price is the weight of example and authenticity. No one can share the risk and fine-drawn pride and pain with the coach, not even most of her athletes. If the whole thing wasn't so much your own creation, your baby, it wouldn't bring such incredible tension: the chance of high-flying consummation, the looming possibility of defeat. Sometimes it's like riding a bike at breakneck speed down an immense hill—without the possibility (likelihood?) of a crash, there couldn't be so much beauty.

Coaching seemed to me then a commitment to care—about life and its living. I privileged the team experience. The quality of our togetherness would take us through a very long season. At the same time, I believed strongly in individual effort and responsibility. Each athlete had to do her job in the throwing circles, and on the track and jumping aprons, and live with whatever the consequences turned out to be. If this team was my baby, then I saw my job as helping it to grow up.

In company with many parents, though, my joy and caring at times slid into a protective anger. College coaches by tradition enjoy almost complete autonomy in their work with their team members; outsiders' interference with discipline or training schedules is serious trespass, analogous to walking into someone's living room and telling her children what to do. Nevertheless, at HSU the athletes and I soon began to receive unsolicited advice. One community member, a man, told a frosh that the weight workouts I'd written for her training were wrong, and pressured her—an inexperienced young athlete— to follow a strength program used by pro football players. Another man, this one a visiting high school coach, walked up to a group of us at practice and simply interrupted me to criticize an athlete's running form. Unasked-for guidance from male students, faculty, and staff became a constant sore point. As the months passed, I grew adept at warning them off. And more and more angry.

May 1977

If as a female you lose, men laugh at you contemptuously and treat you patronizingly, even if they themselves are losers. ("After all, I can beat her.") If you win, you are considered subnormal, a dyke, "too muscular," and probably a bad lay in the bargain. Bets are laid on you, males crowd around offering advice—something they wouldn't think of doing to a male winner—and everyone tries to get a piece of the action, to build his ego on and from you. ("Yep, I can *still* beat her.") . . . The insidious effect of all this is that women listen to this pompous patronizing and let it ruin the joy they gain from improvement . . . How many times has a fledgling female athlete, spreading her new wings, had them clipped by the coarse and unfeeling remarks of a self-styled Mr. Superstar, himself by all outward indications a "failure" in athletics? It's time for women to say "to hell with you" and turn their attention from the color and cut of their uniforms to the incomparable grace and beauty of the female body in disciplined motion.

These particular men—not every man, I hasten to add, and not often those associated with the HSU men's track team—insulted the athletes and me by assuming that their expertise was more valid than our own and that we would be grateful for their help. Even harder for me to accept were the female athletes who asked if they could travel and compete as team members but train with their boyfriends or a male coach. (One simply said she just couldn't get used to obeying a woman.) Curiously enough, the man in question was never our own assistant coach, a highly competent grad student and former wrestler named Lloyd Wilson, who combined an intuitive understanding of people with a well-known penchant for hard work.

Where I once loved sport for the fun, the laughter, the physical highs, I became fierce in pursuing the wins which would show the men and women who rejected my coaching that I could be competent on their terms.

Each season at HSU began with a scramble for athletes. Phone calls, letters, recruiting talks in PE classes, bulletin boards extolling the pleasures and challenges of taking up track and field—Lloyd and I did everything we could to make five months of hard work sound special. We didn't have scholarships or a strong tradition, so we sold the sport on its merits, often to women who had not competed in athletics before. Our you-can-do attitude perforce extended year-round; the bulletin board in the locker room became a long collage of photos, pictures cut from magazines, our own and rivals' results. I typed every quote I could find which modeled the approach I wanted "my" athletes, as I called them, to take.

Some of those slogans came from mimeographed cards my own college coach handed out after practice: "Luck is what happens when *preparation* meets *opportunity*." "Enthusiasm *creates* momentum." "Act as if it were *impossible to fail*." Athletics still seemed to me a moral world, one which rewarded effort. Except for my increasing brusqueness toward male would-be "colleagues," I taught what had been taught to me.

And—following yet another sporting custom—I placed myself in charge. I knew just two models for women wielding authority. The first I thought of as the "do as I say" method, the one my own teachers and coaches used with me. It wasn't ideal; I knew being told what to do kept me for years from taking responsibility for my own training. But it worked in the short term. While I hated the idea of ordering other women around, and wondered sometimes about my fitness to lead, I needed something effective. The second way I'd seen women use power involved the self-sacrificing, nurturing-as-service paradigm of the proverbial mother, which seemed soft in comparison. Soft was something a too-young head coach with eyes upon her could not afford to be. Authoritarian got things done, reached the measurable goal; it seemed safer, especially in the face of aggressive masculinity. Everything in the athletic world, right down to the HSU locker-room bulletin board, supported my choice.

My notebook for the 1977–78 track and field year still contains every training plan and result. An athlete readying herself for practice on Monday read one of these mimeographed schedules, pinned of course on the bulletin board. There she found her personal plan for the next seven days, detailing what to run, how fast, and where, accompanied by goals, perhaps "constant effort" or "concentration." A typical March workout for half-milers and milers might consist of a mile or more of easy warm-up running; stretching; five repeats of 1,000 yards (just over half a mile) run faster than a specified time and separated by a timed rest period; then 1.5-plus miles of easy warm-down followed by more stretching. Sprinters added hopping and bounding drills designed to build speed. Throwers drilled for speed and strength, the components of physical power. Most athletes lifted weights two or three times a week.

Much of this activity took place under a coach's eye. My tension about the workout to come began to build in mid-morning, as I lectured or read student papers. By two or two-thirty, I stood on the track with watch and clipboard in hand. For the next four hours I encouraged, teased, cajoled, browbeat, and criticized people into choosing to perform. In any fifteen minutes I might jog from the track to the practice field behind the stands, there to instruct a discus thrower in "blocking," the strong bracing and extension of her left leg which would enhance the whiplike sling of her right arm, resulting in a longer throw. Then back to the track to time a mile repeat, watching closely for the slight wobble and too-hard breathing which signaled overexhaustion while shouting encouragement and at the same time looking out of the corner of my eye for male kibitzers and checking to see that athletes finishing their workout stretched their muscles before escaping inside. Up, again, to the practice field, to work with javelin throwers on the crossover steps taken to bend the body back—draw the bow—just before the spear sails into the sky. At the same time,

Lloyd performed his own circuit, moving between jumpers, hurdlers, and sprinters. Evenings and weekends we met, or I pored over pieces of paper, making lists comparing our distances and times to those of athletes from other schools. Computer-generated tables awarded points for each result in competition, which allowed comparison rankings across events; lines on a big chart I posted for all to see showed an athlete's relative position on the team, and across the weeks her rise . . . or fall.

On paper, all the effort paid off. By my second season we had a team of twenty-two young women, including nine who had never competed in track and field before and eight frosh; among them were three national-class athletes, a shot-putter and two distance runners. Although we would again finish last in the conference, we won two meets—the first in five years—and broke school records forty-one times, setting fourteen conference marks. Five of us traveled to Tennessee for the national championship.

Told simply, my coaching at HSU sounds like success. It was and it wasn't. A month or two into my second season, an athlete thrust at me a hand-lettered Notice of Declaration. It served notice from "the plebeians of the Humboldt State Redwood Runners" to the "czar" that the latter's "autocratic tendencies" in requiring weight lifting endangered "the femininity of the female populace." This, coupled with the amount of time practices took, "might increase the spinsterhood rate," and so, I was to understand, the "peasants" hereby took the "evanescence of decision-making" into their own hands. Laughter graces my memories of almost all HSU team interactions. But I'm quite sure the Declaration's authors had a point or two to make with me, their czar. Points I chose, finally, not to heed.

The athletes who gave me the Declaration took sport very seriously; at the same time, their understanding of femininity formed a barrier beyond which they could not easily step. This bothered me, to say the least. What we should be about, I felt, was not a mere expansion of gender roles (by being that unusual thing, female athletes) but a radical recasting of them. A new definition of what women could do. For me back then, in sport, that meant everything honorable society labeled "masculine." All the leadership advice I'd received or read—coaching how-to books, articles in *Sports Illustrated*, and male-authored sport and war fiction—told me never to let my subordinates see me sweat. So I laughed as I read the Notice of Declaration, its authors' eyes on my face, and treated it thereafter as a joke. I did, I thought, something new, even radical, for a woman. I played it tough and aggressive. Just like a man.

The ultimate challenge to my authority, when it came, didn't play out prettily. I posted on the board our list of entries for the conference championship. One team member, a senior I'll call Connie, told me she would not run the races in which I'd entered her. My decisions had been based on probable team points and were subject to adjustment on meet day, but in her final season, Connie wanted to run well in the races she enjoyed. I saw that as selfish and, despite her exemplary year of team leadership and very hard work, refused to let her compete. The situation passed beyond fixing.

I understood quite soon that the lines I'd spoken as the authoritarian female coach came from a much larger script. Sporting conventions of obedience to leadership can teach— had, in fact, taught me—a certain relationship to power, one benefiting those who already have it. As power's representative in this situation, I showed those watching what can happen, and too often does, to a lone individual with courage enough to voice a challenge. I wonder now, too, about the dynamics of power among us women. We'd all internalized certain expectations about the way coaches and athletes interact. At the same time, most of us carried scars from power expressed and experienced as domination. Would Connie have argued with a male coach? When he argued back, would she have listened?

We lost the meet anyway, and would have even had Connie run the races I wanted. Some part of me knew that even before it played out. Our argument had been partly about the team's best interest, but also about our individual, unmatching expectations and my ability to win by acting tough. I still feel badly about it.

Yet of course power was part, a large part, of what I loved about coaching. The athletes were "my" athletes; the team, "my" team. I saw sport then as a wager, a gamble; mainlined adrenaline. Coaching appealed to me because it upped the stakes. Suddenly, I had many more cards to play than just running my own races. And much more to lose. But aren't the stakes part of what makes the game? As long as I filled that central role in our small corner of sport—where I *mattered* (rare for a woman)—I could win. For even while I hated the sexism and misogyny in sport, and despite all my talk of blazing new trails for women, I remained a bona fide member of the sporting world. And very, very angry. I was in charge, responsible. Winning, I see now, was damn near everything.

At least in public. Privately I wrote about power's cost, envisioning coaching at times as a predator sucking away my energy and creativity. I worried that, like those men I could not abide, I simply wanted an ego massage. And without much support for the difficult task of teaching women to value their own strength when too many others did not, I wondered why I bothered.

March 1978

There is a raw power in coaching that both excites and frightens me in the sense that the team is an extension of me, dressing, behaving, competing according to my rules and wishes. Who am I? Others' rules and ways are just as good . . . Track is incredibly fulfilling to me in a way classroom teaching is not, yet what is it? Teaching women to run with grace and strength—in meaningless circles on an artificial surface . . . Training someone to jump backward over a bar into a foam-rubber pit. For what?

This need to question would, years later, bring me to answers. But first it fed my shame. As we mingle before the Homecoming Hall of Fame banquet, people ask, "And are you still coaching?" I mumble, eyes downcast, some unmemorable answer. I tell no one the truth: four years after leaving HSU, I simply realized one day that many of my actions as coach, despite the best of intentions, furthered inequities I'd come to abhor. The whole thing was much, much bigger than I felt able to change. I quit coaching the year the team co-captains skipped our own regional championship to cheer at a race their boyfriends ran. Twenty years after my own introduction to organized sport, not much had changed, except that it was now by choice—not solely for lack of options—that young women sat on sidelines watching boys and men play.

I had so wanted to make things different for women. The sport creed's slogans and myths taught me that we control our own fates. I was the leader; if I found myself unable to teach women a sense of free agency, to pursue athletic excellence regardless of parents' or boyfriends' agendas and actions, then the fault must lie in me. What I took away from coaching, besides this haunting sense of my own failure to effect what truly mattered, were only more questions. How, specifically, does muscularity threaten a female's "femininity"? Why would women's pursuit of sporting excellence jeopardize relationships with men? And what, in any case, are issues of women's relationship to men and men's judgment of women's physical appearance doing in *women's* sport?

My banquet speech sticks closely to fact. I don't find it easy to joke, as do other speakers, about those years. I hope what I do say conveys the affection and respect I feel for the woman I'm presenting, the first national-class athlete with whom I was privileged to work. I want my words to honor her guts and persistence. Before arriving at HSU, she honed her talent by competing directly against boys and men, usually finishing near the back of the pack amid tolerance rather than celebration. During that time, if she wanted to be taken seriously as an athlete, she had no other choice.

What I don't say at the banquet is what survival in those

years of no options cost many sportswomen. I want to recognize women's successes. So I try to mask my contempt for malesport, a contempt for so long now my shield against anger and pain. But internally I have few illusions left: I know it is precisely women's competence, our claiming of our own physicality and of our right to direct it toward our own ends, that prompts remarks meant to fan women's worry about their "femininity."

I teach now at a small experimental college, where at our best we manage to look through (not ignore) gender, race, class, disability, sexual orientation, and other differences to see the human being within. Faculty are co-learners with our student colleagues; we strive to give up the authoritarian power of age, privilege, and position, and replace it with shared powers of expertise and curiosity, joined with responsibility. From my vantage point away from coaching, it occurs to me to ask: At this turn of the century—a time when women thrust shot puts, run marathons, hurl javelins, push weights, and fold themselves backward over a high jump bar as skillfully and seriously as men—what's really happening? Isn't it time to drop the labels and admit that all the positive qualities we've ceded to men and called "masculine" belong also to women? How will sport be different when we take pride in sharing the components of power? How will doing so change our world?

I remain angry about what we women suffered in sport. But the more important legacy I carry comes from sliding into home plate during a junior high PE class: a few pieces of gravel under the skin of my hip. I remember the actual play quite well. I slid safely around the tag, and the teacher and a few teammates gathered nearby in admiration. Others groaned, exasperated at my insistence on taking sport seriously. But what I did mattered; I scored the winning run.

Sport should be about being a hero. About grit and gumption and taking life seriously. I'd just add more to "hero" now.

I'd talk about sportspeople, not sportsmen and sportswomen. I'd say that when we do our genuine, thoughtful best as human beings possessed of integrity and mindful of others, we each earn the right to speak our piece and shoulder our share—of the work *and* the glory. What's at stake here isn't our gender or our sexuality, or even a mark on some achievement-oriented ruler of worth. What matters are our abilities to care, to take risks, and to own our own bodies, as each of us pursues her or his healthiest self. We're all heroes when, together, we get that job done.

A couple of years ago, I revisited the Redwood Bowl. The occasion was nonceremonial, just regular HSU track practice. The present coach and I have corresponded, most recently when the school's women's cross-country team placed at nationals. But in my hotel room the night before, I decide to stay an anonymous observer. I think for a while about how some students and I started the cross-country team as a non-varsity sport, raising entry and travel money on our own and traveling crammed together in my sagging Toyota to and from meets.

March 1996

> I'd like to believe it all lives on—that Redwood Bowl still holds our will and desire like a cup, to slake our own and others' thirst for significance. For meaning. That's certainly what I looked for on that track: the exact circumstances in which my effort and courage had meaning, for myself and others. That special alignment of earth and sun in which I *mattered.*

When I walk into the stadium the next afternoon, a group of young men and women are gathered around an older man with a clipboard who stands exactly where I always did to start practice—at the finish line. I take a seat on the spectator side and look around. The track itself is different, pitted black asphalt replaced by a softer, leveler red. Gone too are the weeds in the long-jump pit, though flowered vines still twine along the far turn and redwood trees brood. A sudden longing for my companions, those twenty-two young women and Lloyd, that good, patient man, pushes away lingering anger and guilt. In trying circumstances, we did the best we could. Memories of them continue to teach me. Although some of us disagreed about crucial issues, and at difficult junctures, together we all formed a team. Every one of us mattered.

Below me the group around the coach breaks up, and the complex chaos of a track team in action begins to spread out. Two men with the hungry look of distance runners circle the track on the infield grass; one says, "Chemicals are really hard on my body," and the other nods, clears his throat, and spits. A woman dressed all in black sits alone, staring, at the far end of the straightaway, then curls into a long set of crunches, the more difficult version of sit-ups. A short, powerful-looking man wearing a black baseball cap and green sateen shorts attaches a pulley apparatus to one football goal post, turns his back, and reaches over his shoulder, palm up, to grasp the elastic tubing. He pulls as hard as he can, then relaxes, strengthening javelin-throwing muscles but looking like an ant gone mad with the need to haul home a huge and oddly-shaped trophy. Cries of "track" clear the way for two women running one-lap repeats; as the coach yells, "Come on, ladies, pick it up," younger male voices cut through his admonition with warm encouragement.

This once was my world; I feel completely at ease. The sun crosses slowly over the Bowl. A steeplechaser stops for the first time in his forty-five-minute series of recovery jogs, alternated with half-mile repeats over hurdles, to chat with the coach. Tiny red letters on his T-shirt read "Track and Field Championship." A muscular woman slowly jogs by, her bare feet and easy motion a sharp contrast to the snap she displayed a few minutes ago, the spiked shoe on her left foot leading her over flight after flight of hurdles.

I try but can't remember a time when we shared this track with the men. The two teams trained, traveled, and usually competed in their own separate orbits. I still strongly oppose combining programs unless the number of female athletes who come back each season holds steady or rises, and as many female as male administrators, coaches, trainers, publicists, and officials hold jobs. Even in the late 1990s, this rarely happens anywhere in sport. But these HSU women do display knowledge and experience visibly greater than in our day. If that comes from moving into sport's center of public significance—the previously all-male enclaves—I'm willing, at least, to consider the value. It's hard to let go of the suspicion born of my own experience; I'll believe sport is truly beginning to change when sportswomen no longer endure harassment, when sportsmen regularly enact the positive qualities we've for so long called "feminine," and when sportscasters and marketers stop emphasizing coaches' and players' heterosexuality. In the meantime I'll try to notice milestones. Who would have thought, for example, that men would ever cheer openly for women at practice, in front of their peers?

More athletes come out of the PE building to start their workouts. I watch until the scene seems to recede and lift. Then for a ghostly moment, it is as it was. Throwers strain in baggy green sweat clothes, rasping breath steams in cold, shadowed air. Two hands grasp the top of a hurdle. Coaches' shouts ring out over laughter. A lean figure in gold and green breaks the tape in a championship mile. All of our gear bears indelible stains, marked by the sweat and the tears of our shared aspiration. And each of us, including the women and men actually before me, looks quite a bit like a hero.

As shadows darken the field, a young woman wearing a clean white T-shirt and baggy green shorts begins to run methodically up and down the long stairways in the stands where I sit. She passes near me on her fourteenth climb, breath pushing out in time with her foot strikes. We didn't require female athletes to run stairs much when I coached here; their inexperienced and previously undertrained legs simply couldn't handle it. This woman moves evenly through her four circuits of the grandstand with no signs on her face but those of discipline and hard work, the same sweat and fixed resolve I saw around her predecessors' eyes as they ran sprints on level grass.

When she moves back out onto the track to finish her workout, I shiver once in the chill, empty stands, and acknowledge the significance of what I and others did here. The flame we passed. To now.

learning to swim at forty-five

COLLEEN J. MCELROY

> *I could not whistle and walk in storms*
> *along Lake Michigan's shore . . .*
> *I could not swallow the lake.*
> >   —*Clarence Major*

Having given up hope for a high-wire act
I've taken to water and the quicksilver
Danger of working words hand over hand.
At the edge of the pool I am locked in gravity
And remember the jeers at girl scout camp
Where *catfish* meant anyone who lived in a ghetto
With no pools and no need to tan and everyone
Spent more time learning how to keep their hair
From *going bad* than they did learning breaststrokes.

And yes, Clarence, I learned to swallow the lake
Including all that it held and what I was told
By Mrs. Fitzsimmons of Harris Stowe Teachers
Who later said I couldn't hold the elements
Of tone or the way words break and run like rain,
The *Hecates* and *Africs* filling the page
Until it grows buoyant under the weight of sonnets,
A feat she believed so unconsciously automatic
It arrived full blown at birth.

For forty years I've lived under the pull of air,
All the while knowing survival meant learning

To swim in strange waters. *Just jump in and do it*
They yelled at camp, then tossed me heels over head
Their humor an anchor dragging me down.
There I defied training films and descended just once,
My body stone weight and full of the first primal fear
Of uncurling from the water belly of a mother country.
There I could not whistle in the face of the storm
And even my legs were foreign.

Poetry like swimming cannot be learned
Fitzsimmons insisted as I rubbed the smooth skin
Behind my ears where gill flaps had failed to appear.
Now years later, I voluntarily step below the surface
And there beneath the chlorine blue, I am finally reptilian
And so close to the Middle Passage, I will pay any price
For air. If silence has a smell, it is here
Where my breath fizzles in a champagne of its own making,
Where I must learn to sing to the rhythms of water
The strange currents and patterns of moons and tides.

Fitzsimmons, it doesn't happen all at once. To swim
You must learn to labor under the threat of air lost
Forever and hold fear close to you like a safety net.
You must imagine the body, the way it floats and extends
First like an anchor, then a lizard or a dead leaf.
Direction is some point where the sun is inverted and sweet
Air hammers the brain with signals that must be ignored.
You learn to take risks, to spread yourself thin,
You learn to look *through a glass darkly*
And in your darkness, build elegies of your own rhythms,
And yes Fitzsimmons, you learn when to swallow
The lake and when to hold to the swell of it.

seconds

TERESA LEO

In high school my life revolved around running. There wasn't much else to do in 1981 in Carbondale, a once-vital coal-mining town in northeastern Pennsylvania. By the time I turned thirteen, the mines had long closed, trains no longer rolled through town, and draglines crouched frozen in time at the slag heaps, as though the miners all went home from work one day in 1957 and never returned. In a town without any real industry to speak of, a person's worth was measured by his or her ability to excel at sports. The local newspaper devoted three-quarters of its pages to every sport imaginable, from ladies' golf to the Knights of Columbus basketball league to peewee football. Being a star in a particular sport meant you had a chance of getting out of town.

My chance came during my senior year of high school, when a university in central Pennsylvania began scouting me for a track scholarship. By then I'd distinguished myself as a runner: I was captain of the girls' track team, a three-time MVP, and held the league records in both the mile and the two-mile. I ranked twelfth in the state in the two-mile, my strongest race. No one in my family had attended college, and I knew that only a scholarship would get me there. My mother was a hairdresser and my father used his Air Force training to work as an electronic technician at an army depot an hour away from our house. They didn't quite understand my desire for college, especially since a year's tuition at a private school added up to more than half their yearly earnings. Especially since others in my family who'd had opportunities to leave had chosen to stay.

My grandfather had his chance one Sunday afternoon in 1937. He stood five feet seven inches with a slight build but, from working as a coal miner, had the forearms of a much bigger man. His good throwing arm won him a stint as third baseman for the Scranton Miners, an AA farm team. His big break came when a scout from the Philadelphia A's approached him after a game. They wanted him to move. He knew my grandmother would never take their young son (my father) away from Carbondale, never leave behind the family members who had immigrated from Italy. The choice came down to my grandmother or baseball. He made his decision on the spot, and continued to work the mines until they closed. I wanted to have the same kind of choice. I wanted to choose differently.

I didn't have the build of a long-distance runner. Most girls I ran against were tall and lean with bounding, elongated strides; at five feet two inches, I had to take two strides to match the distance the taller girls could cover with one. Local sportswriters said I won races out of sheer desire, and began calling me the Two-Step Two-Miler.

I didn't train with my teammates, since I'd put myself on a regimen of ten to fifteen miles a day, and no one else wanted or was crazy enough to run that far. I ran for my life: the backwoods paths that led up around the slag heaps, the narrow country road out of town up to the four corners, the railroad tracks that had rusted and overgrown with weeds, the footpath that ran precariously next to the riverbank. The running hurt and was lonely, but I just blazed on, hoping that if I ran far enough and fast enough I'd find my way out; but wishing, too, for someone to run with me, someone who understood.

Then he showed up.

One day after practice I walked by the weight room the boys' track team used. I glanced in and stopped cold. There, talking to the coach, stood the most beautiful man I had ever seen. He wore a dark-blue sweat suit with three white stripes down the sides of the arms and legs and matching Adidas running shoes, and had hair like Bruce Jenner's, but blond and messy, as though he'd just finished a ten-mile run. His body looked taut and muscular, but it was his face that drew me: it was a child's face on a man's body, kind, but a little sad, and if not for that hint of sadness, he would have looked exactly like the leading man in an '80s soap opera. But the sadness made him more human, and after five seconds of standing there, water bottle and school-issue blue-and-red cotton sweats in my hands, I recognized him. He was John Kelly, a four-letter varsity athlete who'd graduated from my high school five years earlier and attended college on a football scholarship. His football jersey still hung in the glass case by the gym. I'd heard he'd dropped out of college to join the Marines, and figured his tour was up so he was back in town. I stood and watched him for a few minutes, but, unable to think of anything to say, I left before he saw me.

A few days later he showed up at the track. He introduced himself and told me he'd been following my progress in the local papers. I'd often made the headlines, since during each meet I ran an unprecedented four miles: the half-mile, the mile, the two-mile relay, and the two-mile. Most meets I would make a clean sweep and win all four events. But it turned out he'd been following my progress because of my name itself—I had the same name as his high school sweetheart, the woman he had dated for seven years in high school and college. She was my cousin, a second cousin the same age as John. He couldn't believe that another person had the same name, so he'd shown up at the track to see who I was, then asked my coach if he could become my trainer.

Delighted that John wanted to run with me, my coach thought it a miracle that I'd have my own personal trainer, a local hero who, perhaps, could get my times down and move me up the ranks at the state finals. I thought him a gift, not only someone who could keep me company on the long runs that made my insides burn but another athlete who knew what it took to win, someone whose ability in sports had gotten him noticed by college scouts.

My parents had become jaded. Since I won races so often, they seemed compelled to make comments only when I didn't break my own records. So I imagined John waiting at the finish line, ready to drape a jacket over my shoulders and tell me how well I'd run, then sweep me off in his 1972 Plymouth Duster while the rest of the team took the bus back to town.

Every day after school, John met me in the gym and, without much talking, led me through a series of stretches and then out for our run. As the weeks passed, my times improved. I even broke my own two-mile record at my high school stadium, a loosely packed gravel track around the football field surrounded on three sides by towering black mountains of slag. But at the same time, I began to develop a crush on John, and seeing him every day became increasingly difficult. I grew overly concerned with my appearance. Running alone, I hadn't cared much about how I looked, mostly wearing an old, washed-out Green Bay Packers T-shirt and baggy shorts. I started to coordinate my outfits, pairing brightly colored cotton tanks with skimpy nylon running shorts slit high up the sides.

My hair became a ritual unto itself. Loose, it hung long and coily, and before John I just pulled it up into a tight ponytail for utility's sake. Now I found myself spending an inordinate amount of time in the locker room holding my head under the wall-mounted hand dryer and wielding a large round brush in an attempt to straighten and feather my hair to look like Kate Jackson's in *Charlie's Angels*. After the first mile, however, I'd start to sweat and my hair would kink and frizz, so I'd end up pulling it back anyway with the rubber band I wore around my wrist.

By mid-season John thought I should continue my training with him on weekends. He'd pick me up at my parents' house on Saturdays and drive the Duster to some remote, wooded trail, park the car, and push me to run anywhere between ten and eighteen miles. We talked and joked around on these runs, but when I asked him personal questions, he'd steer the conversation to my running form.

"Stop clenching your fists," he'd say. "You're tensing your arm muscles by doing that. You have to keep your hands open. Think." Or he'd tell me to stop talking and concentrate on my breathing. "Don't breathe like you're hyperventilating; take deep breaths and fill your lungs. You have to expand your lung capacity." Then he'd move on to my posture, which he thought a little too slouched, or he'd catch me swinging my arms from side to side when I got tired. It got to the point that he could catch any small deviation from the perfect posture within seconds.

My parents became curious about John, since I disappeared with him for hours every weekend. My mother asked me to invite him to dinner. I brought it up on one of our Saturday runs and wasn't altogether shocked when he said, "So, is this a date?" I'd been shamelessly flirting with him for weeks, saying things like, "You know, Italian girls have that hot Mediterranean blood."

I had no idea what I was talking about; all I knew about sex involved the awkward teeth knocking I experienced in the back seat of a couple of cars and the ritualistic fumbling with my bra hooks that made me think all boys hopeless and crude. I wanted a man, a real man, someone who could make me see colors with my eyes closed when we kissed.

We planned to have dinner at my parents' and go to a movie the following Saturday night.

My mother made eggplant Parmesan, vegetable lasagna, rolled pork-and-beef meatballs, and sauce from scratch. I came from a long line of Italian women who loved to cook from secret recipes. Any occasion could be turned into a lavish celebration of food. I hated to cook and steered clear of the kitchen that night, spending two hours trying to transform myself from girl-jock to something approaching my version of feminine sophistication. John had never, in all the weeks we'd been running together, seen me in anything more elaborate than a sweat suit.

I showered and shaved my legs and underarms, and

attempted to work a miracle of early '80s styling on my hair. My mother's beauty shop, located right in our basement, contained every tool imaginable: curling irons and blow-dryers hung from wall mounts like the tools at my father's workbench; shelves held gels and mousses, rollers and bobby pins, and the kind of spray that shellacked hair permanently into place. I knew what to do from having watched my mother work her magic on women's heads, their hair poked or teased, fluffed or straightened, until they emerged from their comb-outs with souped-up versions of styles from ladies' magazines. I blow-dried the back straight and forced the ends to curl under through incessant yanking with a large round brush. Then I used a curling iron to make symmetrical ringlets that twisted away from my face from the center part down to the ends. I slipped on a pink blouse with glittery pinstripes, puffy shoulders, and a matching ribbon to tie around the neck, and tucked it into a tight pair of Sergio Valente jeans with little silver zippers over the rear pockets. Brown platform shoes and a clear plastic belt pulled the outfit together. Then I borrowed my mother's makeup and lined my eyes, brushed the lashes with blue mascara, dusted my cheeks with blush, and colored my mouth with pink frosted lipstick, a shade lighter than Pepto-Bismol.

I thought I looked beautiful.

When I answered the door John said, "Look at you." I couldn't tell if this was a compliment or a neutral remark to mask disappointment. I told him to come in, and as soon as he entered the house, my parents went into overdrive, as if Joe Namath himself had dropped by for a home-cooked meal. My father, a lifetime athlete and sports fan said, "Hey, Kelly, remember that pass you threw in the fourth quarter against Lakeland? Where'd you end up? I thought you got the big football scholarship."

Everyone who had ever tried to make it to the big leagues and failed knew everyone else who had tried and succeeded. My father tried in 1954. As a senior in high school, he was one of twenty-five ballplayers invited to a tryout camp for the St. Louis Browns. But he didn't have a great throwing arm and couldn't hit a sidearm curve ball. The manager who cut him saw his name and hometown on the tryout roster, and asked if he was related to the Leo who played ball back in the '30s. When he said yes, the manager told him it was too bad he didn't have his father's arm.

My father's questions hovered over the room like an infield fly before it drops between two players. John looked uncomfortable and smiled his boyish grin. Before he had a chance to answer, my mother grabbed his hand, led him to a seat at the table, and started piling lasagna on his plate. And for an hour and a half I was invisible. I'd never seen my parents so starstruck. They obviously thought him perfect son-in-law material, and a part of me thought this, too, the part programmed to believe that girls got married after high school, the part that wanted to please my parents.

Out in the Duster, I arranged myself as demurely as I could. Usually I just flopped in the car after a ten-mile run, immediately taking my shoes and socks off, and put my bare feet up on the dashboard. John wanted to take me to the Viewmont Mall to see Richard Dreyfuss and Amy Irving in *The Competition*, a film about two virtuoso piano players who compete against each other at a recital but end up falling in love.

Since we were too early for the late movie, John pulled off at the Sleepy Hollow bowling alley so we could play video games. I couldn't bear to lose at anything and played pinball as if it were an Olympic sport. While I wildly banged the flippers, John, who stood behind me, unzipped and rezipped one of my back pockets. "Pretty fancy," he said, and I froze for a second and lost the ball.

At the movie theater, John looked nervous when we walked in, and only when the lights dimmed did he seem to relax. We both sat bolt upright and watched the film without speaking. About halfway through, his hand brushed up against my leg. He hooked his pinkie around mine, then wrapped his hand around my pinkie and the next two fingers, then grabbed my whole hand and pulled it over to rest on his lap. He held my hand like this for the rest of the film. I hovered somewhere between abject joy and outright fear. I convinced myself that if I moved slightly or turned to look at him he would realize what he was doing, think better of it, and drop my hand. I sat motionless and kept my eyes riveted to the screen.

After the movie we walked outside, and when we got to the passenger side of the Duster, I turned to look at John's face while he fumbled for the keys. Depending on the light, his hazel eyes vacillated between blue and green. In the bright parking lot lights of the Viewmont Mall, they appeared to be green, but I kept staring to pin down the exact color. He pulled the keys out of his pocket and I stepped away from the door. It took him a few seconds to locate the right key, and, singling it out from the rest on the ring, he moved his hand toward the lock.

At the last second he dropped the keys, grabbed my head with both hands, and threw me back against the car. I'd seen this move in championship basketball matches, right at the buzzer, when the star shooter looks like he's going to pass off the ball, but fakes instead and takes the jumper that wins the game.

He held my face, then slowly ran the thumb of his right hand across my mouth and back again. He leaned toward me and lightly brushed my lips before he opened his mouth. Then he pushed his tongue in and ran the tip over the tops of my teeth near the gumline. He pulled his tongue out for a second, then thrust it back into my mouth. I had never been kissed like this before. My brain trailed one step behind my body, and, by the time I processed his tongue-to-gum sweep, he had already pulled back and squatted down to pick up the keys.

"That's a technical foul," I thought, as he opened the door.

After our date, John disappeared. He stopped training me and didn't show up for my next-to-last meet of the season, an away game at Abington Heights. By then the university had offered me the track scholarship, and I wanted to finish the season at the top of the league. But I was so preoccupied with John's absence that my four-year undefeated stretch in the two-mile came to an end. I lost to a tall, skinny sophomore from Abington named Eileen, who had her hair pulled up high into two cascading pigtails that snapped behind her like twisted wet towels when she ran.

When the gun went off, two of her teammates sprinted out from the starting line, one cutting me off and nudging her way into my lane to take the lead. The other rushed up on the side and boxed me in, running elbow to elbow so I couldn't get out. I literally ran on the heels of the girl in front of me, short-stopping each stride so as not to trip. Halfway around the track, Eileen raced up alongside us, passed our moving boxlike formation, and took the lead. Seeing her ahead made me panic, like a swimmer tangled in weeds whose frantic struggling only tangles her further, until she exhausts herself trying to escape.

We ran like this for half a mile before the girl on my side faltered a bit and dropped back. I edged out into the lane and sprinted up to pass the other girl. Both of them fell back almost immediately, sacrificial runners whose whole purpose had been to burn themselves out in an attempt to advance their star teammate.

By the time I got a clear view of her, Eileen had a 100-yard lead and I simply gave up. No one knew that I was a "front-runner," someone who sprinted when the gun went off and kept running hard until comfortably ahead of the pack, when I could settle in and run at a calculated pace. No one knew, because in all the league meets I ran during high school, no one ever attempted to pass me in the two-mile.

I spent the last mile of the race chugging along in second place. I lost focus on my stride and breathing, ignored my coach when I passed the stands, and thought about my future. I began to worry that losing one race might be reason enough for the university to revoke my scholarship. I pictured myself working in the sporting goods department of Sugerman's, a K-Mart–style store in town, with the rest of the once-famous local athletes.

Joe Spitzarri, Sugerman's sporting goods manager, graduated from high school with my father. Everyone remembered Joe as the star quarterback of the football team in 1954. He followed my running career in the papers and gave me discounts on sneakers, T-shirts, and shorts based on my performance in the last track meet, 5 percent off for every event I won. Once, while I shopped for a new sweat suit, Joe came up from behind and slapped me hard on the back, saying, "How's the little Two-Stepper?" The force of his hand knocked me off balance and I stumbled forward, taking a couple of steps to recover my footing. Joe thought that I did this on purpose, to demonstrate my famous stride.

"You know," he said in all seriousness, "when you graduate high school, there's a job waiting for you here at Sugerman's."

By the time I crossed the finish line, a good twenty seconds behind Eileen, I could see myself in one of Sugerman's red polyester smocks with the little name badge over the left breast, shotgun shells in one hand, shoehorn in the other.

I was glad John wasn't there to witness this race.

The last meet of the season was the Lackawanna League Finals, held in Scranton, where all teams in the league competed against each other as in a mini-Olympics. Only one girl from each team competed in a given event, and the winners received individual trophies. I knew I'd be running against Eileen in the two-mile, the last event of the night. I tried to put John and the scholarship out of my mind, and just focus on the race.

Fans from area towns, reporters, and twelve girls' track and field squads crowded the stadium. It had huge bleachers, the kind I'd seen on TV for major league sports, with towering stadium lights and numbered seats painted in three equal sections of red, white, and blue. The track was tightly packed dirt sectioned off by precise lines to mark the lanes, and would be a joy to run on compared with the loosely packed gravel one at my high school. A judges' box loomed over the finish line, where an announcer called events over a loudspeaker.

I asked my coach to pull me out of the mile, because I wanted to be in top form when I ran against Eileen. I then ducked under the bleachers, where I spent most of the meet crying about the race. For the first time in my high school running career, they seeded me in second position, and I felt humiliated to take the track in front of that crowd. At nine o'clock, when the announcer called us out for the two-mile, the stadium lights blazed full force. White glare blanketed the track, but the stands remained dark and hard to see. I felt like a mannequin on display in a store window.

As I approached the starting line, someone called my name. I couldn't see him, but I recognized John's voice. While the other two-milers stretched, I ran to where he stood behind the wire fence at the 100-yard mark. He immediately went into coaching mode. "I heard what happened at Abington," he said. "Tonight she's on her own; she doesn't have her teammates to box you in. You can do this. This is your race."

At that moment, I didn't care why he'd been away; I wanted to climb the fence and throw my arms around his neck. When he said, "Good luck," he hooked his fingers through the openings in the wire and leaned a little against the fence. Something came over him then: for a second the sadness lifted from his face. I grabbed his fingers and stuck my lips through one of the diamond cutouts of the fence, and John leaned in and kissed me hard, like a convict in a prison movie. A voice came over the loudspeaker and said, "Will the runner in lane two please get into position."

I broke the kiss, unlocked my fingers, and said, "I'll win this because I love you." I backed up and waited. John stared at me and said nothing, then the sadness returned. His face reminded me of a runner who pulls a hamstring during a race, whose expression changes from deep concentration to painful contortion in a matter of seconds. I turned away partly because I couldn't bear to see his face like that, and partly to see what was going on at the starting line. The starter raised his pistol, so I ran up into position without looking back.

When the gun went off, Eileen bolted from the starting line

and sprinted hard into the first turn. She hugged the inside of the track, trying to keep me out of her lane. She set a ridiculously fast pace, more like the pace of the mile than the two-mile. I tried to pass her on the turn, but she had longer legs and the inside lane, and I couldn't get the full stride on her to cut in legally. I almost dropped back, but to me this seemed like admitting defeat. Instead I did something no long-distance runner should ever do: I moved into lane two and ran at her side.

On the turns I stayed half a step behind, just over her right shoulder, then moved up alongside her when we got to the straightaways. This meant that I actually covered more ground over the course of the race, but in my mind I had no choice. Each time I tried to pass she picked up the pace, so for seven and a half laps we trudged side by side, like a mismatched body and shadow.

During the third lap, I began blocking things out one by one: first the lights, then the noise from the stands, the pain in my lungs, the legs that felt like weights were attached, and finally Eileen's pigtails, which snapped in my face as we rounded the turns. When everything vanished I thought about John standing at the 100-yard mark. I figured he would see my strategy of running an entire race in the second lane either as a dramatic attempt to show how I felt about him or, from a coaching stance, the worst tactic he'd ever seen. I wanted my title back. But I also wanted to make it a race he'd never forget.

I caught my right foot on the inside of my left shin at the 220-yard mark, just a half lap from the finish line, and snapped back into the race. This was the point in the two-mile when I usually picked up the pace and my stomach turned into a volcano. Running as many miles as I did, I'd experienced every possible injury from the waist down: tendinitis over my right ankle, shinsplints, charley horses, and every pulled muscle imaginable from the groin down through the backs of my legs. None of them compared to the pain I felt at that moment.

First I stumbled a bit, then my breathing went out of sync with my stride completely. I gasped for air, taking quick, short breaths from the top of my lungs. By the time I headed into the last turn, my arms and legs were nothing but a frenzy of spastic movement.

Eileen moved three or four strides ahead, and I finally gave in and dropped behind her. My body shut down piece by piece. I lost my posture and hunched my shoulders, and instead of lengthening my stride to try to force my body back into position, I shortened it, moving off the balls of my feet and pounding the track with flat-footed steps. Eileen picked up the pace, and began her kick toward the finish line.

I thought it was over, but when I hit the straightaway I remembered the sprinter's training my coach incorporated into my workouts over the last four years. She'd made me run the 50-yard dash and taught me how to do the "sprinter's lean," an upper-body tilt into the tape at the finish line. I'd thought it pointless, since in the two-mile, winning the race never came down to a single shoulder.

At the 100-yard mark I ran in a diagonal from the inside lane right toward John, who must have thought I'd lost my mind and was going to run right off of the track. When I hit the fourth lane, I pivoted back to face the finish line, pressed my elbows tight against my body, took a deep breath, and sprinted with everything I had left.

About ten feet from the line I was half a step behind Eileen, who must have been shocked because she broke one of the cardinal rules of racing: Never turn to look at your competitors. This slight turn threw her off stride for a split second, just what I needed to close the gap. We ran neck and neck for the last few steps, and when we reached the tape, I literally threw my upper body into it, leaning so far I lost my balance. I took two steps and collapsed on the dirt past the finish line.

Eileen fell, too. As we both writhed on the track gasping for air, a voice came over the loudspeaker saying the judges were conferring to decide who won. I rolled onto my back to look at the sky, but could see only the bright stadium lights. I stared into the glare and thought about the choice I'd have to make: either college or John, and with him Carbondale, the beauty shop or sporting goods department, too many recipes, the mountains of useless slag that rose up and over the town like trophies on a mantel gathering dust.

I shut my eyes and squeezed them so tight tiny bursts of white dotted the blackness. When the voice came back on the loudspeaker and announced my name, I opened my eyes to John standing over me. Even as he smiled and held out his hand, I knew I was headed to central PA. John looked strange against the light, like a composite of images at the end of a dream, a snapshot of what it is to be broken in one-tenth of one second, on a track or a ballfield on a Sunday afternoon.

sidelines

AMY IRVINE

The fake wall is ugly, and totally unlike the canyon walls I am used to climbing. Crudely made pressed plywood perches on its skeleton of scaffolding. The wood surface is fleshed out with a coating of resin to give it the feel and look of stone. Measuring forty feet in height, the wall looms high above the audience. Attached protrusions will be used as hand- and footholds by the climbers. Whoever climbs highest wins.

It has been a long time since I competed at anything. Competitive sports took flight from my world when my father began drinking and driving his way from one bar to the next, dinging a car door in the parking lot of Green Street, bending a fender at Lumpy's Sports Bar. There were hit-and-runs. Late at night he'd come into my room and cry, his hands stroking my shoulders, my arms. I could smell the alcohol swirling through his system, nearly hear it blowing the veins in his nose, eating his stomach and his mind. And then my father evaporated into thin air, like a fine November mist over wetlands. With him went my appetite for competition. I was seventeen years old.

But here I am, about to climb a wall in front of hundreds of people. At twenty-four, I think I am finally prepared for this: more balanced, and a reasonable shape and size. Under glaring lights I turn and squint out into the audience, where faces are nested in ink-blue shadows. For the first time ever, I feel confident. *He's gone*, I tell myself.

The 1990 American Sport Climbing Federation's National Climbing Competition is being held at the Berkeley Theater, in California. The women will go before the men and judges will watch to see how high we climb. As each of us ascends the wall, hot white lights will illuminate the lines of our bodies, define every move, note every mistake. I want to test my worth, pit myself against other women again. I think of the vicious young girls on my childhood gymnastics team, flocking around me, pointing and laughing at my corpulent body and my graceless movements. The women here have treated me differently, with respect. I run my hands down the sides of my hips. *No need to do that now*, I tell myself. I turn back to the wall, take the rope from the judge, and tie in.

My father loved to tell me how I came thundering into the world, weighing nine pounds and three ounces, nearly splitting my mother in two. Through sweat and blood and animal howls she expelled me from her body, cursing me for my size. I don't know how my father knew this last part; at the time, he was squatting in the silver-blue marshes of the Great Salt Lake, hunting ducks as they flew overhead. He said their wings sounded like shirts flapping on a clothesline. My mother blamed my father for my size. My father blamed me for her leaving.

The head climbing judge gives me the signal. I chalk up and step onto the wall. I adjust to the vertical world by smearing the sticky soles of my climbing shoes on the footholds, for maximum friction. With a deep breath, I look at the methodical, linear path of holds. There is no lovely chaos of features, like you find on real rock. The moves at the bottom of the wall are easy. But I save my strength; the route will become more difficult as I progress.

I have promised myself there will be no tears. I had cried on my first and only deer hunt, which greatly disappointed my father. On the eastern slope of Utah's Wasatch Range, my father shot a sleek young buck with a budding rack. I followed him through dense oak brush and up an eroded gully to retrieve it. The creature had collapsed with its head bent awkwardly down the slope—half of its nose shot off. Blood ran red as rubies into patches of early October snow and pooled in the dark mud. I had not been prepared. On the spot I vomited, then wept. My father grabbed my arms through my orange down jacket.

"Lighten up, Amos."

Through clenched teeth, he called me by my nickname. He let me go, walked a few feet away, then turned around. His voice was softer this time, but more menacing. He promised me a lifetime of loneliness if I didn't play by his rules.

"I don't ever want to see you cry again," he said.

I did cry again, when I invited him to my first gymnastics competition. I was ten years old. He hadn't shown when the notes of my chosen Tchaikovsky symphony began to fill the gym. Taking one last look around for him, I kneeled on the marine-blue carpet, the lights above bright and warm on my head. A series of sweeping motions with my arms began the routine; I imagined myself with great white wings, the Russian composer's swan, swimming on deep-blue water. Chalk dust from the uneven bars and vault fell in motes around me. Through the lights, they looked like snowflakes. For the first time ever, I felt pretty and slender, perhaps even enough to please my father.

He appeared as I rose from the floor, a swan in flight—like those I'd seen rising out of the marshes where my father hunted—his favorite bird. He climbed up onto the highest bleacher and watched, his face hidden by shadows. I whirled around to face him, squinting to detect even the smallest gesture. Soon I was out of sync with my music. Charlie, the coach, went unnoticed. If I had looked to him as I did in practice, I would have seen his gray-haired head nodding to the tempo, lips counting silently, *"One, two, three, four . . . "*

My neck craned too far out in front of my body. A desperate, too-cheery smile spread across my face, lips stretched like taut rubber bands. My belly defied the fabric of my purple leotard and spilled out unrestrained. Red-faced and huffing, I fumbled my last tumbling pass: a run down the middle, arms drawing back for the setup, then a cartwheel into a round-off. I went into the last move too slow and came up short. My hands then my knees crashed into the floor, *ka-boom.* The sound vibrated across the gym.

Fighting the tears, I spun to my last pose and finished, my rubber band smile snapping into a limp O. I plodded off the mat, reached past Charlie's outstretched arms for my sweat-shirt, and ran past my teammates, who sat in a neat row along-side the mat. I heard them begin their chant:

"Elephant Girl, Elephant Girl, she's too fat to tumble or twirl . . . "

The girls got up and fell into line behind me. They swag-gered their thin little legs to mimic my bowed walk. Hunched over and stifling giggles, they clasped their hands together and held them straight, their noses hidden between barely formed biceps. Their arms swung back and forth like elephants' trunks, their feet stomped loudly, *ka-boom, ka-boom.* Suddenly Charlie was on them, scolding. I kept walking, tears falling.

Halfway up the climbing wall, the holds are farther apart. I step my foot as high as my waist and rock onto it. Pushing through, I can just latch the next handhold. I rest there, drop my other hand down, and shake it until the blood returns. I look ahead; still I feel pretty good. I glance down at the audi-ence. Until now, I had forgotten about them.

"Elephant Girl . . . "

The song twirls through my head. Why *now*? I see my father standing in the cold March sunshine, just outside the gymnas-tics academy. He smoked a cigarette and with his boot squished ants as they scurried through his shadow on the side-walk. I ran to him; he inhaled and studied me as if he didn't recognize his own daughter. Finally, he smoothed the hair from my eyes and sighed.

"Amos." He flicked away an ash with his free hand, the other resting on my head. *"You've got to be lighter."* He tried unsuc-cessfully to hide his anger, his disgust, his pity.

My foot slips on a small hold. The audience gasps as I catch, then steady myself. I am more than two-thirds of the way now.

Fly . . . I tell myself. My arms are like lead; it takes so much effort to keep them above my head. I have to stop, find a way to shake them out. Then I read a sequence wrong and struggle to reverse the moves before I topple into space. Desperation, then humiliation sets in. These are old and familiar feelings, courtesy of my father.

I retreat down to a large hold, where I can shake both hands, one at a time. I put on the dry-eyed poker face of my high school days—days when I marched around the volleyball court with clenched fists, a short-haired jock who after every play spit on the floor and said *fuck*. I imagine the thin, aggressive boy I became then—when I successfully whittled away my curves, becoming all the lighter for my father. And he'd be there, right on the sidelines, squatting, eyes squinting as the serve was launched. He'd never been that close, that involved. It hadn't mattered to me that at fifteen I began the season as starting server for the varsity team and ended it on the bench, my weight in the double-digits and my body too weak to play. My eyes were bone dry. My father was proud.

The audience beneath the climbing wall begins to stir. I have been in the same spot for some time. I have to move soon, continue upward before my hands uncurl from the holds in exhaustion. I finger this former high-school-jock image of myself like a scarf in a department store: I try to wrap it around my neck, but it slips through my fingers, fluttering away. I have no other image of strength. I am losing faith.

The announcer's voice is melodramatic and ricochets off the stadium's metal beams and bleachers.

"*. . . five foot four and one hundred and fifteen pounds . . .* "

Now I feel completely exposed, my body larger than life, like a giant clown balloon in the Macy's Thanksgiving Day Parade. I would give anything to be off this unnatural, hard-angled, contrived joke-of-a-wall, instead to have my palms on the natural curves of glacier-kissed granite, to lean my body into the crevices of the wall, to feel wind on my arms and hear silence punctuated only by the spiraling call of the canyon wren, nesting high on the cliff tops . . .

Nearly thirty feet above a crowd of strangers I realize: This is my father's world. No matter how well-proportioned my body becomes, no matter how much time I spend with a therapist, no amount of learning to accept my body, learning to feel okay, would ever change the truth of this moment.

From below the wall, I just barely comprehend voices. One of the women competitors has called my name. Another joins in, and soon another. An entire chorus of women is calling to me.

I think of my gymnastics teammates, swaggering along the sides of the mat, and of my father, scrutinizing every action. I am certain that the women are ridiculing me and I feel the impulse to push away from the wall and just fall, all the way to the floor. In this tenuous position, hanging on with just my fingers, I even wonder if I can untie the rope from my harness.

But then I remember arriving in the staging area before the climbing competition began. The other competitors were slender, well-defined women clad in turquoise, fuchsia, and bright yellow Lycra. As they chattered among themselves, they stretched their limbs and bent sleek torsos gracefully—trying to stay warm and loose until it was time to climb. In their vibrant and social state, they looked like a flock of tropical birds. It had been a good feeling, being among them.

The women's voices are louder now. I'm amazed at what I hear from them.

"Come on, you can do it . . . "

I imagine Charlie, bent over with old-man hands on his knees, nodding hopefully at my every move, believing one day I'd get it right, counting for me.

"One, two, three, four . . . "

The women continue to coax. I look down. I see in their faces that they mean it. Tears come with the realization that I do not have any women friends. That I go climbing with men in whom I can endlessly seek my father's approval. I look up at the last section of the wall, and I promise myself one thing.

This is the last time . . .

I close my eyes and count, finding my way to a better place. Now my fingertips are pressed to cool, smooth stone, and the damp metallic smell of mountain soil, rich with minerals, fills me. I open my eyes just barely and begin to move. I look ahead, targeting a small handhold, and reach. Grasping it, my fingers are like talons, wrapping the branch of a tree. I move with the rhythm of my breath, which I count in my head the way Charlie taught me. I soar upward.

Beneath me, I imagine the white and brown fluttering of their hands, like dove's wings, as the women continue to applaud. I climb, and imagine the graceful rounding sidelines of my hips, my thighs, my belly. I look at my outstretched arms. Spread like the wings of an eagle, they carry me upward.

turning it up
BETSY CROWFOOT

Twelve pounds of rubberized clothing and gear lay bunched around my ankles. I squat on the toilet, which swashes with icy seawater as the boat lurches and surges ahead. In the opaque darkness every groan, squeak, thump, and shudder is amplified.

We are pounding in choppy green seas, in the first few days of the Transpacific Yacht Race, a 2,225-mile voyage from Los Angeles to Honolulu. Nine women on one 50-foot sailboat versus 166 million square kilometers of Pacific Ocean.

Offshore racing is not a glamorous sport. This thought inevitably comes to me at 2 a.m., when I'm roused to go on watch.

My stomach convulses and a flush of fever radiates over me. I hurry through my business. It is difficult to wipe, stand, pull up the layers of thermal underwear and foul-weather gear while the boat thrashes from side to side. Flicking the lever, I pump the head, and teeny bioluminescent sea creatures sucked up from the ocean sparkle down the insides of the toilet bowl. I stumble up the steps of the companionway. The nausea is in my throat now.

Buckling on the last of my gear I paw into the open cockpit and—*whomp!*—a direct hit nails me in the head just a moment before I pull on my hood. Chilly brine trickles down my back. I'm wide awake as the others scamper down to bunks still warm.

I actually worked my tail off to earn a place on the sloppy wet deck of this boat. Women, more often than not, are passed by when race crews are chosen. So we create our own opportunities to answer the call of the open ocean.

I began sailing only nine years ago and at once felt surprisingly at ease and invigorated. Never graceful or swift enough to compete in tennis, volleyball, or the like, I found my niche in yacht racing, which has a place for beefy women with some strength and tenacity. When my daughter came along, Saturdays at sea became my "girls' night out." As my career changed, from mobile sales exec to very rooted mom, I looked to my racing adventures to satisfy my compulsion for excitement and accomplishment: a sharp contrast to a drab office job girdled by diapers and baby food.

Begun in 1906, the Transpac was designed to lure tourists to the tropical paradise of the Sandwich Islands. Organizers promised a warm aloha upon landing, hospitality, and parties with exotic "hula hula" dancers. Since World War II the race has been held on the odd years, providing a challenge for thirty-five to eighty boats, 30 to 150 feet in length.

Ninety years after the first Transpac, we are still enticed by the promise of welcome in Shangri-la. Our reward for a fast passage will come in the form of endless parties, the first when we tie up at the docks. Relieved family and envious friends will greet us with garbage cans full of mai tais, fresh fruit, and other delicacies we have missed at sea, and the velvety soft petals of fragrant leis stacked around our sweaty necks.

It is this picture of paradise that helps us press on.

The night is black. We have set sail with thirty-eight other boats during a moonless phase. The billions of stars that normally light the sky are shrouded in dense clouds. Driving blind, using only the compass and wind instruments, I struggle to hold a favorable course, not knowing when a peculiar wave might lick up the side of the boat, or the sea might fall out from beneath the bow, at least just for a moment. The yacht volleys, yaws from side to side; sails flutter, and the trimmers—one each on the main and the jib—inch the sails in and out. We constantly tinker with the sheets, lines attached to the loose corners of the sails, and the halyards that hold the sails up, while we tweak the outhaul and leads which control the "belly." All to define the shape of the sails to get the most speed out of the velocity and angle of the wind at that particular instant. The first few hundred miles our sails will be set tight to help us race into the breeze; days later we'll set a spinnaker for the sought-after downwind rush to Honolulu.

There is nothing between here and Hawaii. We are self-sufficient: our own commissary, hospital, power plant, social structure. Aside from one mandatory daily check-in via radio, we are on our own.

We sail day and night, night and day. Our assignments: four women on deck, four off watch below, and one housekeeping. We call her the Bitch of the Day. Each of us will rotate off for a turn as B.O.D. to prepare meals, hang up wet gear, keep the head clean, and sort the garbage (biodegradables get minced into little bits and thrown overboard; other trash gets smashed and stowed). The B.O.D. keeps our water bottles full and sunscreen handy and dispenses painkillers as frequently as the directions on the Aleve bottle will allow.

We are nine women between the ages of twenty and forty-seven. Although four of us have done this passage before, it is the first time for us as a team. The first day out we were stunned at the last-minute withdrawal of our skipper, Linda. Just five days before the race start, after a full year of preparation, Linda had a relapse of ovarian cancer. From her hospital bed she commanded us to go on.

An offshore skipper is unique: in what other sport does the captain assume responsibility for the *lives* of her team? And Linda is the one of us most familiar with *Bay Wolf,* the yacht she's chartered (taking out a second mortgage on her home to do so). We feel her absence, we miss her skill as a sailor and driver, her warmth, humor, and management style. Weepy at the onset, soon we are forced to push aside the thought of her lying in a hospital bed, being fed intravenous fluids along with daily race results. She is fighting for her life and we, now out on the ocean, must fight to sustain ours.

Two all-women crews have campaigned this year, a first in

Transpac history. In its inaugural year there were no representatives of the "weaker" sex on the three boats that sailed. By 1908 women started showing up on crew lists; usually it was the wife of the owner or the occasional cook. In 1933 a Los Angelina was invited to sail with her husband and a crew of six men. She hardly got to see more than the galley and cabin. During the torturous journey the sails were torn and tattered so many times, Mrs. Radcliffe sewed her way across the ocean, cutting up her aprons when she ran out of spare canvas.

After World War II women became more active in the competition. Lady skippers have run the gamut from the brassy Peggy Slater, to Beverly Hills socialite Sally Blair Ames, to Martha Baker, a 1950s single mom who brought her twelve-year-old kid along because, hey, who can afford a baby-sitter for three weeks? It wasn't until 1979 that the regatta saw its first all-women crew. And here we are in 1997, finally with two expert women's teams on highly competitive boats.

Each of us is limited to what we can carry in a yellow sixteen-by-twenty-four-inch Gore-Tex duffel. In addition to standard offshore sailing gear—foulies, rubber boots, fingertipless gloves, a self-inflating harness and tether—I have thermal underwear, a wool hat and socks, nylon shorts, Lycra leggings, a tank top, two T-shirts, a swimsuit, and sneakers. This ensemble, although hardly fashionable, will suffice during the extreme weather conditions we'll see, whether the trip lasts ten days or twenty.

Two years earlier when I did this race I sailed on a seaworthy but older boat. It proved to be one of the slowest Transpacs on record. For one solid week we drifted over glassy seas, clocking a total finish time of just over seventeen days. Had we not gotten along so well we would have killed each other. Eight women on a 40-foot yacht in the scorching sun with diminishing water and food stores. But we survived the frustration— nearly more threatening than an angry sea—reading, writing, spying on sea life, and watching one spectacular sunset after another . . . and another . . . and another. I even caught a jellyfish with a spaghetti strainer, I was so crazed.

But this year has been different. The weather reports are rosy, showing a strong and steady breeze all the way, and a tropical depression brewing near Cabo San Lucas. And for once, the weather we find offshore is as surly as the forecast.

As a result, when dawn slinks through the woolen clouds the second morning out, we are met with another setback: in the night our mainsail has developed a tear near the top. We douse it at once, but repairs can't be made until the sail, wet with dew, dries. There will be no race to Hawaii without this powerhouse of canvas. Our new skipper, bumped up from navigator to captain by default, agonizes—and is finally convinced to let us carry on another twenty-four hours. If we can patch the sail, if it holds, if the wind clocks behind us a bit, if . . .

In near silence—abetted by an epidemic of mal de mer in all but two of us—we push ahead, knowing that each fraction of distance we struggle for we may have to retrace tomorrow.

In each of the past thirty-eight Honolulu races there have been boats that turn back, and others that limp into Ala Wai Yacht Harbor with broken spars, missing rudders, shredded sails. Some arrive short a crew member or two—evacuated because of medical emergency—but no competitors have ever sunk during the race, and no one has ever died.

Three days out and the wind has circled behind us. It's a blessing. With the sails cracked off a bit there's less pressure on the main. Hoisting the repaired sail, we are ecstatic when the decision is announced to go on. Despite an insurmountable loss in mileage, we are going to Oahu, not Catalina—the booby prize offered, had we been forced to drop out.

As we advance south, the weather warms up a touch. Seasickness phases out. Our bodies adjust to the schedule of four hours on, four hours off. I am part of a machine. My life, typically intellectual, is now purely physical. I sweat, groan, struggle, and coax my body to its limits. I eat, we all eat, like pigs. Off watch we sleep the sleep of the dead. We share one purpose: to push this ship to Hawaii.

The wind this year is ceaseless! Tricks on the helm, trimming, or grinding are kept to thirty minutes. Then we rotate through the cockpit. Driving requires physical stamina, practice, intense focus. The helmswoman holds everybody's fate in the grip of her two hands, skirting the seas, following that just-perfect angle to the wind. As you catch a wave—the boat we sail was designed to do just this, skim along the huge Pacific rollers like a 50-foot surfboard—the wind moves forward. It's an art. If you pinch too much you collapse the chute—a 2,000-square-foot nylon spinnaker pulling the boat along at 15 to 20 or more knots (18 to 24-plus m.p.h.) of speed. Drive too low and the wind crosses the back of the boat. Sailing by the lee is lethal, sweeping the boom and mainsail 180 degrees across the stern with such force it can take out the rigging and lop off the head of anyone in the way.

Like Sisyphus of ancient mythology, condemned to heave a boulder up a mountain in Hades for all eternity, the trimmer's job is never done. I continually ease out and trim in the sheets with hands gnarled from clutching the slippery, skinny synthetic rope. My job is made possible by a grinder whose sole purpose is to muscle in the line on hefty winches. After half an hour, we trade.

Sunshine is scant. There are few of the stunning sunsets or sunrises I've seen in previous Transpacs, and the omnipresent dolphins, pilot whales, and sea turtles are obscured by rambunctious waves. Now and then an albatross glides unerringly over the ever-moving profile of the sea, and as we approach the islands, tropic birds appear.

Nighttime is sheer hell.

As the sun sets, the wind rises. Lines of squalls, dastardly storm-laden cumulonimbus, are hard to detect in the dense night. The combination of no moon and the sparkling starlight shrouded by clouds creates the blackest pall. Mesmerized by the LED instruments on the mast, the wind whipping past my ears, the sensation of speeding, swirling, I am overwhelmed. Vertigo is not unusual in these conditions; neither is just plain fear. I beg off the wheel.

Four of our drivers turn out to be better suited for this "simulator" sailing. But stints are short.

Lying in my bed—not really *my* berth as we are hot-bunking, just whatever sack is free—I hear terror in the voices of the women on deck. A squall has hit and the wind has increased. If possible, it is even darker. The traveling storm system sends the breeze from a new angle and kicks up the seas in its path. We careen into the wind: a roundup. Eyes closed, I still can see and anticipate the sequence of events. We're flying enough sail area to carpet a barn, and the gusts blast us with tremendous force. The driver knows she's losing the fight to keep the boat headed down and shrills, "Ease! Ease!" Already the trimmer is letting the sheet run to deflate the spinnaker, but the boat has chosen her own course. She crashes up into the wind and on her side; water pours into the cockpit.

I slam shut the little windows above my head so the sea doesn't cascade in. I know that in two hours it'll be me on deck, hip-high in water, grinding like a son-of-a-bitch, trying, at times in vain, to keep the boat upright and on track. Eventually the boat will tip enough so that the breeze spills out of the sails, and she'll right herself. In the meantime, I turn up my headphones, roll over, and try to rest.

I dream odd dreams, people out of place and out of context. I think sweet thoughts of my daughter, almost six years old. On my first offshore race, I remember lying shivering and crying in a bunk, weary from a long watch in stormy seas, uncertain of our fate, terrified I would never see her again. We tore the main in an accidental jibe and struggled with a contorted and ineffective sail. Our navigator, I suspected, was way off. And the promised glide down the California coast transformed into a hellish ordeal through 35 knots of breeze on a confused sea the size of a roller coaster. As a final insult, our batteries ran low and we had no power for running lights or radio communications. We couldn't even call for help.

I kissed the dock when we finally straggled into port. Then I refused to sail for nearly three months. But eventually I realized that offshore yacht racing is at once arduous and exhilarating. It's a matter of who can show up most prepared, with the best-conditioned equipment, then stick with it the longest, with the most focus.

Halfway to Hawaii, and life on board is rough. A number of problems befall us. Our water-maker refuses to work and we drink lemon-flavored tank water with unidentified floating objects. A hairline crack appears on the mast. Our instruments, so crucial to our night driving, are about to croak; one repeatedly flashes "no data." Tensions are evident: the two watches snipe at each other. The B.O.D., now adoringly and rightfully called the Goddess of the Day, referees. We make too much noise while the other watch tries to sleep, they make too much noise while we are trying to sleep. In truth, no one gets much sleep at all. Jibes—positioning the sails from one side of the boat to the other to get a better angle to our destination in the ever-changing wind—call for all hands on deck. The sails are kept flying while the boat and spinnaker pole are swung in a perfectly orchestrated maneuver . . . at 18 or 20 knots of speed. Think: changing the tire while driving down the freeway; we are racing full-bore and there is no stopping allowed. Sail changes (we use heavier or lighter sails for a heavier or lighter breeze), the replacement of chafed and worn gear, and the mandatory hoisting of Pam to the top of the mast to check the rig mean no shut-eye as well. Even when we are "down," it's impossible to sleep with the screeching of the on-watch crew, the moaning of sheets as they slip on the drum of the winch, the shuddering of the rig when the boat comes off a wave, and the incessant rush—like a flash flood—of water along the hull.

I have never felt more alive.

A friend who has sailed more than one-quarter of a million miles points out, *"It's like turning up the volume on life."* My senses heighten. There is wind in my hair and the taste of the salt spray on my face. My body feels toned and fluid. The sound of the rooster tail off the stern is deafening; the laughter of happy, strong women is music. The tropical heat warms my skin; I smell sweat, a delicious dinner cooking, and—at last—a puff from a sugarcane fire which has journeyed far out to sea.

Mostly I feel in place . . . because the ocean equalizes my sensibilities, too. I realize how small and insignificant I am. And with this comes relief. In this greater arena, I remember that life is to be enjoyed.

A spectacular lightning display hovers above the Hawaiian Islands as we approach the final leg—and challenge—of the Transpac. Thousands of miles of ocean and wind converge at the Molokai Channel, shimmying between the towering peaks of Oahu and Molokai. This is the scene of many dismastings, blown-up spinnakers; where the race has been won—and lost.

At nightfall our instruments are declared DOA. The captain appears on deck, her eyes rimmed red with agitation and lack of sleep. This is not the program she's signed on for. She growls, but mostly we disregard it. My personal experience has established that all skippers turn into werewolves at the entrance to the Molokai Channel but transform back into humanoids upon docking, with the assistance of a mai tai or two.

Our practiced crew pulls off the final jibe in 30-plus knots, and the quartet of hotshot drivers take turns helming the boat through the passage. As the lumpy shapes of the islands rise up from the sea, the crew clusters in the back of the boat to keep the bow from burrowing into the waves. Everyone is hooting and hollering like banshees. I join the driver and a trimmer, I straddling the winch on the low side, mostly submerged, as we scream through the channel on our ear. It's strenuous and eventually Jeanie steps in; I take her place high and aft.

We pick off navigation lights as the glow of Honolulu City outlines the profile of Koko Head. As is required, we radio in our arrival so a squadron of boats can greet us. Around the corner the unmistakable silhouette of Diamond Head appears. Its light dances around and we look for the adjacent bell buoy that marks the finish line, and also the dangerous reef to its north. In the night, with so many lights on shore, it's easy to miss—as one competing yacht did eight years ago, running aground just a few hundred yards before the finish.

Lights spill down the surrounding canyon roads like necklaces of lava; wind cranks down these ravines, too, and buffets us with tremendous gusts that knock us repeatedly on our side. Our skipper decides to douse the chute early. Four of us move gingerly forward, harnessed and tethered to jack lines which run the length of the boat. We carry knives, in case we get tangled up in the sail or sheets and need to cut ourselves free. In a matter of seconds we are all soaked to the armpits as the captain brings the boat up into the wind, luffs the spinnaker, and the halyard is let loose—then thrown overboard to ensure it runs free.

There is too much wind in the chute—it refuses to come down. For at least ten minutes we grab on to it, only to have the brilliant nylon sail fill and rip out of our hands again and again, even though four of us—all pretty hefty—are hauling on it with all our weight.

My fingers are raw; I am barely on the boat, suspended by my tether. I am fully aware that if either the stanchion or my harness fails, I am lost. History. This is terrifying.

I am also delighted that it is night and the ESPN camera crew is not out to document our clumsy finish.

Finally we muscle the sail down and stuff it, along with gallons of water and possibly a few unsuspecting fish, down the hatch. We finish quietly, lining up the buoy with the lighthouse and popping a chilled bottle of champagne (our only booze on board), after nine days and nineteen hours. It has been a record-breaking race, a twenty-year Transpac standard broken, and we are the fastest-ever all-women team.

Then it is finished. The crowded skyline of Waikiki unfolds in front of us, as first light creeps up. Despite the hour we are surrounded by boats packed with indecipherable forms but familiar voices. We tuck away the sails and tidy the boat, change our shirts, and enter the Ala Wai Harbor.

"A-looooooooo-ha!" a voice booms across the PA system, even though we have arrived in the wee hours. Each member of the crew is welcomed by name, and a throng of people, alerted by a relentless, sleep-deprived team of volunteers, begins to take form along the docks lining the canal. Figures rise ghostlike from the seats of the yacht club. One is bobbing up and down like a jack-in-the-box. It's Linda! Her doctor has determined she'll recover much more quickly from surgery in Hawaii, as opposed to lying agitated in bed at Long Beach Memorial Hospital.

The tears that have been waiting for ten days finally fall. We have arrived, ranking fifth in class (comparable boats) and seventh in the entire fleet. Six boats have turned back because of difficulties, including three dismastings, a broken rudder, and illness.

I feel strong and alert as pink clouds cluster to the east and we turn into our slip. The plumeria leis placed around our necks are the most fragrant you can imagine. The drinks are icy cold, sweet and strong, and the fruit is so fresh, it must have been picked yesterday. Linda looks ravishing and the men are more handsome than even I remember. The Hawaiian music that plays has the sweetest melody; as my friend promised, the volume of life turns up—to "high."

losing baseball, **the** 1950s

SUSAN EISENBERG

for Connie Wong

Except for fat Peter picked
with the girls and Connie
chosen before even the
best boy, teams were already
boys-first-then-girls when

puberty demanded absolution
gym teacher as priest denouncing
all we had worshiped—
    arms that cracked balls over
    the left fielder's head, legs
    that sailed around bases
    and carried her home before
    the ball could reach infield . . .

The gym teacher's taunt
Not feminine! landed two stories up
where fifth-grade girls grouped
at the window batted the epithet
among us like a live grenade
no one dared hold. Below, Connie
scooped a softball out of the air,
whirled it toward second. Double play.

memoirs of a would-be swim champ

ANN GERACIMOS

Once when I was very young I nearly drowned. I remember going under in a shallow lake, curling up helplessly, and sinking before being rescued by my frightened mother. Doubtless the incident sent off shock waves in my subconscious, but it was not until much later that I connected water with life's momentous events and understood that, inevitably, in swimming as in other measures of performance, one faces them alone.

Perhaps more than anything this explains my fascination with the sport, my complete identification with it from an early age. Of course, it also counts that a great-uncle, the man who helped raise me, was an athletics "professor" and owner of a prestigious New Hampshire boys' camp, whose sister institution, Interlaken, some sixty miles away, agreed to take me in. I was a "scholarship case," determined to prove my worth. At camp, at the age of ten, I was destined to learn about the territorial imperatives of the great outdoors, about the even greater imperatives of the body. I was scared to death.

It is a shock coming from the sneaky doldrums of a Lancaster, Pennsylvania, school where there is no swimming pool and sports activities consist of all-girl hockey games and tumbles on a gym mat amid tittering about the boys at play on the other side of the curtain. Camp is sun-washed log cabins bordering leafy paths, a whole lake to play in, empty mountains to hike around on, the smell of pine, the sight of white birch, the sound of crickets, loons, frogs.

My cabin is a cool dark space, a square box with a pointed roof made of plain wood set on raised supports over a pine-needle ground cover. At night the branches of the trees sweep against the cabin walls, and in the distance I hear frogs mingled with the sound of waves lapping on the lakeshore. Such solitude is strange, but I do not confess this to anyone, even to myself. It is the solitude of the water, too, that both attracts and repels me.

At the lake, I am uncertain, not knowing the water's depths, not yet able to swim. The bottom is cold, dark, and full of mud between the stones. But the texture, when I gain courage enough to slide into the beginners' section between plank dock supports, is wonderfully smooth. Slowly I immerse myself up to my neck, paddling chaotically with my arms, raising my feet up from the bottom. Cautiously at first, until I can control myself, I am suspended this way in liquid, free of gravity's pull for minutes at a time, feeling freer than I have been before. All sense of time is lost, as are all notions of guilt. Tiny fish dart between my legs, treading in place with their tails. I follow them through shafts of sunlight, and gradually, by lowering my face more deeply, holding my breath, I learn to submerge, pulling in my arms and legs until I am a floating fetus.

The bugle blows at seven each morning, making the air sing. We are in swimsuits and towels, lined up for "body exercises" before the mist has cleared the lake. The soft-green shoreline a mile away is barely visible. In the foreground, like a glinting stage, are wooden buoys on ropes, red markers on white turning boards, the depths of green-black water shot through with the morning sun. There are bloodsuckers in the depths. I look at the lake through sleepy eyes.

Shrieking, we wet our toes to test the temperature and wade in slowly for the risks of immersion. More advanced swimmers—among them a distant cousin of mine—walk by to the far section with a bare nod in passing and fling themselves out boldly across the water. I return to the lake each morning determined to do as well as or better than my cousin. It is the start of an ambition I do not call by name. It isn't a word that anyone, apart from our coach, the "swim director" (he spends his winters at the Harvard University athletic department), ever uses.

Nevertheless, camp is an aggressive, competitive place. We are divided into two tribes—Mohegan and Iroquois—and work two months each year racking up points, medals, skills. It is the best way to learn, we are told; dutifully, we obey—although the object lesson is never spelled out.

Swim sessions are strenuous. Our bodies become machines. Happily, greedily, I steal time from other sports to be able to spend time in the lake—a fluid, charging object counting turns.

Swimming is a clean sport, well suited to the classically long-limbed bodies and clean minds of young American girls. It is a very singular occupation. All that sleekness and sublimated aggression made respectable for a few hours under a "sporting" sky. Forgetfulness, team spirit, sensuality, monotony, absurdity—and utter sexlessness. It suits us perfectly. Novitiates of ascetic religious orders don't undergo the ritual chastisement by water that we budding swimmers do, kicking one and two miles a day, routinely doing laps, arms flailing, neck twisting. Like chasing your tail and being chased by it at the same time.

Do we work for the feel of working, or for the sake of winning? We understand—we are told over and over—that it is not who wins but how each girl plays. But when, each year, the camp enters the New England Swimming and Diving Championships (for girls' camps only), our team carries home a spread of trophies.

How we worship the inexorable spin of the silent seconds that pace the swimmer's journey! Our eyes are fixed on the circular silver mechanism resting in the palm of the referee's hand like a silver dollar of rare vintage caught in the gleam of a collector's eye on auction day. All of the weak sun's rays this day seem drawn to the spot. Light gathers there as though fixed by gravity.

There will be two events for me, plus diving. A full program; exhausting in view of the pressure.

My hands are hot, my feet cold. An intermittent drizzle has wet down the dock. I shift the towel from one hand to the other. Different parts of my body keep changing temperature.

I stand as firmly, as confidently, as possible. Silence in the bleachers. The crowd likes the tension, appreciates the drama. They are waiting for familiar chaos to break through the order.

A sudden burst of sun sends streaks of color across the lake's dark surface. Boats outline the competition area, anchored haphazardly. Surprisingly, the bleachers are filled; who would bother to come see a group of campers exercise? The judges are in place; the starter waits. I take off the itchy green wool bathrobe and step up to the starting block.

I shake my fingers loose, a cool flutter like a swan shaking its feathers. Deep breaths of air, hyperextension, more shakes of the fingers. The race belongs to me, what is there to worry about? My pulse charges. Six contestants in this heat, a medley event. Our lanes are covered with oil slicks, just enough to taste bad if a swimmer accidentally gets a swallow.

I push breath into my lungs and throw my chest forward, keeping my shoulders level. If someone had come up to me then and asked what I was preparing myself for, I could have answered: Childbirth or murder.

Real control is in the pelvis, slung low and back, ready to force the plunge. The downward pull is in the fingers. My neck, however, responds first when I hear the shot. I spring. Cool slippery wet embraces me.

Too late for escape, I am aware only of flight.

A thousand different thoughts hang in the sky overhead— in the instant before hitting the water I see a split-second silhouette of a bird. "I am that bird," I think. "I sing without sound, fly without wings . . . "

The ropes on either side are like wet rough snakes. I swerve on landing to avoid them, losing half a second, cursing as I dig in deep from the shoulders, arms taut, fingers groping, grasping for the turn ahead. The water unfolds like soft silk; a boat in the distance floats toward my mouth. I breathe in the horizon as I raise my head. The shoreline falls away; I breathe again. Water dissolves against me. My breath is the wave, I am the sea, I am floating, my eyes are my fingers, my feet are the sky . . . breathe, relax, every muscle awake, ready to work.

Spring and soar, take possession of space: that is what this sport is about. The head leads with a minimum of direction, arms forward, ready for the plunge, eyes open on recovery, staring hard . . .

Below, churning the water, the swimmer's body adjusts to the pull of weight underneath while keeping enough balance to stay in touch with the air. The motion is a constant bending and yielding flight through water, the reflexes tuned to subtle changes of sight and sound, pressure and temperature. Swimming is a way of freeing the mind; only by preoccupying the body so completely does the mind come alive. Weightless, nearly nude, out of physical touch with all other human beings, the swimmer is an elemental force. The sureness of the limbs as they cut through the water in regular rhythm is comforting. The muscles are smooth and lean, their action directly related to their function. The course—a few feet wide by fifty feet long—is a universe of several dimensions within which the swimmer maneuvers as fast as possible toward a destination, simultaneously keeping watch on either side. Thus vulnerable and exposed, she takes her chances.

The turn. Into a backstroke now. Two lengths to go.

What is that speck on the horizon, between the trees? Birds? A balloon? Are the spectators cheering? What do they do when all of us are knocking our hearts out in this crib? Do they sit on their hands or what? What are the other swimmers up to, bunched up in towels and robes, their skin gone to goosebumps, little prickly fingertips and all?

There is some cheering, a smattering of applause. I hit the turn again, faster than I expected, catching the slime below the waterline, then around and out again with the sound of a gun to signal the last lap.

The clouds are gaining; they seem to be advancing with jagged edges, snaking overhead under the gray cover. What is the girl in the lane next to me doing now? No time to look. I grab the water voraciously. My body is weak—a moment of danger. Heavy arms, short breath, nervous legs. Shoulders up and around. The final push. Where is the girl on the far side?

Then cheers, yells, no time to check out anybody, head down for a long breath and twenty last strokes. Quick down the middle, a touch of the hand at the end of the course (another shotgun blast, more cheers), I am home.

The last night of my last year the whole camp gathers for award ceremonies in the dining room, dressed in identical blue-and-orange sleeveless pullovers and blue shorts, regulation equipment like the smiles, the songs, the speeches. It is a well-lacquered, clean, bright room. Previous campers' names are written in black on pinewood boards against the rough pine walls. We have tradition, excitement, fellowship. When the Best Camper Trophy is handed out, I am chosen over my cousin, who seemed to me to be so superior long ago. My tribe wins the most points for the season; as chieftain I collect the prize. Our swim team has had an unbroken string of victories; the team members stand up with their coach. Afterward he tells me that I should think about training seriously for Olympic tryouts four, eight years away.

But there is a conflict: camp is a play world that has nothing to do with the rigorous dedication of a "serious life." This is, after all, a girls' camp where we are being trained up carefully to be "young ladies." Most of us eventually will take our rightful place at the head of the family dining room tables across America, like our executive director. Summer is for fun and games; no one really expects the experience to relate directly to decisions in the "real world." It is a period of life in which I feel I lead two lives. Whatever happens in one seems to bear no relation to the other.

This was a double bind: camp wasn't "real," yet the evidence of my senses told me otherwise. For about the age of puberty, every girl in America learns that to survive she must compete, that to compete she must be strong. And, as always, there are rules.

Such rules, of course, depend on the status quo, which said that competition for the sake of character was good; but competition for its own sake, as a game or sport to be played without a moral imperative, was not. It wasn't ladylike . . . Real rules had to do with etiquette, with knowing how to please others, with being a "good girl."

Back home in Lancaster, I join the Middle Atlantic YWCA Swim League. I swim the fifteen meets per season with growing awareness of my abilities.

Our coach's nickname is Angel, a booming rush of sound surrounding a mass of curly black hair and rippling muscles on a tall broad frame. Angel is a philosopher: he would like to be able to move water by words. Sometimes his words exceed the limits imposed on them by the dictionary. He talks about our "corporate welfare." Other times he does not bother with a dictionary. His dual nature keeps us in thrall; his body and mind seem to be at odds with one another. (Years later, I am not surprised to discover that Angel has become a business entrepreneur operating a chain of swimming pools and the "Y" has appointed a woman in his place.)

"Hey you guys, whatsa matter in there? Whatdaya think this is, some picnic or something?"

Angel stands just outside the locker-room door leading to the pool, hesitating. He has been inside just once, when he wanted to congratulate us on winning a home game with a rival team. He was excited then and forgot the rules; the newspaper had just taken a team photograph.

Generous and unpredictable in his speech, he is never boring. The orders ring out like tremors on a seismograph. It is the prelude to his weekly pep talk, half jokes and half teasing. We file out in high spirits. He puts his arm around the shoulders of one of the girls, so her soft skin brushes his chest. She giggles; a tiny blush spreads over her face. Then he releases her with a hearty slap on the back and the noise reverberates against the ceiling. We work in an echo chamber. He stands on the perimeter and gives orders:

"Go on in there, get 'em. Don't be shy. Show your stuff. *Push* that water."

We push it. The water's agitation actually creates sound waves against the walls; the pungent chlorine smell burns our nostrils. No one stops to rest in the first round—six lanes, six girls following six others, ten laps, slow-slow, quick-quick. Angel watches, cheering us on.

The rituals of our sport demand instant response. We strip souls and bodies alike for each fresh assault on the man-made pond; we follow our instincts without thinking and are rewarded with the sense of continuity in time. Possibly it is the most absurd activity in the world, confining oneself to an airless cement chamber full of the nasty smells of human sweat and toxic chemicals, throwing oneself headlong willy-nilly upon a quivering body of water no more than twenty-five yards long and ten yards wide and eight feet deep at the far end. Make a flip turn in the shallow section and your hand is likely to develop a rough patch on top like a newly mown hay field. To do this over and over and pretend it's fruitful, constructive, mind-expanding demands mindless diligence and a total absorption in the spirit of the occasion.

Next we practice turns and racing starts, forward dives and backward plunges. Ten each. Then ten with the starter's whistle. It is no wonder that at least one girl will drop out of the team because she is ashamed of appearing in a swimsuit. Her chest muscles have expanded unnaturally; her breasts have grown "too big." The rest of us have "Angel wings," as we call them—stretched shoulders. Strong, powerful, all-American shoulders on long limbs, a chorus of blue nylon virgins, one-hundred-pound imitation Esther Williamses lined up under the bright lights in the basement of the converted Georgian-styled, white-trimmed, red-brick mansion next door to Snyder's Funeral Parlor, opposite the Central Presbyterian Church.

We are all innocent abandon, unself-conscious achievers full of meat, tea, peas, toast, breathing exercises, and lots of sleep. Or pretending to be. I mention one day to Angel that I expect to go on to a liberal arts college. He is puzzled, not being accustomed to hearing women talk in terms of "college and career," and asks if I am going to study painting.

To his credit, Angel treats us like members of a family. "Persevere," he says. "You gotta build endurance. The more time you spend in the water, the more natural it becomes." He talks about Amateur Athletic Union meets, assaults on local, regional, national levels, ignoring the fact that most of the team by then will be either pregnant or married or both.

I swim the required lengths, concentrating simultaneously on arms and legs like a bug awash in a dishpan, the state of doing instead of being. Forget to do your homework one day and it becomes that much harder the next. Muscles have to be forced one-tenth of a second faster each time.

My lungs are filled with the steamy air. Hyperextension exercises stretch my tank suit to capacity. I step up to the edge of the pool in a crouch, poised like a cat on a tree limb eyeing a bird on the branch: taut, mindless, determined. Angel's commands echo like cannon shots. I fling arms and shoulders forward into a giant arch, dropping my head in anticipation of the splash, the welcoming sting—the signal for life to begin. Gravity's rainbow is within reach as I spring. A single swallow of air lasts a full length. I don't hear it when Angel calls out my time.

Lengths completed, I move to the diving board. I'm ambidextrous: Angel's words. Swimming and diving. You never know when they will come in handy: my uncle's words. The bug has found its way out of the tub and become a bee in a tailspin, dipping into a flower. I bend my knees and grab with my toes for balance, feeling for the right stance. Instinctively, almost magically, the toes know their job, holding the body upright, intact, tense, primed for the fall.

Five or ten times warm-up on the approach, then a jackknife into the pool. Five, ten jackknifes. Then somersaults, forward and backward. Back jackknife, back dive, forward one and one-half twists. I climb out for a towel. It smells of ammonia. We take turns; each girl watching the others carefully, measuring the performance against her own.

It's a short board, and the water beneath is comparatively shallow. We have to hold out our hands each time on entry to protect our heads from hitting the bottom. For some reason during the next round I miss.

My mouth bangs down hard on cement. My hands come forward. Too late.

On top of the water, my fingers cupped to my mouth in fright, I grab for the towel and press it against my face. My tongue feels bloated. Angel pulls me aside for inspection. I see red on the towel. A jagged piece is missing from the side of an upper front tooth, a diagonal break, one-eighth of an inch at the bottom. I poke a finger into the gap. "Just a baby break," says Angel. "You can hardly see a thing."

But the accident, I feel, has destroyed my privacy. I have been singled out for punishment by the Fates, with whom I previously felt on equal terms.

"Back in the pool, kids. Nothing happening on the side." Angel waves his arm grandly, a call for order. Black curls fall down the center of his forehead as he leans over with an arm on my shoulder:

"Do it again."

"I'm scared." I'm shaking.

"Never mind, it'll go away."

"No."

"Yes. *Now.*"

I have no choice; disobeying him scares me more. Wiping the last bit of blood off my chin, I mount the board. Wet feet have made the rough matting slippery. One, two, three steps, feet together in the air. Think! No, don't think. Act, don't react; don't anticipate, don't imagine the dark. The body is resilient. Now breathe in, relax. Another breath. Tighten the brain, the muscles. Forward with eyes down and out, taking possession of space. Spring, soar, fold in the neck and roll with arms clasped around knees bent to the chest; turn around and kick the feet out as the arms move forward on entry in a perpendicular pose, eyes open on recovery, staring hard.

"Okay, that's better. C'mon here a minute."

I drag myself slowly out of the pool, Angel offering a hand.

"Can you get a little higher?" he asks. "Your feet weren't together on that last entry. Try it again."

That night at dinner I keep feeling my tooth, saying how peculiar the accident was. I feel peculiar. My uncle scoffs.

Attributing my condition to shock, Mother cautions me not to chew too hard, to rest after dinner.

I undress for bed early. Taking off my underpants, I notice a brownish-red stain. Connecting it somehow with the accident (had they brushed next to the towel?), I drop them into the clothes hamper and climb into bed. Mother comes in soon afterward, awkwardly holding out to me a bundle of bulky cotton pads and a book called *Baby and Me*.

She tells me not to be alarmed, that I have reached "a very significant stage" in life. Has she been looking into the hamper nightly? For how many years? She says I should read the book carefully and ask her questions later.

My innocence about the human body could be explained by my years, being barely at the stage where I understand that women function differently from men; that it is a difference in the number and function of holes. But how many holes and which one for what? I am not sure about it in spite of information passed between lavatory stalls at school. I expect the book will tell me, but it does not; the minds of young girls do not easily accommodate news from sources other than their own. Discovering that the body makes its own decisions has a religious dimension, to be sure, but it is never news passed out in Sunday school. I have a mirror and examine my choice. The hole for blood is one of three. The center one seems logical; I aim for that. I take the pads and place them between my legs according to directions and never mention the subject to my mother.

Next day I am up early preparing a surprise for my English class—painting bright red letters on a poster in honor of Mephistopheles, the devil, Satan. All the names that represent the figure of evil I write on the sign. Our class is studying Macbeth's dark deeds. I am moved by the spectacle of power in Macbeth's mind and wish to reproduce it in color. I carry the poster to school and carefully unfold it for the teacher to examine. Pleased by my initiative, she comments on my "ingenuity" and fastens it to the outside of the classroom door to the accompaniment of giggles: "Satan lives." Red marks, printed boldly in scraggly letters, lick the edge of the paper like flames of the inferno. I feel proud and the rest of the morning am unable to concentrate on any part of Shakespeare, who, if not exactly a stranger to us, is not known either as a close friend.

My exaltation is short-lived. The school principal sees the sign, which has caused a commotion in the hall. He notifies our teacher on the intercom system to take down the decoration immediately and henceforth be more diligent in her duties. This is a Christian school, he reminds her; devil-worship is banned. The teacher, a fragile dark-haired young woman with painted red fingernails, turns the poster over to me gingerly, one adult to another. She thanks me for my effort and, covering her embarrassment, encourages me to continue my interest in art.

My notions of the devil's power are confirmed: The world, the flesh, and the devil are one. I am a sinner, a sufferer; good deeds alone will clear my name.

Too alarmed to confess my confusion, I go home that night and thank Mother for her book, reassuring her that, yes, I feel fine. No pain, no discomfort: only tiredness and wonder. My body has become A Responsibility. But if the body has a mind of its own, how is one ever to become fully acquainted with it? I have already glimpsed the truth. We float with the current—an accident here, an operation there—worrying about our sexual capacities, trying to shed the fat. The real world has come home to me. I am a fully conditioned woman.

Friends of my uncle mention a swimming scholarship that might be available for me at a private girls' school in the state. Nobody in my family pushes the opportunity. I hold back, claiming pride in the "democratic principle"—a glib phrase stolen from my history class—and say, no thank you, I'll stick to public school. I enter a single AAU meet and then withdraw from further competition. It is a slow turning off; the mysteries of life and the mysteries of the body are irretrievably mixed up in my mind. I have learned my lessons well: To glory in sport is vain and unladylike.

Today at the ocean's edge, I feel an immediate, predictable threat. My compulsion is to run and at the same time to move closer. The rhythm of the waves is a release, but one that seems to doom me. I stand paralyzed, thinking I will drown for sure if I continue to wait. Admitting the fear offers some relief. Still, I wonder, had I pursued the course of ambition when I was younger, would I feel such a cowardly emotion; had I been able to take my chosen sport seriously, would I be standing there at all?

sneakers

ALISA SOLOMON

As some girls ached for their first brassiere, I pined for a pair of cleats. It's not that our field hockey pitch was so smooth and sleek that I really needed them for traction—indeed, the piece of Illinois ground assigned to Highland Park High School's girls' team was rarely mowed and not even flat—but I knew that those plastic protrusions underfoot would proclaim my seriousness as an athlete. I could see myself loping to practice on lumpy soles, my legs bowing out over their uneven but certain purchase on the earth.

Truth is, my legs bowed anyway, even in my everyday flats, my Converse All-Stars. And though I was not as emphatic as my best friend, Fran, whose annual new pair of All-Stars were always black high-tops, I had well understood the fashion fundamentals drummed into every teenage female: Shoes make the outfit. And the outcast. Risking ridicule, we eschewed femmy pointy-toed Keds, and sauntered with preconscious defiance in sneakers that could be bought only in the boys' department. Other girls rebelled, they thought, by primping in fuck-me pumps. Our Converse, and more so the cleats we coveted, said fuck *you*.

Miraculously, I got a pair. One August night, just before the new practice season would begin, I blew out candles and my mother handed me a card that concluded: "When it comes to ways of dressing we have such different views. Still, for your 15th birthday, you get a pair of hockey shoes." The next day we made the pilgrimage to the sporting goods store, where I was giddily fitted for a pair of black leather Adidas by a salesman who kept smirking at his colleague in the storeroom. I noticed; my mom pretended not to. As soon as we got into the car, I took the fragrant shoes from the box and fingered their jagged white stripes as feverishly as any fetishist ever stroked a set of T-straps.

It's a little hard to stomach that twenty-five years later— and as many years after Title IX went into effect—the only folks taking unabashed pleasure in the feminist frisson of athletic footwear are the marketing strategists at the big sport-shoe companies. Hard to stomach, that is, that the courage to claim jockdom's challenge to gender conformity comes primarily from the connivings of capitalism. Meanwhile, even as more girls join teams, more women work out, and more elite athletes gain the adulation—and endorsement contracts— once reserved for men, their coaches and promoters, and with rare exception the athletes themselves, strain ever more strenuously to insist that girl jocks aren't butch.

Some years ago I attended a banquet sponsored by the Women's Sports Foundation, honoring top women athletes. The climax of the evening was horrifying: when her name was called, each athlete walked across the stage in a gown and high heels, as if prancing down the runway in a beauty pageant. Some practically stumbled, and two men were stationed on either side of the steps leading off the stage to help the women down to the floor. Never mind that these were women who could run miles in less time than it takes to poach an egg, or that they hoisted hundreds of pounds overhead and dashed through the wilds of the North on dogsleds. In heels they were helpless. (Only Martina Navratilova, bless her, wore slacks and sensible shoes.)

Even the 1996 Olympic preview stories on the U.S. team's "better half" couldn't help taking on the astonished tone of Dr. J. extolling his dancing dog. The most egregious example was Frank DeFord's condescending cover story for *Newsweek*, "The Year of the Women." He noted, for example, that girls who participate in sports are less likely to "get . . . themselves pregnant"—as if that were something girls did by themselves.

Ad agencies, however, aren't buying. After all, as is well

known, they sell image, and "Just Do It—As Long as You Don't Break a Fingernail" won't wash. You can't colonize Planet Reebok by flipping the flounciest hair. With soccer growing almost as quickly among girls as boys, Nike figures that 42 percent of the young players they hope to woo into their first pair of cleats—and brand loyalty—are girls. It's a massive market. The number of women's NCAA soccer teams has leapt from 80 to 446 since 1982. And with the advent of two professional women's basketball leagues over the last two years, that consumer base is only expanding. In 1997, Spalding's top-selling item was its WNBA basketball, orange and oatmeal and pared down to 28.5 inches. Advertisers will use what sells, even if it flies in the face of the image promoters prefer to pitch.

Indeed, the promoters are doing backflips to pull athletes away from old amazon stereotypes, and to present them as wholesome, heroic, and, above all, heterosexual. A director of a sports marketing firm recently bragged to *The Atlanta Journal-Constitution* that the U.S. women's soccer team "has done a lot to erase that misconception in a lot of people's minds, especially men running corporations, that a woman athlete can't compete at the highest level without being masculine" (code language, according to the die-hard stereotype, for "lesbian"). And players on the team who have husbands, boyfriends, or babies parade them more proudly than their 1991 world championship trophy. Here's how *Sports Illustrated* led its report on the U.S. women's gold-medal victory in Atlanta: "Joy Fawcett stood transfixed under the stands of a college football field turned Olympic football field. She had a gold medal around her neck and her two-year-old daughter, Katelyn, in her arms." (Of course, Fawcett was subsequently referred to as "Joy" in the story.)

The WNBA handpicked its superstars as much for their ability to stay on-message in feminine looks and perky personalities as on their prowess in the paint. Each has a dramatic story to tell that will draw in fans and help push products: a mother surviving cancer; a new baby; a modeling career. And never, ever, a girlfriend.

Nike, Reebok, Adidas, and some other companies are starting to talk about backing a professional women's soccer circuit. While their experts may blab about the "lovely ladies" of sports—a means of counteracting the fear that strong, independent women would be equated with lesbians—their ads look like nothing short of promo spots for dykedom. A recent Nike commercial features an uppity gang of three little girls sneering at Lisa Leslie for wearing a pair of pumps.

Fran sent me the premiere issue of *womenSports* in the mid-'70s, after we'd gone away to college. (I joined the field hockey team at my school; Fran, as those black high-tops might have predicted, went out for rugby at hers.) The magazine's brazen motto in those days was "Women's Sports Has Balls," and it promised to cover the emergent pro women's basketball league and other competitive sports, as well as to appeal to athletes on college and community teams with training tips and tales of glory. As the basketball league foundered and the antifeminist backlash gained ground, the magazine got a quick makeover. It soon became the less threatening *Women's Sports and Fitness*; photos of muddy ruggers with hairy legs were replaced by airbrushed beauties in shimmering Lycra. While there were still updates on the greats in track and field and other sports, the emphasis turned to how-tos for first-time marathoners and tight-hammed aerobicists. This year, since Condé Nast took over, the magazine has featured articles revealing how supermodel Rebecca Romijn stays fit and exalting the U.S. women's soccer team for sustaining their femininity in spite of their rugged play. The message of strength and independence still glints off the glossy pages, but the sweaty glee of jock culture has been purged.

Except in the shoe ads. Recently I faxed Fran a copy of one I tore out of *WS&F*, figuring it would strike the same chord that it had sounded in me. On a bright-blue background, U.S. national soccer team star Julie Foudy soars above a moonlike terrain, her right leg parallel to the ground below, her body torquing into the sky. Her left hand strains upward with veins bulging in her forearm, as she levers her taut torso into a twist and her extended right foot toward an airborne ball. She's wound up to whack it right out of the picture.

You can't see the logo on her blurred kicking shoe, and the other is tucked tight under her butt. No brand name appears on the page. But there are seven lines of white-lettered text. It reads: "Tomboy. Alright, call me a tomboy. Tomboys get medals. Tomboys win championships. Tomboys can fly. Oh. And tomboys"—here there's a mid-sentence line break—"aren't boys." You have to turn the page to see that this tribute to butchness pitches Reeboks.

But what else? At the very least, the ad pumps up the nostalgia of *WS&F* readers, women whose sustained interest in exercise suggests they might have been hard-core as kids (and, if the magazine's adventure-travel features and ads are any indication, now have plenty of disposable income). A much-publicized poll recently reported that 80 percent of women in top positions at Fortune 500 firms identify themselves as erstwhile tomboys. So the pugnacious text, like a sultry song from the '60s, stirs memories of bygone pleasures, not least of which was an unself-conscious ease in the body. Like the gender-bending tomboy, the ad is at once naughty and nice, appealing to a subversive impulse still lingering beneath conformity. "And tomboys / aren't boys" may seem to rein in the gender disruption of the flying, medal-winning champion by reminding us of her femaleness, much as the weddings at the end of Shakespeare's comedies of cross-dressing promise to return their heroines to their maiden's weeds. But just as those heroines were played by boys, rendering the containment incomplete and ironic, the ad's naming of the disruption celebrates it. Foudy, after all, is no twelve-year-old. And that interruptive "Oh" insists that the point that follows is not to be overlooked. The pause before "aren't boys" clinches the reversal—the ad's appeal comes not in the assurance that at the end of the day the athlete is a lady but that as an athlete she need not be. She's sexy not because she fails to assume "masculinity" totally but because she refuses to assume "femininity."

A queer reading is unavoidable, at least for the likes of Fran and me, athletes from the generation that took to heart the '70s quip "Feminism is the theory, lesbianism is the practice." Past forty, we still play the game of seeing the incipient lesbianism in the overdetermining activities of our adolescence, which we couldn't recognize at the time. And then we project it onto everyone else. We know Foudy is married to a guy, but that doesn't make the ad any less lesbo in our eager eyes.

A more recent Nike commercial confirms our suspicions that advertisers are tapping into the submerged forces that drew us out for hockey, volleyball, basketball, softball, and even badminton teams every year in high school. We measured the season by the type of shoes we took to afternoon practice, tying their laces together so we could sling them conspicuously over our shoulders as we made our way to the locker room. We reveled in the pure joy of unfettered movement, of the wind slapping against our moist T-shirts, of feeling our speed and strength and adoring it in each other, of hollering and sweating and slapping high fives, of blending together so perfectly we'd blur into a new organism, a team. Beyond evoking these visceral pleasures, the Nike commercial knowingly lays bare the homosocial fact that made all that even possible, and then hints at the eroticism pulling beneath like a ferocious undertow.

The spot is barely thirty seconds long, but with fast cutting packs in more than fifty spectacular slo-mo feats. A player bounds into the sky and backflips midair, smacking the ball as she uncoils; another, like a base runner sliding into home plate, drives her body along the ground toward the ball, sending up a gorgeous spray of earth in her wake. A goalie bursts from the ground like a missile to make an impossible save; a forward leaps up and heads a pass into the twine. Close-ups of the players' faces in the huddle are intercut among these amazing action shots. In an almost flat voice-over, one player declares a vow; then it is repeated in chorus by the entire team. And this is what they are saying: "We are flesh and we are blood and we are bound together. For better or worse, in sickness and in health, through thick and through thin, in good times and in bad, till death or the world championship title do us part."

Pegged on the 1995 world championship, where the United States was hoping to repeat its 1991 victory (instead they took third, losing to Norway in the semifinals), the ad aired during sports programming featuring women (a four-Sunday ABC special on women athletes and the NCAA basketball championships) and men (the NBA finals). It even got some prime-time play, showing once on *Seinfeld* and on *ER.* An official at Wieden & Kennedy, the agency that produced the ad, told me that the "soccer vows" appealed to women because "we all dream of getting married." However, that some of us (maybe all of us, to some degree) dream of getting married to each other was not a message, she said, that they had intended—or even considered. Incredulous, I rephrased my question: Didn't this commercial maybe remind anyone of, say, the debate over gay and lesbian marriage? "Oh, no," said the ad exec. "That really wasn't such a public debate in 1995. We were stressing their commitment as athletes and as a team."

For a presumed audience of traditional sports spectators, the emphasis on team spirit calls forth a more innocent time when players were loyal and so were fans, a time before pro athletes became best known for grabbing more millions, going on strike, getting arrested on charges of rape. Indeed, in a *New York Times* report on the Olympic soccer victory, sports columnist George Vecsey wistfully compares the U.S. women's cohesive playing style to the way "the New York Islanders used to be, like the old Boston Celtics." Later, he sighs, "[Mia] Hamm chases the ball obsessively, the way Pete Rose used to pursue base hits." Male columnists covering the WNBA in the dailies rhapsodize constantly about the purity of the women's game, untainted by the greedy excesses and solo slam-dunking strategies that have overtaken the men's game. As yet uncorrupted, women's teams return honor and camaraderie to the field of play, glorifying sports for sports' sake.

Conveniently, women's sports does all this without demanding entry into a male preserve. The WNBA gets accolades in part because it plays during the summer, not daring to tread on the male turf of a winter season. (The American Basketball

League—the pro women's basketball league that does play during the winter—is virtually ignored by the media.)[1] As for soccer, at least in the United States, it just doesn't rank with the male bastions of baseball, basketball, and football. Indeed, women are tolerated in soccer here in part because the game is not considered American—and neither, these days, is teamwork. Network nationalism, and commercialism, dismiss Vecsey's vision as quaint. Not surprisingly, the nascent men's Major Soccer League is already promoting players as individual superstars; meanwhile, the U.S. women's team considered getting identical tattoos to indelibly mark their gold-medal unity.

Little wonder that NBC barely showed any Olympic women's soccer (or basketball or softball)—not even the gold-medal finals, despite a record 76,481 fans attending the match against China in Athens, Georgia. To do so would have jangled the jingoism. In these welfare-bashing, social-contract-busting times of sink-or-swim individualism, exalting women's teamwork is downright commie.

As usual, nationalism lines up with sexism—and heterosexism. As cultural historians have long demonstrated, nationalist narratives cast men as protectors of the homeland and women as its procreators. Especially amid the frantic flag-waving that passes for Olympic coverage, to celebrate the tenacious teamwork of women would have challenged the deep assumptions of American chauvinism. Focusing on the adult athletes on women's teams would also have meant relinquishing recourse to the reassuring images of male control—like Bela Karolyi cradling Kerri Strug in his brutish arms, Bobby Kersee pulling Jackie Joyner-Kersee from the heptathalon—"A Concerned Husband Ends His Wife's Quest," according to *The New York Times*. By contrast, a team's real authority comes from its collectivity. And that means women—strong women—in charge of themselves. Prime time can't cope. Especially because the majority of TV viewers of the Olympics is female. You don't have to be Brecht to recognize that NBC's much ballyhooed "feminine" melodramatic narrative strategy, encouraging sympathy with individual athletes, lulls spectators into uncritical acceptance of the grand old narratives. When even shoe sales-folks see the subversion in soccer, the network knows to keep it out of America's living rooms.

I had been tempted to call Fran during the Olympics to squeal about the new inclusion of women's soccer and, even more so, softball, Fran's master sport. I have no doubt that if there had been women's softball in the Olympics, say in 1980, or even '88, Fran would have been on the team. She can prob-ably still peg the plate from the deepest reaches of left field. And then, of course, I was tempted to call to rant about NBC's jilting of our beloved team sports for its fixation on the prepu-bescent pixies of gymnastics who don't even wear shoes (but all the same walk with the arched backs and mincing steps induced by high heels).

But I didn't bother—in part because it would have felt too sad, but also because I wondered if maybe their not showing these sports kept them safe from the "feminizing" forces of peacock and patria. Let soccer and softball remain suspicious, dangerous, beyond the pale. Where else would Fran and I have gone as girls to find our rowdy refuge, if even on the field frilli-ness had carried weight?

Yes, yes, it's grand that so many more girls are playing sports nowadays. It's thrilling that cleats come in girls' sizes. And I can't even imagine how it would have felt to plaster Mia Hamm or Teresa Weatherspoon pix on my wall instead of Gale Sayres. Yet, my jock-heart cries, don't let them make sports normal, unthreatening, as hetero as ballet. Not until they've run some windsprints in my shoes.

1. The ABL went out of business in December 1998. Founder Gary Cavelli was widely quoted as attributing the league's demise to lack of adequate media coverage. Eds.

q: why **do** you **want** to **race?**
a: because **my** name
comes apart

GRACE BUTCHER

Loading up the motorcycle. Tugging on the tie-downs to secure it on the trailer. Heading through the countryside, through a little town: Main Street with the teenagers hanging around the pizza place staring at my bike, the racy little white Yamaha RD250. I am proud to be the driver of this car with the bike on the trailer behind it. People don't expect to see a girl driving the car.

A girl. Am I not supposed to say that about myself now that I am forty-four? My body is a girl's. My long hair is a girl's. From a distance people think I am a girl. From inside I think I am a girl. In bed with my lover I am a woman, but here, now, driving this car to the racetrack, I am a girl.

When I was indeed a girl, I pretended to be an auto racer. My balloon-tired Schwinn was my race car, my Indy car, my blue No. 5 Offenhauser. I lied intensely to my little friends about being a real auto racer at night when they were in bed. For some reason my mother aided and abetted me in this lie; she *almost* verified it, never scolded me, allowed my friends to believe me by not telling them anything different. Now I think maybe my mother *wanted* me to be a race car driver. Or wished she were one herself. People used to gasp when she drove our family car 50 m.p.h.! She loved it. You see? My mother was skinny and loved to drive fast. She was always a girl.

My motorcycle is not a race car, but it is what has come into my life now. It is almost the same thing except that I ride it like a horse. It can go so incredibly fast with a flick of my wrist that it could leap out from under me. I lean over it, wrap my legs around it. I am perhaps in love.

I pull in through the gates at Nelson Ledges, the road-race track. "Hi, Grace!" Ah, they know me here, seem glad to see me. I park the car, make myself stroll casually into the big barn for registration. I want to run, to leap around saying, "I'm here! I'm here!" I happily sign all the papers that deal with death and damage and destruction and disaster and doom. (Whose? Not mine, surely.)

And being with my bike-race friends in the shadowy tents and vans of the darkening infield, sitting by the bike-race campfire in my bike-race chair, toasting my bike-race hot dog . . . yes, I am here among these people to do this amazing thing, to ride the 100 m.p.h. I am afraid to ride on the street where cars and dogs and loose gravel and chuckholes all leap out to bring me down. Here there is a clear clean track for me to go fast on, and corner workers who speak to me with silent sudden flags of many colors that tell of oil spills and accidents ahead and one lap to go—corner workers who will run to me if I should fall. Here there is an ambulance, sleek and quietly, quickly coming just for me should my body explode onto the pavement in that terrible surprise of knowing I have crashed.

And tech—the late-night laughter in the brightly lit building where we've pushed the bikes through the ruts and dark and dust of the infield. The bikes go through tech inspection. They are declared safe, for look here—here is proof. This is safety wire so nothing falls off the bike except the rider. My leathers, my skintight road-race suit, is looked at. It is declared safe, for here is all the padding that rounds the angles of my skinny body and here are all the zippers that zip me into this additional layer of brown leather skin that has my name on the chest in white letters. And my helmet that may bounce on the pavement so my head does not. Ah yes, I am safe as long as I do not fly over the crash wall and drown in the swamp or cross paths with the woodchuck who ambles across Turn One at least once on every race day. Push the bike back through the dark voices of my friends, through the dark summer night with its red jewels of campfires, through the dark butterflies that rise from somewhere with wings so gentle they seem almost not to be made of fear but of summer wind, through the dark rows of trucks and vans and families and babies and dogs and children. This would be like a picnic tomorrow if it were not for what some of us are going to do.

I pretend to sleep and morning pretends it is never going to come. But finally we stop pretending and I do and it does. Riders' meeting. I am a rider. I am amazed by this, every time. I am again going to do this unreal thing that only incredibly brave young men seem to do. Am I therefore brave by association? I am the only girl in this boisterous gathering. I listen intently as the race director explains the upcoming practice session to us. I look serious or keep my face carefully neutral but laugh at the jokes.

Instructed in the protocol of practice, we leave the hot, crowded little room in the stands. The track shimmers and curls off into the distance like a thick gray snake in the sun. At my campsite in the infield I struggle and wiggle into my leathers on this sticky hot Ohio morning—like a snake myself now, writhing around to get back into my skin. Now my loins are girded, my feet are booted, my hands gloved, my head helmeted, my pigtails tucked in. *Now.*

Kicking my bike into action I ride slowly through the pits to line up for practice. Where are my friends who also ride this class, the 250 Production class? I keep looking for the big X taped on the backs of the leather jackets of the beginners, the first-year racers. My own X in silvery duct tape from shoulders to waist seems to burn into my back: a reminder. Veteran riders will watch out for me, be aware that I might do something squirrely out there, something they wouldn't do. While I am waiting, I pray. I also pray while I'm riding: "Please, dear God . . . " (hurling the bike around the 80 m.p.h. first turn), "Keep me safe . . . " (scraping my toe in the fast left-hander), "Let the light be around me . . . " (speedometer needle touching 100 m.p.h. on the back straightaway).

Practice session. Another one. And the first race. As I line up on the track with twenty other bikes, all of us revving it up—that shrill, sharp, racketing two-stroke howl drowning the pounding of my pulse, drowning all my thoughts—I am turning my throttle, turning it . . . turning it . . . till the green flag swoops suddenly down and I am doing this wild and crazy incredible thing. Going as fast as I dare, feeling good, true lines through the turns, hauling my bike down nearly on its side to keep my line, to stay on the track. Getting passed, being whooshed by better riders as they go by. Amazed that I'm going as fast as I can and they are passing me. No, I'm not going as fast as I can, only as fast as I dare.

Spot a friend ahead of me, concentrate on moving up lap by lap, maneuvering, passing him at last when he goes a little wide on one turn. At last! Ah! A small ecstasy finds room to flower, pushing through the dense layers of concentration. Must stay ahead now. No one to tell me how; I'm on my own. He stays right behind me. Oh lord. I lean more tightly over my tank; my neck aches from fatigue; my engine and the wind scream inside my helmet.

Rider ahead goes wildly down, went too high, caught the edge of the track. He is rolling across the track and away out of sight as I pass him, an object suddenly gone like scenery streaming past the window of a train I'm on. I feel neutral about his fall. I don't know who he was. I felt neutral about my own fall once, and I certainly knew who *I* was.

Oh beautiful for checkered flag! I sit up, slow down, ride an easy lap back to the pits. I think this is one of the most real things I've ever done. I've raced well, smoothly, not been last, not crashed. I ride into the pits, kill the engine, lean the beloved little white bike on a box, dismount, unzip my brown-and-white road-race leathers, let the jacket part flop down around my hips. My T-shirt is soaked with sweat. The wind and sun start to dry me off. I try not to swagger as I walk a little aimlessly, unwinding, feeling as if there is a glow all around me.

Then I grab my stopwatch and head for trackside to time laps for a friend in the next race. "Okay, Grace! Looked good out there!" a white-uniformed track official hollers at me as he hurries by. There's that feeling again, that sort of blossoming, as if I'm leaving flower petals behind me as I go, or a little trail of golden sparkles in the air.

Yes, thank you, and please, I *want* to look good out there. Like a real motorcycle racer. So far, so good. Motocross for three years on a Suzuki 125—the ruts, the jumps, the mud, the foot-down turns; the jolting, slamming speed; the dust so dense I'm riding blind; the aching biceps and forearms and thighs; the wrenching around of my whole body. And now road racing, sinuous, graceful, the track a steady gray blur of speed, the little Yamaha 250 two-stroke shrieking beneath me as the tach climbs to the red line—

Motorcycle racing in my forties. I've always liked going fast: running; horseback riding; driving on long, empty highways. On the street, on a motorcycle, going fast is not cool; it's too dangerous. But on the track the distance opens up into an endless horizon that I can speed toward as fast as I dare. I would call this *ecstasy*. I seek it out again and again.

After the checkered flag says I am through, I feel drained and exuberant, grateful to whatever turns of fate have led me to this track in this lifetime, grateful even for my name, which may be why I do these things. Funny, the way my name comes apart like that: Grace—race—ace. An echo. It tells me what to do, what to be. My parents named me Grace. I must have heard just "race."

"Okay," I said.

ernestine bayer

LINDA LEWIS

Early on a brisk December morning in 1984, nine women took a borrowed shell from Philadelphia's Vesper Boat Club for a short row on the Schuylkill River. The women had all been inducted into rowing's hall of fame the night before in an emotion-filled ceremony. The chill of the morning air and the mist rising from the still waters of the river provided a delicious contrast with the heat and excitement of the previous evening. The moment just before the row began was particularly sharp and poignant for the woman sitting in the number-two seat of the shell. This woman did not look like the others in the boat. She was smaller and considerably older, by about fifty years. The other eight women—the coxswain and seven rowers— were Olympic gold medalists, having swept with power and precision to that honor just four months earlier. The white-haired woman had never rowed in an Olympic event or even in any kind of elite national competition. Yet, the eight gold medalists felt that they owed what they had accomplished in rowing to her. They had impulsively invited her to row with them the night before when they were all celebrating how far women had come in a sport that was closed to them for so long. The eight Olympic gold medalists had used all the words they knew to thank this white-haired woman for insisting, nearly fifty years earlier, on women's right to row competitively. Now they wanted her to feel with her body what a force she had unleashed.

The Olympic eight wanted to perform exquisitely, to show the woman in the number-two seat the level of athletic accomplishment that she had made possible. There was some hesitation, though, out of deference to the woman's age. The eight wondered how much of a display of speed and strength they could put on without pushing her too hard. After all, they were in their twenties and thirties, the best rowers in the world. She was seventy-five and primarily a recreational rower. If they took the stroke rate up too high, would they turn what was meant to be a triumph into a disaster?

As the coxswain considered what cadence to call after the warm-up, the woman in the number-two seat yelled out: "Let's do a start and a ten."

She was asking to feel the boat's explosiveness off the starting line. A start is five rapid strokes designed to get sixty feet of shell and 1,500 pounds of bodies moving. The ten strokes after the start are full power strokes at the high rate set in motion by the start.

The coxswain stopped the boat and got the rowers ready for a start. All eight moved forward on their sliding seats, planted their blades in the water, and breathed deeply, preparing for the quick burst that would get the boat going. The coxswain gave the traditional French starting sequence: *"Etes vous prêtes?"* (Are you ready?) Every body was at the same angle, knees bent, back forward, arms extended, compressed, poised to release maximum power.

"Partez." (Go.)

All eight oars pulled as one. The shell heaved through the water as the rowers rammed their legs down and pulled through on the oars to pry the boat forward. All eight brought the oars out of the water together and slid forward on their seats together to begin the next stroke. After the tenth power stroke, the coxswain told the rowers to "weigh enough" (stop) and let the boat glide.

For a moment there was only the rush of water and the sound of hard breathing. All nine women floated in a cocoon of suspended time. Then from the number-two seat again came the call: "Let's take a start and a ten."

The other women in the boat came fully awake. They

understood immediately what the tone of that request implied. The honored guest in the number-two seat was saying to them, "Come on, you gold medalists, show me how it *really* feels." She was challenging them to row as hard and as fast as they could. That first start and ten had not been at full pressure. The Olympians had held something back. They had been quick and graceful but had not turned on the explosive power. The woman in the number-two seat had kept her part of the bargain, staying right with them. Now she wanted to see what more they all could do.

The second five-stroke start and ten high on that December morning was charged. All eight rowers moved up their slides into the starting position determined to hold nothing back. They buried their blades in the water and shook the tension out of their shoulders. They were coiled and ready to explode when the starting command came: *"Partez."* The boat flew, slicing through the placid waters of the Schuylkill. With every stroke, the rowers translated their muscle into motion. They took every stroke as one flawless unit, achieving a power that transcended their individual efforts and lifted the boat over the water. When the rowers stopped and feathered their oars so the boat could glide, Ernestine Bayer, in the number-two seat, wept.

solo shoot (from *in these **girls**, hope **is** a **muscle***)

MADELEINE BLAIS

1995

Kim pulled out of the driveway of their ranch house and headed up Route 116 to Crocker Farm, where she had been an elementary school student along with numerous other Hurricanes, including Kathleen Poe, Emily Shore, and Rita Powell.

Wearing a T-shirt, shorts, and her game sneakers, she pulled into the dark parking lot and backed the car up so that the headlights would throw the greatest light possible on the hoops she had used as a child.

She got out of the car and gave the empty courts and fields a sweeping look. Good: she was alone.

She walked onto the court and dribbled in a fashion that might seem aimless to an outsider; but in fact she was glancing at parts of the pavement, imagining:

This is where Jen will throw me the ball, here is where Jamila will pull up and dish it off, here is where Kathleen might miss a shot, and this is where I have to be for the rebound.

She moved carefully, methodically, trying not to stress either of her ankles. Surgery was inevitable, but she wanted to make it through the 1992–93 season first. She inched her way closer to the basket:

Eight feet is too far away; shoot from eight and Coach will put me back on the bench just like he did in that last game against Hamp. Six feet. That's better. Right side off the back-board, through the chain-metal net. Left side, rattle it through. Over and over, spin right, dribble, jump. Drop step, pivot, shoot.

Applauded only by the mosquitoes and the crickets, she would take the ball and pound it on the asphalt and set up and shoot. Despite the noise from the bugs and the drone of traffic on Route 116, she heard nothing except the thud of the ball and the pulsing inside her chest, the steady beat of pride and exhaustion, the old brag of the athlete's heart.

what goes around, comes around

FRANCES K. CONLEY

My alarm clock sounds at 5 a.m. Monday through Friday as it has for more than twenty years. It is time for my daily run, an hour of "physical culture," a time for me, before I am challenged by the daily demands of my work as an academic neurosurgeon.

In the winter it is dark. Often it is also windy, rainy, and cold. But the dog, ecstatic, runs ahead of me, using her superior eyesight and magic nose to lead her gracefully through the tangles of downed limbs on the nighttime trails. She knows that my nose, as well as my eyes, are worthless, and that I depend on the beam of a flashlight to guide my stumbling steps.

Unlike human running partners she does not require conversation, so I have mental time for plans and dreams. I can think through a difficult surgical case and take it step-by-step to its successful conclusion. Or an elusive diagnosis suddenly becomes clear. And how will I—or can I ever—convey my utter frustration, my empathy, my caring, and, yes, my grief? What words will I use to gently, compassionately, ever so softly tell the forty-five-year-old lawyer that his MRI scan, which I saw as my last chore before heading home the evening before, reveals an unresectable, malicious, ugly brain tumor that will take him in the prime of his life?

In the spring the dog and I are even, and as the days lengthen, my eyes tell me what her nose tells her. At that hour the faces of the spring wildflowers remain hidden from the emerging light, tucked behind tight curls of petals which relax into glory only much later in the day, when touched by the direct warmth of sun—a time when I am at work in an air-conditioned operating room. I often win our race in the summer when the day-old air remains along the trails and there is no cooling fog to obliterate the oppressive heat that leaves the dog lagging far behind, and both of us wilted, panting, and sweating.

Young women of my era were not supposed to sweat, at least not heavily. Physical education classes provided our gentle "sport," mandated but hardly demanding. Modesty prevailed—we changed clothes in separate cubicles, showered (when forced to do so by an instructor) in individual stalls, and hid our developing bodies from the critical gaze of our peers, as well as from ourselves. Girls were not expected to enjoy physical activity. After all, how could one attract boys with wet, sweaty hair that inevitably dried into unruly waves and curls? Even in college, competitive sport for women was very low-key. However, I played intercollegiate lacrosse and swam freestyle and backstroke on the swimming team, and gradually became addicted to the endorphins produced by active physical exertion.

As a reward to myself for having successfully completed the first year of medical school, I bought a ticket to the 1962 USSR-USA track meet at Stanford University. I watched the American women javelin throwers lose badly to the Russians, and decided, "Why not." I had never seen a javelin competition before, had never held a javelin, but the day after the meet visited the practice track to see if someone would teach me how to throw. There I found a singularly handsome man named Phil who had javelins, international competitive experience—he represented the United States in the Olympics in 1956—and a willingness to teach. And, glory be, he was single. We were married the following summer after I had learned the fundamentals of javelin throwing and, more important, how to keep up with an elite athlete and his friends in their heady world of obsessive, competitive athleticism. To compete on a national level in any sport requires extensive physical conditioning, and my increasingly demanding medical studies did not allow sufficient time to train. I had started working with the javelin too late, and was willing to give it too little.

In the early years of our marriage Phil and I communicated through exercise and athletics. As his ability to throw with the very best began to wane, we started to run together on the weekends, gradually increasing the distance we covered. By the time I was learning hands-on how to care for patients, our runs became my escape from the endless, exhausting routine of the hospital. The open air and vigorous activity permitted a brief return to that world where people delighted in health and physical capability—where obsession with pain and disability seemed distant and out of place.

Yellow-orange-red dawns, intruding through floor-to-ceiling windows at the end of a long hospital corridor, color depressing memories of "all-nighters" from years as a neurosurgical resident. In the intensive care unit a patient, one of far too many, is on autopilot. During a night of work the pressure from a blood clot and fragments of fractured skull have been removed from a bruised and battered brain. The fragments of broken bone rest in a freezer, waiting for the brain swelling to decrease, when the pieces of the puzzle can be reassembled, wired together, and implanted back into their rightful place. For now, only a thin scalp and thick layers of white gauze dressing protect the delicate, damaged brain. Written in large black letters on a strip of adhesive tape is an ominous warning: "NO BONE"—a message that succinctly describes the broken head and life that just hours before had been functional and intact.

The beauty of those early mornings so frequently was lost, not only in the all-consuming fatigue but also by the knowledge that this life, if it survived, would never see or appreciate this dawn, or any other, in the same way it had previously. By the time the sun began its daily commute from the eastern edge of the earth, it was usually quiet, and my immediate decision lay between a run followed by a quick shower, or getting an hour and a half of sleep before rounds and another day of work began. I learned the day would be better if I chose the life-replenishing run on the wet grass of the university athletic fields.

In 1966 Phil and I ran the 7.8-mile cross-city race in San Francisco, the Bay to Breakers—he officially, I unofficially, as race organizers did not allow women to enter. At the start I threw my coat to a friend and took off with the pack in my running outfit, protected by Phil and other male friends from officials who would have stopped me. Along the race route, a little girl noticed my hair ribbon and yelled excitedly, "Mommy, Mommy, look! There's a girl out there!" It would be another eighteen years before women would run an Olympic marathon.

In 1971, the Bay to Breakers race officially opened to women. Unexpectedly, I won the women's division. Reporters covering the race asked me two questions after I caught my breath: Where do you live? and Are you married? A "Palo Alto housewife" won the women's race, one newspaper reported.

After that, for the next year Phil and I competed in road races virtually every weekend, running distances ranging from three miles to marathons. I won the women's division in almost all of these competitions. Lacking formal training as a runner, I have but one pace. It operates at the edge of short-of-breath misery, but is sustainable over varied terrain and distance. A repetitive pattern developed. A few miles into a race I would begin overtaking other runners, most often men. There would be no change in a man's stride, until I drew even and passed. The sight of a feminine butt and hair ribbon would kick in a misogynistic acceleration, and I would rapidly be overtaken, in turn, by a blurry maze of pistoning arms, heavy breathing, and pounding feet. I usually drew even again within half a mile. Only rarely was a second burst of masculine adrenaline available, unless the finish line was clearly in sight. A closetful of trophies and ribbons rust and gather dust from that era.

Toward the end of my short racing career a woman competitor told me, right after I arrived at the start of a race, "I was so hoping you weren't going to show up today." Obviously she thought I had won my fair share of these events. My being such a competitive threat to her took the fun out of racing for me. Besides, it was time to get back to making myself into the best neurosurgeon I could be.

At age forty, when my academic career was well established, I joined Phil at masters track and field meets, where both of us won our share of javelin competitions. I enjoyed being with Phil in *his* world, making new friends, and competing against women who hailed from many different walks of life. One I had seen before; she was among those defeated by the Russians in 1962 at Stanford. All of us throwers competed to win, but we also commiserated with each other over our common experiences of aging—sore, aching muscles, the occasional ankle sprain, neck and back tightness from a hard throwing workout. We also shared our pleasure in increased fitness, pride in accomplishment, mellowness of mood, and the ability to eat whatever and however much we wished. All of us still felt young and pliable. A luxurious soak in a hot tub, along with a glass of wine and a good night's sleep, would repair our still-almost-perfect bodies. The hospital, operating rooms, and clinics, where day after day my life is surrounded by neurologic injury, damage, and death, remained a very separate world.

However, the aging athletic voices gradually changed and began talking incessantly, at every track meet and workout gathering, about serious structural injury, unremitting pain, and relentless loss of competitive ability. Instead of pleasure, a hard workout became a biweekly chore. Injury became reality—a broken foot, a ruptured Achilles tendon, a torn hamstring. My two worlds collided, and now neither offered me an escape from the other.

I find that athletic competition is no longer important. After all, every day at the hospital I compete against disease, disability, pain, and unyielding demands from a vast array of worthy constituents. I fight for operating-room time, I fight to get my papers published, I fight for research funding. I struggle constantly for the very right to be myself, a woman, in a distinctly masculine, hierarchical environment.

But I could never give up my morning run. Now when the alarm goes off at five in the morning, my thoughts less often are about distinct, cohesive events, or even patient-care concerns. On most days they are nebulous and simply celebrate the glory of the emerging daylight colors and shadows. The gray silence brightens with single and then harmonic notes as birds awaken. I am reminded how close God's world of nature is to that of civilization as a silent airplane with silver wings, coming from some distant place, materializes high over the ocean, to circle down to the bay and the safe embrace offered by the firm asphalt runway. Muffled sounds of automobile traffic waft upward from Highway 280 to the redwoods and meadows, and an increasingly dense necklace of bright lights shimmers across the two distant bridges that link the east with the west. My early morning run serves now, and probably always has, as my personal oasis of peace and tranquillity.

by atoms **moved**

DIANE ACKERMAN

1998

On cool summer mornings, as the pool steams,
Persis and I slip our curves into its
and crawl toward an invisible shore,
churning half an hour into half a mile
of blue, arc over arc. Then we arrive
glad as immigrants at travel's end—a place
we've come to know but can't describe
except with the soft machinery of our limbs.

My mind's abacus always floats away,
so Persis counts the laps, glad to oblige,
since, by day, she hurls the minuscule at speed,
ramming electrons until their guts spill free,
then using numbers to read the entrails,
at the particle accelerator down the road.

When fatigue tugs, we like to rest halfway
and share the odd, busy news of our lives.
It's still a little early for deeper truths.
But swimmable mornings will pivot right
into fall, despite the chill, until leaves fly.
What better place for poet and physicist
to meet than astride waves, dreamily yawning,
somewhere afloat between earth and sky,
on the bright geometry of a summer morning.

from **"the** revolutionary **bicycle"**

ANONYMOUS

The disfavor with which many people, both men and women, look upon the stimulation of this feminine passion for wheeling is not at all surprising. The practise is undoubtedly revolutionizing habits to which women have been tied, and it runs counter to immemorial prejudices as to the sphere within which feminine activities should be confined. It is giving them self-reliance and overcoming the timidity which used to be considered so appropriate to them as beings who needed the shelter of seclusion and the protection of manly courage. It is making them the comrades of men in sports and employments from which before they had turned as unfeminine. It is accustoming them to publicity. It is inciting in them the ambition for muscular development. But, after all, are such results deplorable?

ready, wrestle

HELEN VOZENILEK

No amount of practicing and real-life sparring could have prepared me for this moment of pure competitive terror. Less than
six inches separate my body from that of a stranger. Her eyes
pierce mine. Sweat flows from every gland on my body: each
tiny hair follicle glistens and triples in weight. I fear I will be
sick.

My sole purpose here at New York University, in front of
hundreds of spectators, participants, and press, is to throw this
woman down and pin her shoulders to the mat. That, too, is
her only mission.

Dimly in the background I hear, "Ready, wrestle!" and we
are upon each other. Our bodies entwine. We both struggle for
dominance. Somehow in that huge galaxy of time between the
match's beginning and end I manage to execute some of the
moves I've spent months rehearsing. Just as often I revert back
to the survivalist wrestling maneuvers I'd used as a kid against
my older brother, trying to overpower my opponent any way I
can.

Mistakenly, I think this panic will lessen in my next three
matches. No chance: I'm terrified that the wrestling command
will be given and I'll just stand there. Or turn and run off the
mat. Strategies race through my head, more as electrical
impulses than as cogent thoughts. Do I make the first move,
and she counters? Or do I defend against her initial attack and
use her momentum to my advantage? Should I make a mad
leap and pull her legs out from under her? And then hurl my
body on top? The only constant is this prancing figure in front

of me. Her intentions are clear. My vigilance cannot flag. The amount of time it takes to go from an upright position to lying flat on my back is literally seconds.

By the afternoon's close, I am completely drained. Three wins and a loss earn me a bronze medal in my weight class. I am happy to have done so well. But, more than anything, I am relieved to be done with wrestling for the day. Now, from the relative comfort of the stadium's bleachers, I can watch my teammates in the evening finals. As the Gay Games' first female wrestling participants, we've made history. As first-time competitors, we are delirious.

I didn't grow up wanting to be a wrestler, the way some girls grow up knowing they want to discover radium or fly solo across the Atlantic. Role models did not pop out from the sports pages or beckon from hopscotch squares. I watched my brother wrestle a few times, but it looked like a lot of adolescent male groping. My only images of women's wrestling came from late-night TV: scantily clad gals wrapping troughfuls of oozing mud around each other's exposed body parts and the buxom, blond hulkettes of GLOW—Golden Ladies of Wrestling—scratching and clawing their choreographed way through the ring. My brother and I flipped back and forth between the GLOW gals and Roller Derby's ferocious babes. They were certainly fun to watch, but hardly cause for emulation.

It wasn't until my mid-thirties that I discovered the thrill of throwing women to the ground, jumping on them, and earning points for the whole endeavor.

An ad in one of the local gay papers caught my attention: "Be a part of the first Gay Games women's wrestling event." Intrigued, probably as much by the idea of pioneering as by women's wrestling, a friend and I showed up at the San Francisco gym.

Initially I was kind of skeptical. I'd played a lot of sports in my life, basically anything that involved a ball or that could be done outdoors at a pitched pace. But wrestling seemed in another class entirely. It certainly didn't bespeak a love of the great outdoors. In all my time wrestling I don't ever remember looking out on a sunny day and thinking, Wouldn't it be nice to be smashing my, or someone else's, face in a mat somewhere? No. And it certainly didn't have that sense of leveling and inclusivity that comes with some other sports. I'm thinking now of softball or volleyball, in which the least athletically inclined can participate.

Friends were titillated by my newfound sport. (They'd probably also stayed up late at night watching the Golden Ladies of Wrestling.) Their knowing winks and barely concealed smirks were impossible to avoid. I'm not sure exactly how the sport of wrestling became connected in people's minds with the sport of sex. Maybe it's the vocabulary—"taking someone down," "moving in," "being the bottom"—or maybe it's the sustained physical contact that invites sexual commentary. This repartee seems especially lively when directed toward lesbian and gay wrestlers. "After all, isn't it kind of what you do in bed anyway?" goes the thinking.

But in truth, my libido has never been activated by having my legs jerked from under me or my shoulder wrenched upside my earlobe. Maybe I'm just too vanilla to appreciate the possibilities . . .

A larger question hovered in friends' minds, only occasionally voiced. Is wrestling really an appropriate sport for women? It seems so violent, so masculine. Where, they wondered, is the sisterhood in the gut wrenches, the half nelsons, the cross faces? How is this different from drag racing, hydroplaning, and spinning out on two wheels in a crowded intersection?

At first I, too, grouped wrestling with other testosterone-based activities. And while wrestling may have started out as a war preparation rite among the Greeks and Romans, evolution does, on occasion, move to a higher form. The more I learned about wrestling, the more I came to appreciate it as the ultimate fitness and conditioning activity.

One of wrestling's appeals is its earthiness, and I'm not just talking about the smell of the gym after a practice session. The equipment intensiveness that characterizes numerous other sports is missing from wrestling. Nor is there much emphasis on spending all sorts of money to "look the look." Fashion coordination extends to matching the colors of one's singlet and one's kneepads. What you weigh and nothing else determines who you will wrestle.

The action itself is a supreme combination of stamina, strength, and style. Matches typically last five minutes. After thirty seconds your chest wall is banging and you are sucking up any and all available oxygen. It's impossible to distinguish your heavy breathing from that of the body next to you. And it only gets harder. Long-distance running is good training; long-distance sprinting would be even more useful.

Most of wrestling practice is spent going over and over the same movements until they, hopefully, become second nature. The last twenty minutes, the sparring, makes it all worthwhile. This is the thrilling part, like shooting the rapids after you've spent time learning to paddle in calm waters. It is these intensive minutes of pure explosive energy that wrestlers live for. They kept me coming back again and again.

You can spot good wrestlers by their instinctive, polished textbook techniques. There is no flailing about, misdirected movement, or wasted energy. However, nothing came easily or instinctively to me. "Left hand over, right hand under," our male coaches would repeat over and over again. I'd get it right about half of the time. One coach patiently explained that learning a sport can be like learning a new language. It's a heck of a lot easier when you're younger. There are also more opportunities for practicing a new language than a new head hold.

Early on I realized that repetition was not only the best but perhaps the *only* teacher. "Go home and visualize the proper techniques," the men urged, not a hint of exasperation in their voices. But often, all I could see was a bottle of Motrin and thick flannel bedsheets.

The road to New York was painful. Thick swirls of black and blue appeared in odd and embarrassing places on my body. I discovered muscles and sinews hitherto unexplored on anatomy charts. The morning after practice, I'd wake certain that I'd been struck by a large moving van sometime in the night. As I slogged through the day, I'd amend that nocturnal visit to include several large vehicles. I had to alter my wardrobe to include buttons and zippers, since for at least half of the week pulling clothes over my head was out of the question.

Thankfully, after a few months of continuous physical contact with a continuously inflexible surface, my aches began to diminish. And usually by the time the next practice rolled around, I'd forgotten my earlier pledge to take up lawn darts or croquet. This process of memory and forgetting is, I think, a good tool for survivors of high-impact sports.

As I contemplate the upcoming Amsterdam Gay Games, I'm painfully aware of an added four years of body aches and of muscles that don't spring back quite so fast. But as long as my fellow teammate Barbara keeps wrestling at age fifty-three, I don't really feel I can throw in the towel. I'm just hoping there will be enough entrants for a masters category. That way us over-forty gals won't show up the younger things.

up for **the** count

LOUISE A. SMITH

Slam dunks have shattered backboards; a simple "brick" destroyed mine. It happened on Christmas Day 1986, when I was twenty-six and in my first year of graduate school for writing. I was shooting around in my parents' backyard with my father and grown nephew. The Catalina cherry trees shimmied in the warm breeze as Dad gloated about the superiority of winter in Los Angeles. The basketball bounced with the familiar *thud-thud,* the same perfect music that had once driven our neighbors to demand a 10 p.m. curfew on my constant practice. The nylon net, still stiff, welcomed each shot home with a crisp shout-out. As I rebounded for my nephew, though, I cast a disapproving eye on what else had become of my court. AstroTurf covered its concrete; broken-down chairs and tables cluttered its driving lanes. There was no denying the passage of time. Old folks had reclaimed their territory.

The brick came from my nephew's hands. Though he'd frequently watched my high-school summer-league games, I had obviously failed to imprint him fully with the soft touch. His shot rattled the rim, careened hard off the backboard square, and bounced into the trees. Then, as if in slow-motion tribute to its eleven years of service, the standard fell gently toward us. My nephew caught the white wooden pole, and together we eased it and the backboard down to the ground.

As a young girl, I begged long and hard for that hoop. The game had courted me in the driveway of our first house, ensnaring me with its most basic charm: sinking a basket felt joyful even if the street was almost dark and everyone else had gone home. That first rim was rusty and lopsided, but when I was six its imperfection didn't matter. The hole could have been a discarded toilet seat as long as I learned to shoot a ball through it like my older brothers. We moved when I turned nine, exchanging the basketball court for a sloping driveway and a swimming pool. There was no space for a hoop, Dad insisted.

There was no space because in 1969 there was no future for a girl in basketball. No college scholarships existed for female hoopsters, let alone professional ranks. Although my parents applauded my proficiency in a wide range of sports, Dad reserved his active encouragement for tennis and golf. In addition to being moneymakers, those sports had the cachet of being ripe for a black girl like me to break into. Black kids playing basketball came a dime a dozen, but tennis and golf were nearly all-white sanctuaries, their doors barred by more than just a talent requirement. At our dinner table, much of my family's conversation revolved around black firsts and what so-and-so was accomplishing for the race. Names of pioneers such as Althea Gibson, the first black to win the Wimbledon and U.S. singles championships, were held up for emulation. As much as I wanted to bust barriers, though, nothing felt finer than sliding down the hillside across from our house into the backyard of my only white classmate. We played as many two-on-twos with her brothers as I could instigate.

My friend's family eventually moved away like all the other white families in our grammar school. And I was again without a nearby hoop—until the day I returned from basketball camp after my freshman year of high school with the news that I could earn a college scholarship if I learned to shoot with one hand instead of two. The year was 1975; Congress had passed federal legislation, Title IX, which mandated more money spent on girls' and women's sports, three years earlier. Dad called the handyman. The handyman poured concrete over a twenty-by-seventeen-foot lawn that had never grown well in the first place, and the pole was raised—a symbol of my parents' faith in the seriousness of my play.

The court became a model of self-sufficiency. I taught myself to shoot correctly from a book by UCLA coach John Wooden, then methodically added moves. The house's shingled roof doubled as my point guard. The threat of the rebound bouncing off the edge of the concrete, over the juniper, and into the pool encouraged me to follow every shot. I could only have been more satisfied if the court had come equipped with weekly matches against Lusia Harris, college basketball's first great center. For that, I had my imagination.

The day the backboard took its final bow, it had been four years since I'd had a reason to practice. After a record-setting career at Beverly Hills High School and a sun-setting one at Stanford University, I'd chosen not to chase more double-doubles overseas. Hesitant to head off to a foreign country alone, I convinced myself that it was time to grow up, to leave childish games behind. I had no more use for post-move repetitions or 100-free-throw nights. When I'd travel home in the years immediately after college graduation, shooting hoops in the backyard provided meditation, not preparation—a reconnecting with the one thing I knew I could do right. Now, termites chewing through the base of the pole had ended even that.

I touched the dull-red rim as I hadn't since one high-flying afternoon during college when a regimen of running up hills increased my leap and fooled me into believing I could reach anything. The metal felt hard and cold. I wondered if the pole could be restored, but then, always on the lookout for symbols and signs, I concluded it must not be. The tumbling down marked the final punctuation after a long ellipsis. Basketball should have been long over, its dreams replaced by other possibilities. What could be more clear? The next day, instead of a new pole, I bought my first computer.

I assumed the game's hold on my imagination would continue to wear out like the last of my cardinal-striped game socks. I did not expect that in 1998, twelve years after the hoop's demise, I would still be playing at all, let alone two or three times a week. As I jog up and down the court now, the perfection I once sought beside the juniper is but a distant memory. An air ball off a baseline move, a rebound stolen because I forgot to protect it, slow help defense—sometimes I'm able to make more mistakes in three minutes than I used to in a whole game. Few of the athletes I compete with are in their prime, though. Tendinitis vies for as much attention as 3-pointers. Attrition ends our games as often as exhaustion.

After a recent evening of pickup I returned to my parents' house. My mother looked at my fresh bruises and commented, "You're not going to be satisfied until you break something, are you."

My battered left knee complained in agreement. I sagged in a chair in the kitchen, slowly flexing a sprained middle finger, as Mom walked to the sink. "There's always golf," she laughed, offering up Dad's game as a more appropriate lifetime sport.

"Maybe so," I replied, unconvinced, gazing beyond her shoulders. Through the window I could see the yard where I used to spend so many solitary nights. Back in high school, I traveled across the city to attend mostly white and Jewish Beverly Hills on a multicultural permit. The first two weeks not a single classmate talked to me. The silence was excruciating. At basketball tryouts, though, the chatter of other girls who also couldn't wait to play ball each day replaced the silence. We became a team. I never hung out alone again, at least until I rode out of their world each night and back into mine.

I wanted to be a star, but nothing was more fun than combining efforts with four other intense athletes. The thrill of good teamwork has enticed me back several times after long stretches away from the game. A 3-on-2 fast break with everyone touching the ball or a back-door pass for a reverse two creates as much lightness of being as it ever did.

"Mom," I said, "do you remember when our basketball hoop fell down?"

"Yes," she said. "I took it as an omen. Better it than you."

I laughed, an echo of the merriment earlier in the gym when one of the less experienced women sank the winning basket. I stood and joined Mom at the kitchen window, my long legs appreciating the chance to stretch their hardened muscles. Outside on the AstroTurf, outlines of cardboard boxes and rusty exercise equipment crowded among the chairs. As far as Mom was concerned, the backboard had fallen so that I might stay healthy, but I took her words another way as well. The backyard hoop used to be a taskmaster, demanding perfection. It allowed no slack for mediocre effort or goals unobtained. But the hoop was gone now. In its place stood the ability to treasure good plays and discard the rest. Symbols and signs are what you make of them. Despite the pain, despite the blown 15-footers, basketball still equaled joy.

tournament-tough

BARBARA BECKWITH

The fifteen of us huddle under the dome of Terminal A at Boston's Logan Airport, swapping rumors. Rackets slung over our shoulders, we're sharing what we know about the teams we're up against. Portland's team from the West Coast looks like the strongest, with players mostly in their twenties or thirties. We're at least a decade older.

My squash buddy, Trish Johnston, is forty-one, and I am old enough to be her mother—sixty. We're both past the age when people tend to give up strenuous sports. Yet here we are, en route to the national women's squash team championships in Minneapolis.

"Attention, ladies and gentlemen," announces Eve, Trish's eight-year-old daughter, to the all-women crowd. She grips her mother's hairbrush like a microphone. "We're taking bets," she proclaims, "on who gets here next."

Eve's broadcast is the only media coverage our Massachusetts team's departure gets. Squash is not a high-profile sport in the United States. Until fairly recently, it was played almost exclusively by men in prep schools and private clubs. Few Americans have played the game or even watched it. I myself did not see squash played until after Title IX widened opportunities for women in school and college sports, and women joined clubs where they could learn traditionally male sports.

Trish and I did not go to prep school. We've played squash for only four years. This is our first national tournament. We'll be up against the best amateur players in the United States. I tell myself that I'm going to learn, but I'm as eager as any other player to win. I want Trish to win, too. And I want Eve to see her do it.

Staying cool is my goal. Squash is a head game as well as a body game. Power and speed count. But strategy and placement count more. That's why I managed to take up this sport at midlife and do well. I have beaten players half my age. When I place the ball strategically, my shots are ungettable and I win the game.

Trish wins, too, especially when she's in the right mindset. But competition has not come easy to either of us. We women over thirty-five did not grow up competing. To win, we must get tournament-tough.

"I'll play—but only if we don't keep score," Trish declared when we first played squash four years ago. I, too, wanted to play "just for fun." I'd just learned the game but, like Trish, was leery of competition. We both assumed it would spoil our pleasure. Side by side on adjacent courts, we played solo squash, ignoring each other's presence.

Our club's pro urged us to play together. I liked Trish's Aussie accent, her flyaway hair, her graceful strokes. Her daughter, Eve, watched us play and called me "Gramma." Still, we refused to count points. We didn't want winners and losers.

The pro pressed us to play "real games." Once we dared keep score, we discovered that we liked it. Counting points made us want to win, which made us run faster, leap farther, and hit deeper. We focused more. We started to hit balls *away from* instead of *to* each other—the point, after all, in squash. We learned and then perfected strategic shots—high cross-courts, tricky boasts, and feathery drop shots. We realized that scoring improved our game.

Warming to competition, we challenged other players. But we soon noticed an odd gender difference. Women players at our club—at least those of us over thirty-five—tended to play the sport differently from men. Male players vied to dominate the game by staying in the center of the court. We women gave our opponents too wide a berth, placing ourselves at a disadvantage for the next shot. We let the loser of one game start the next, defying the rule that gives the service advantage to the winner. We replayed the shot if a player got hit; protocol says the struck player is at fault and must give up a point. We rarely called "let"—interference—and lost points as a result.

When we played "soft" like this, our game suffered. So, Trish and I vowed to play the sport tough and right.

We started to play male players to give us experience in returning hard fast balls. We challenged women players rated at higher levels. We jockeyed for center court. We lifted weights. We cross-trained. We played to exhaustion and then said, "Let's do two more games for stamina."

Trish eventually pulled ahead of me. But I stayed close at her heels. I fought her speed with my wits. We stayed squash buddies. Each of us wanted to win; each of us wanted the other to win as well.

When a poster announced a round robin—with prizes for the winners—we signed up. It was our first official competition. Trish's stomach churned before her first game, but she managed to calm down and win a trophy. I reached the semifinals—no trophy but a slot on the winners' roster. The next fall, we organized a women's team. We played against six other clubs around the state. By the second season, our team won the tournament.

Statewide contests are one thing. The national competition we're en route to is another. In addition, Trish will play a step above the level at which she usually competes. Just before the trip, a more advanced player dropped out. The state captain asked for someone from Trish's level to fill the slot. One by one, the players refused to be "bumped up." Trish, ever obliging—she's a mother, after all—volunteered to bump herself up.

When she's at her best, Trish plays a fluid and strategic game. She relaxes and moves with ease. She lobs balls so high that they kiss the wall and die in a corner. She feints impressively, setting up for long drives, then switching to tricky corner shots.

And she outsmarts other players. "I never know what she's going to do," her opponents say. When Trish is "on," she's graceful, unpredictable, and elusive.

Trish wants to inspire Eve. She hopes her daughter will see her win—or at least play her best. The idea of being trounced bothers Trish. But the competition she and I face in Minneapolis—players both younger and more experienced than we are—will be tough.

Our first morning in Minneapolis, Trish and Eve join us for a pre-tournament breakfast. Trish had a bad night. The rest of us are bunked together, but because Eve brought Trish, they'd been shunted off to a private room. Trish had looked forward to gossipy swapping of training tips and shampoos. She needed that banter to lighten the tension building inside her.

What's more, Eve's "gigapet" electronic toy started beeping in the middle of the night. Trish pushed the "feed me" button to turn it off, then lay awake the rest of the night. She pictured high lobs leading her to victory, then feeble serves leaving her scoreless.

Bagels and banter at breakfast revive Trish. We all trade aches and pains. "My foot is killing me," I moan. "I'm glad they don't do blood tests," says a player on medication for shin pain and asthma. "I'd flunk."

Our talk is an odd reversal of male locker-room bravado. Each of us vies for underdog. "I'm going to be fodder," says a top-seeded player. "I'll get my butt kicked," says Wendy. It's as if talk of defeat will free us to give our all. Eve licks frosting off a Pop-Tart and listens. I wonder what she's learning.

As girls, Trish and I both loved sports but didn't take competition seriously. Trish grew up in Australia, where every town had public squash courts. Squash looked sweaty and male to her. She never bothered to learn. Instead, she played field hockey just for fun.

Growing up in New Jersey, I thought of squash as an almost mythical sport, like polo, that rich guys played. I, too, played hockey, and won "good sportsmanship" awards because I didn't care if I won or lost. As an adult, I hiked, biked, rock-climbed, skiied, and jogged—always for fun. In my forties, back pain slowed me to a walk. At fifty-six, I joined a sports club, determined to recover my athletic self.

Trish, meanwhile, spent her twenties traveling, carrying her hockey stick with her although her only exercise was waitressing. In her thirties, she settled down in Boston, and found herself driving her two kids to after-school sports but playing none of her own. At age thirty-six, Trish joined a sports club. Doctor's orders—her blood pressure was far too high. She planned to swim a few laps, then soak in the hot tub.

On the way to the pool, Trish and I, about a week apart, spotted the row of glassed-in squash courts. For Trish, it was a familiar sight. Except that now she saw women playing the game. Yes, they were sweaty, but sweat was "in"—this was the '90s. Trish was intrigued.

To me, squash was a revelation. I had never seen such an exciting sport. The play was fast and fierce, delicate and graceful. I wanted that grace. I asked the squash pro to teach me the basics. Trish did, too. We both declared we were playing "just for fun."

Trish heads out early for her first match. I come along to support her. Eve skips ahead, swinging a backpack loaded with games. The other Massachusetts players are warming up. Trish checks out the international courts: they're three feet wider than the older and narrower American-sized courts we play on back East.

Our first opponents, the Pittsburgh team, appear with their trainer. Trish and I have no professional backing. Our club dropped its squash pro a year ago. We've been winging it ever since, coaching each other, and training together.

Eve stares at the Pittsburgh players. Their muscular thighs attest to constant lunging after balls. Her mother and I stare, too: their training clearly surpasses ours. Eve pops gum in her mouth and sits on the floor by Trish's court. Taking Crayolas from her backpack, she sketches the scene.

Trish grips the terrycloth binding of the quality-brand racket she bought when she committed herself to playing competitive squash. She fastens her hair with a pink plastic comb, then slams a series of hard shots to warm up the ball. The hollow rubber sphere speeds up as it heats. A squash ball can travel over 100 m.p.h. in top matches.

"I love this sport," says Trish in a loud voice, as if to encourage herself. A woman in neon-green tights steps onto the court and warms up as well. Her hair is wild and red. Her stroke is controlled and strong.

The game begins. Trish's mouth is open and relaxed at first. It soon clamps shut. The redhead delivers a wicked serve. Trish returns it, but weakly. Her opponent slams a winning shot. Trish panics. She retreats to the backcourt. She hits defensive shots. She forgets her winning kiss-the-wall-and-die lob.

Games between equally matched players can last up to thirty-five minutes. Trish loses hers in under five. "Is it *over*?" asks Eve.

"Think of it as a warm-up," I say. "You have three matches to go." I want Trish to stay positive. A few minutes later, I lose my first match, too. "Ohmygod, they're *good*," I say. So this is what great squash looks like, I think. Discipline, that's what we'll get from this weekend. When we get home, we'll train harder. I tell myself that I did well for a sixty-year-old. For Trish, who is younger, it's tougher to lose.

I remind her that if we're outmatched in muscle power, we can still win by using our wits. Squash is a kind of chess—at high speed. The player who decides, in a microsecond, where to strategically place a shot, can win any rally.

Trish's second opponent trounces her and so does mine. "I

was blown away," gasps Trish, red-faced and teary-eyed. Eve looks at her mother's face, then looks away. Her shoulders droop. She blows her gum bigger and bigger until it collapses onto her cheeks.

Our team gathers at each break to swap tournament tips. "Play each shot as if it's the first." "Play hard, stay calm." Players traditionally use these sayings like mantras, and they often work. Trish doesn't seem to hear them.

Opponents as well as teammates offer advice. A Texan in her forties tells us she plays only men to prepare for the hardest-hitting women at tournaments. She starts her training sessions with 100 sprints up and down the court. I'm impressed. "We can do that," I say to Trish. But she remains glum. "It's humiliating," she says.

Trish considers skipping tomorrow's matches and flying home tonight. Instead, we join our teammates to load up on carbohydrates—and more team talk. "I've had a disastrous day," says one top player, who'd lost her first match, "but outside of that, I'm fine." Trish does not get it—how can you lose and laugh? She's focused on regret: Why had she agreed to be bumped up to a higher level of play? "I was a jerk to play nicey-nice," she says.

The next day, at breakfast, Trish's usually bouncy hair hangs lank—she hasn't bothered to wash it. Her mood has plummeted. She doesn't take her allotted five minutes to warm up on the court. "Why kill myself?" she says.

At the courts, Eve joins a mix of players from different teams as they go through their exercise routine. She copies their movements: ten sit-ups, ten push-ups. To get through the last five, she cheats a little, propping her knees on the floor. "Push-ups are hard," she says.

Eve swims and can dive, she's tried squash and she's starting hockey this year. She may decide to work hard at a sport, hard enough to excel, or she may not. This weekend, she's seeing women exert themselves more fully than she's ever seen before.

She's watching her mother as well. Trish could be a model for Eve—or not.

To let Trish focus on her upcoming match, I say to Eve, "Let's hit a few." She leaps from the floor, grabs a racket, and skips onto an empty court. I feed her balls. She misses the first but returns most others. I'm impressed by her strong forehand, her careful preparation for each stroke, and her easy movements around the court.

"You're good!" I tell Eve. "I can tell you've had lessons." But she suddenly hesitates, her pleasure compromised. "I feel sorry for the guy that teaches me," she says. "He must be bored, just feeding me balls, feeding me balls."

Trish checks the tournament lineup and finds something new to worry about. Her next game is scheduled for a court opposite the bleachers, which means it will draw the largest number of spectators. She now frets about being watched as she is beaten.

I'm getting fed up. "Forget the onlookers," I tell her. "Forget your opponent. The game is between you and the ball." The Texan finishes my rap. "Losing is what you do on the way to winning. Get used to it, Trish," she scolds. "I've played tournaments where I won no points." Trish looks stunned.

Trish's third game unfolds like the first two. Her opponent wins but is gracious, shaking Trish's hand and chatting before they leave the court. Still, Trish exits red-faced and distraught. That evening, she meets up with our state coach in the cramped space of the ladies' room between toilets and sink. "I'm being blown away!" Trish blurts out. "And this was supposed to be fun!"

Word gets out: Trish is demoralized. One player offers to take Eve swimming so Trish can be with her teammates. The next and final day of the tournament, the Massachusetts players find time, between their own matches, to shower Trish with encouragement. "If you're outmatched," says the most experienced competitor, "try to win one game. If you can't win a game, go for one point. If you can't get a point, try to keep the ball in play."

Trish is thinking about everything and everyone but her own game. She now worries that she may not even give her final opponent the workout she expects. She's haunted by the memory of a player at a Boston match who, after trouncing a lesser player, griped loudly to onlookers: "I never even worked up a sweat."

One minute till game time. Trish's final match. Eve sits up front but buries her head in a book. I don't think she wants to watch.

Trish slumps on the bench outside the court, brooding. She stares at the terrycloth binding of her racket handle. "My binding's too fat," she announces. Grasping a corner of her binding she jerks hard. The fuzzy strip falls to the floor.

"What are you *doing*?" I cry, aghast. Trish's handle, shiny with glue, is down to the basics. It's time to play.

Trish grins as she jogs toward the court, hand and racket fused for this one match. "It's a job that's got to be done," she declares to no one in particular. She's found words that work for her.

Five minutes into the final match, Trish is sweating. But so is her opponent. Each rally lasts several minutes. Trish plays her lovely lob—the one she's famous for back home—and wins points. From the bleachers, her teammates yell, "Good shot!" and when she misses, "Good try!" Eve looks up from her thriller.

During each break in the three-game match, a cluster of teammates surrounds Trish, whispering suggestions.

Trish leaps back onto the court. She manages to keep the ball away from her opponent's backhand. She forces the play over to her own stronger side.

Trish loses her final match. But she doesn't mind. She'd returned the ball well. She'd won the serve often. She'd earned—with her tricky corner shots and loopy lobs—almost half the number of points her opponent won. Trish had played her best. "Finally," she tells me, "I was in the game."

"The last three points were awesome," Eve yells.

The next day, we Massachusetts players sprawl across the hotel lobby sofas as we wait for the airport van. Our shoes are off, our feet propped on sports bags, our bodies limp.

Eve, however, has energy to spare. One of Trish's teammates heaves herself off the sofa, shoves a pile of sports bags into a row, and says, "Let's do hurdles." She and Eve leap over them. We cheer. Trish's teammate moves the bags farther apart. "Now let's try this!" she says. And the two leap over the barriers as far as they can go.

longing and bliss

MEGAN MCNAMER

1995

It had to do, in part, with the seasons and the weather. The game peaked at a time of year that was between times, that otherwise felt depressing, with only an occasional tremulous flutter. Valentine's Day, followed by Ash Wednesday. Walking down an alley you would see a sugar-candy heart melting in the slush. The inscription: SUM DISH. This meshes in my memory with all those winters—raw and ugly, sloppy if the wind was a chinook. Life had a dull kind of chaos to it. But inside those gymnasiums it was clean and warm and still. It was whatever I wanted it to be. And that's why I grew up loving basketball.

It all began in grade school with the St. Margaret's Huskies ("Hard to beat, hard to beat"). This was in Cut Bank, Montana, up on the Hi-Line, a series of wind-stripped little towns linked by the railroad tracks and the long ribbon of U.S. Highway 2. At St. Margaret's we were two grades to a room, with no gym of our own and no association with the Public-ers (a word we considered interchangeable with Publicans, Christ's adversaries), so all our games were away. We played kids from tiny Heart Butte or from Star School, the Catholic-run boarding school near Browning on the Blackfeet Reservation. I remember wood-burning stoves just beyond the baskets. They burned any player who reached for an errant shot. I remember another court with only one basket, so the game had to be improvised accordingly. Basketball had limits, barriers. But it seemed full of consequence.

I, of course, was sidelined. It was the 1960s in rural Montana, and I was a girl. By junior high school I acknowledged my position as spectator. But that didn't diminish my interest in the game. If anything it started to take on more weight. I switched my focus from the surroundings to the players.

I watched a Blackfeet player, Jim Kennedy, launch a mid-court shot that left his long fingers milliseconds before the final blast of the buzzer. The ball arced for a silent eternity, then swished back to earth amid a human roar. It sounded as though Lindbergh had landed in Paris. The Cut Bank High School Wolves lost a preliminary game in the State B Tournament to the Browning High School Indians by one pivotal point. My best friend Julie and I cried.

I watched Don Wetzel from Cut Bank—also a Blackfeet, compact and quick—steal the ball at the final moment and dunk it in a victory over the Shelby Coyotes, causing my best friend Shelly and me to cry.

I watched a Conrad Cowboy named Dick Harte make another of those long shots, changing fate in the nick of time. And I knew that the KSEN radio announcer was at that very moment screaming, "Heartbreaker by Harte!" as always, his words bouncing off the stars and down into Canada.

I watched those players for clues to myself. I was concerned with chance, a sudden upset, a ball flirting with the rim. But I was also concerned with certainty. I desired the players, and I desired a certain way to be. Long-limbed and loose. Sweating victory. In this respect, there was something both satisfying and heartrending about basketball. It was charged with against-odds possibility.

We would saddle up with chains and set out—the mother of my best friend Robyn driving—for eighty miles through snow flurries, ignoring the winter-storm warnings, skirting the eventual ROAD CLOSED sign. Homing in on Havre, the B squad game on the radio as our signal, we would have the car heater going full blast, making our wet-nyloned feet stink.

Once there, it was time to head for the bathroom and prepare. Put on our best blouses. Stuff our bras with Kleenex. Take out the curlers and spray the spit curls. Tease and comb our hair into smooth helmets. Erase our faces and apply a ghostly mask of white lipstick and black mascara.

The A squad game would begin, the important game. There were boundaries, rules, it would go on only so long. And while it lasted, the clock ticking away, I could forget the long drive, the rocky night, wind, Lent, death. My own gawky self. I existed within the game, which had an almost organic pattern, a coherence all its own.

From the starting lineup to the end of the bench, the players were extraordinary. In their shiny uniforms (usually something and gold) they were stars, all of them, even Tom, my winter-prom date, who was just getting his growth. When emerging from the mysterious locker room, he had a momentary glow.

This phenomenon wasn't new. Buzz—a guy my father's age, a growly, barrel-shaped, sleepy St. Bernard of a man, now a chef and modestly successful restaurateur surrounded by a hazy halo of cigarette smoke—was in his youth a Hi-Line high school basketball star. He was lean, of course, and flashing. The town fathers, as he tells it, would stop him on the street and give him money. Not to play harder, not to rig the game. Just for being, on Saturday night, Buzz.

My dad was a basketball star for Shelby, as were his brothers. He and my uncle Bob had tight curls that popped back into place after each flurry of play. They would have traded any amount of time on the bench for the pleasure of flipping their hair out of their eyes just once, one smooth swoosh. I guess they sensed something we all knew intuitively: Basketball was only partly about baskets, balls, and the various tactics for getting balls into baskets. It was mostly about bodies.

Poor exposed elbows, winter-pale legs, soft, first-growth hair matted with sweat. Those high school bodies were sort of pitiful. But they were in motion. They kaleidoscoped right past the cheerleaders, who had a physical presence I always found discouragingly at rest.

Cheerleaders in the 1960s wore dress shields. They kept their faces flat. They shouted *V!–I!–C!–T!–O!–R!–Y!*, but their performance didn't seem goal-oriented. They repeated the same motions no matter what was happening on the floor. There was no sense of evolution in their actions.

For a while I wanted to be a cheerleader myself. I wanted the social endorsement that went with being a cheerleader; I wanted the attention. I wanted *something*; and this was what was given me to want. But, for all that, I really didn't want to stand positioned on the center line, traveling neither to the left nor to the right.

Being a cheerleader seemed so static: Be cute and things will come to you. This might sound similar to being Buzz on a Saturday night, but there was a difference. It had to do with desire. Bodies, at their best, are always wanting—in both senses of the word. Those high school basketball players had zits and skinny legs, but they were trained to summon passion. And they were rewarded with a kind of redemption. They were gracelessness turned to grace.

I eventually played in the pep band, a negligible role in the overall mix. Everyone liked hearing our songs. Distorted and stumbling, they nevertheless added jazz to the main event. But we might as well have been a human jukebox or itinerant musicians from the street, the way fans averted their eyes. We weren't in motion, we weren't quite still. We were just something odd in our stiff, hot uniforms with their high-water pants. At tournaments, in the crush of the crowd, pep bands from various towns were positioned here and there in a cordoned-off gulag. Deep within our boardlike band suits, we perspired. But we enjoyed a bit of importance then. We were court eunuchs at the royal palace.

As a member of the band, the closest I ever came to insinuating my body into the orchestrated whole that is basketball was when I performed my solo cymbal crash during "The Star-Spangled Banner." I would take one step onto the floor and clear a little room. "And the rockets' red glare . . . " *Crash!* It occurred to me that I could tamper with the scheme of an evening by being innovative at this point—by executing a modest pratfall or by substituting a triangle's tiny *ping* for the big metallic crash.

But I didn't.

I believed in the drama of basketball; I didn't want to break the spell. And my band position—betwixt and between—was not so bad. It afforded a good vantage point and excellent camouflage. I could become nearly invisible, making it easier for me to dream. And I could really see the players.

Later I had a similar experience while in a community production of *Jesus Christ, Superstar.* There was a rabble-sized cast, dramatic music, an emotional text. I was a leper and had to spend most of my time underneath the stage. I would peep through a little gauze-covered porthole (the stage was built on risers), waiting for my cue. Then I would writhe out at various intervals, along with other strategically placed lepers, to clutch at the Savior's robes.

While I was waiting, I would watch the sandaled feet of the Apostles. Because there were so many bodies, with so much happening on the stage, each second of the show was carefully blocked. The Apostles' every move was scripted and meant to be executed just so. The actors, I'm sure, were thinking mainly about their arm gestures (supplicating) and their facial expressions (agonized), just as I did for those few moments when I twisted into view. But from my porthole I was looking at the Apostles' feet, which were right at the level of my eyes. And I was fascinated with what a good job the feet were doing. They moved so confidently, always doing the right thing to contribute to the overall moment. I suppose that if I had seen the whole supplicating, agonized effect from somewhere in row M, I might have thought, Well, this is, after all, community theater. But at foot level I was in Nazareth.

The basketball players of my memory also followed a script with a limited number of positions and modes of execution. Still, their bodies moved spontaneously, intuitively. Maybe that was why they seemed so full of promise to those of us who couldn't play.

Of course the players yearned to indulge in grand gestures—the hair toss, the full-body prostration, the moment of prayer at the free throw line—and sometimes they did. But like actors or dancers caught up in a performance, they didn't know, or didn't appear to know, what their feet were doing. And so it seemed as if they were involved in the truest dance of all.

"The more constraints one imposes, the more one frees one's self of the chains that shackle the spirit."

Stravinsky wrote that in *Poetics of Music.* "In art," he continued, "as in everything else, one can build only upon a resisting foundation."

By focusing on feet, as gender-equal as any body part can be, I injected myself into the art of basketball. And then the players, with their peculiar constrained grace, affected me. They were, I think now, like male divas of the Chinese opera, women in brackets—beating wings within a tightly defined space. I watched the game, and I was in it; the real actors were me and not-me. We were agents in a combustive play. It was about growing up, death to the present. It was about all of unknown life. For the length of a game, we were an ignited dream.

In my flat band suit I could picture myself any way I wanted. I imagined that I would eventually emerge into the world looking something like them, those leaping players, instead of taking any other form—the domesticated cheerleaders, for example—that I could see.

After high school I stopped watching basketball. I left Cut Bank and considered my departure to be the true beginning of life. All those games had been mere rehearsal. It was time to take the floor.

And then last winter I went to a game, my first in more than twenty years. My six-year-old son, Patrick, and I perched up among the rafters of Dahlberg Arena at the University of Montana in Missoula. I went under the guise of a good mother;

Patrick, I said, should get a glimpse of the world of organized sports. He obligingly sat beside me, content with his plastic pom-pom and tiny megaphone—free, for being cute.

Neither of us quite knew what we would see.

There it was, the gleaming yellow-gold of the gym floor, a warm, squeaky contrast to midwinter muck. And there it was, I felt it, that familiar, light-headed sensation of being inside a large windless space. There was the band duly in its place, having just finished "Satisfaction." (Our warm-up song was always "A Taste of Honey.")

And there were the cheerleaders: Janes of a regimental jungle, each with one sturdy shoulder bared. Some were being flung about by strong and happy boys in sweaters. Some intoned a dispassionate chant before a *very* large crowd—8,000 or so, certainly as many as had ever watched Cut Bank play Shelby.

And there *they* were. The satin-shorted idols of my youth, wheeling stars in this cozy universe, apostles of grace, dancers at the altar, saints on a saffron stage . . . There they were. Working up the same celestial sweat.

Women.

Every one of them.

As I entered the real world to begin my true life, other women, younger women—girls from the Hi-Line—started playing basketball for real.

It began, the thump-and-rush rhythm of the game. I watched April Sather from Havre move methodically down the court, fluttering the fingers of her left hand in a semimenacing signal. I watched Malia Kipp, a Blackfeet player from Browning, assume a stance that was both polite and wary, her legs pivoting in perfect synchrony with the game. I looked at the program. The players on the UM team were all from Montana, mostly small towns. Jodi Hinrichs, from Fairfield, hung her head at the free throw line as if in deep repentance, then slipped the ball soundlessly through the net.

I was moved. I was jealous and joyful. I was filled with longing and with bliss.

I saw the players as high school boys, Wolves, Coyotes. They were Buzz, skinny again, Uncle Bob, his hair straight. They were Blackfeet warriors on horses, Lindbergh landing in Paris again and again. They were stars of the Chinese opera, released. They were loose-limbed and glowing. They were slender men in masquerade, and they were women unmasked. They were me. They were me and not-me.

bench press, **or** becoming a girl **again**

LESLIE HEYWOOD

I meet Billy at the diner. Bill Townsend, thirty-nine, five foot five and two hundred and fifty. Bill with the 465 bench. And bench is what's up this morning, our biannual Elmira Best Bench Championship. Billy's done these meets for at least twelve years, and when he goes out to make his lifts, the announcers always say, "And now our Bill, starting at 440 today . . . " I've trained with him now for two years. Billy chokes down eggs and sausage while I swill coffee, as if my nervous system needs any more kick.

"Gonna open with 440," Billy keeps saying. "You think that's right? Then 460, maybe 465." "You got 460 easy the other day," I tell him. "Think you need to kick it up a bit. I've got 210 as an opener, then 215. Then you think I should go 220? 225?" We go through this until it's time to drive out there, as if saying the numbers will make them so.

Back in the fray. I've been doing this, competing in one sport or another, since I was thirteen. It used to be track, then track and cross-country, then road racing. In the 1980s it was all "no pain no gain," and especially in college, NC fucking double A, Division I, you were only as good as your last win. Sitting here at this old upstate New York diner in the late '90s, staring at the anachronism of cigarette-stained waitresses and plastic booths, so nervous it feels like my stomach's up in my mouth, I keep trying to tell myself that's all changed now. Even the hardest-core sports magazines now advise against "no pain no gain" and preach the necessity of rest.

And I'm not nineteen anymore, every fiber of my muscles, every beat of my heart fixed on winning the race, on keeping my number-one spot on the team. Not a frightened girl struggling to hold fast to the only self she knows, with injuries and a body that is steadily breaking down, struggling to keep the college athletic scholarship that is based on her performances and that is putting her through school. Not anymore. I'm thirty-four, reasonably healthy, good job, four dogs, own house . . . But deep-tissue memories are hard to erase, and the idea of anything athletic in front of a crowd is enough to raise all of it, my heart rate so high I can feel it ramming my chest as I sit there sweating metal-scented fear.

Some coaches used to encourage us to think of it as a struggle for existence. You hold on to your place, your value, what comes to seem like your very soul, if and only if you win. Every practice, every meet. And if you were a girl, you had to compete much harder than if you had that Y chromosome instead, to show that you weren't *just a girl.* You had to choose, because girls don't exist, remember? Girls are *seen not heard, be sweet, just go along with it, give of yourself, don't assert yourself.* Girls are supposed to be nice. Smile a lot, meet everyone else's needs. So if you wanted to be an athlete, you had to *not* be a girl. You can't win a race without asserting yourself. It wasn't a choice for me. I lived to compete. Inside, underneath the smiling blond surface, I murdered the girl.

So twenty-one years later I'm powerlifting, doing the bench press, the one exercise that separates the men from the boys. Billy and I drive to the meet, and walk into the high school gymnasium where it's held. Bleachers fold out over the floor, the bench the very center of the gym. The bin of chalk for your hands and your back, chalk your partners rub over you to keep you from slipping on the bench. The announcer's table. The trophy table against the far wall, its rows of shiny lifters perched on fake wood, smirking. The refs will be on either side, waiting to give you a white light (if you get the lift) or red (if you don't). The audience will cheer in support if you get it. Murmur a disappointed "Awww" if you don't.

Half an hour before we start, people are milling all over the floor, competitors swallowing their last sips of creatine, a powder you mix with grape juice for the fastest absorption, a powder that contains an enzyme that increases your explosive strength. Some down PowerBars, or protein-and-chocolate concoctions with names like White Lightning or Steel Bar, or stimulants with names like Ripped Fuel. The biggest guys, the most intense, tuck their ammonia capsules into their pockets, and will sniff them and hit themselves in the head for concentration right before their heaviest lifts. Some faces are faces you see at all the meets, easygoing, appraising the action, dispensing advice. There are parents and girlfriends in the bleachers. The bathroom that always runs short of toilet paper is directly adjacent to the gym, and the bathroom that always has it is at the school entrance much farther away.

The warm-up benches are in the room across the hall. We all crowd in and listen to a recitation of the rules: Keep your butt on the bench. Lock it out at the top, and wait for the judge to say "rack" before you drop it. No one pays attention. Some of us sit, some stand with our backs to the wall, everyone swallows and tries to keep the tension in: *Let's get going already.* The voice drones on. I scan the room for other women. There, in that corner. A woman maybe forty-five or fifty, middle-weight, though this meet's so small that the women are all lumped in one class, regardless of our weight or age. At the bigger contests, there are three weight divisions: up to 132, 132 to 148, and 148 and above. Usually there's teen, open, and masters, which is anyone over forty. But today we're just women, all the same. So who am I up against? There! Behind the middle-weight woman, Deb, the bodybuilder, from last year. A woman who looks like she must be seventy-five (I find out later that she is). Where's Cindy? I scan. No Cindy of the 280 bench and the national titles, at least not yet.

Then I stop about halfway along the opposite wall. A little girl, with her father. Man! How old is she? I ask the guy next to me if he knows. He does: at this meet, for the first time, there's a very young girl. Thirteen. Exactly how old I was when I first lifted a weight. Could I have been that small, that pudgy?

Could I ever have been that young? She looks at her father and he smiles. Everyone wishes her luck.

The charts that list the competitors' flights, organized according to age and weight, are taped against the far wall of the gym. The women's flight is always first, because the women generally start with the lightest weights. Lately, though, the first flight is a mix, with the strongest women starting after some of the men. In a bench press meet you get three lifts. You open with a weight you know you can get, then have two more attempts. Your final score is determined by the heaviest weight you get, calculated in reference to your bodyweight. The charts list each competitor's opening lift, so you can gauge who your biggest challenge will be.

As soon as the meet director stops speaking, people gather by the charts to check out the competition, and calculate how many lifters are ahead of them in the lineup, and therefore how many minutes before they will take their turn. Rule of thumb says you should try to take your Ripped Fuel about half an hour before, and to do your serious warm-ups about fifteen minutes ahead, making sure to leave time to have your partners help you on with your shirt. Those of us in the first flight stampede to the warm-up benches. You grab a bench, pump out a few, then ask whoever is next what weight they want there. The young girl—who tells me her name is Tracy—warms up with fifty pounds, then sixty. The older woman—whose name is Jean—does about the same. The rest of us rush through sets somewhere in the hundreds, trying to get warm and leave a little more time. Because we've got breasts, it'll take us a little longer to put on our shirts.

Most competitors, those who take the meet at all seriously, wear bench shirts made out of the toughest layers of nylon, or the new denim kind, four layers of fabric thick. To bench without a shirt would be like running the Boston marathon in Keds. A shirt with the right fit can boost your bench by twenty pounds. Your shirt is supposed to fit so tight that you can't pull it on yourself, and many guys—who wear their shirts so tight it often takes three people to get them on—smear themselves with baby powder first to help with the burn.

I've got a red shirt, don't use baby powder, and always get bruised under my arms. Whoever you train with usually helps you with your shirt. After the warm-up Billy helps me, and Owen, this other guy from our gym. First I try to get my arms though the armholes, which are small and placed close together to help with the tightness of the material across the chest. My arms way up over my head, Billy and Owen ease the fabric over my forearms and biceps with quick, efficient tugs. They're pros at this. "Your head!" they yell, and I poke it through a small stitched hole. They work quickly, with short pulls down to the shoulders, and finally my head is out and they're pulling the fabric down over my chest. Owen tugs the back so hard I get thrown off balance, and then spill the other way when Billy tugs the front, which presses my breasts completely flat. I bounce side to side, cased tighter than any sausage. I can barely breathe. "There you go," they say, my shoulders drawn into each other so stiff I can't put my arms down.

This is the desired effect, and made for a startling sight when I saw people walking around in these shirts at my first meet: big guys, a few women, in blacks and reds and blues, walking with their arms in front of them like some Halloween ball or Frankenstein parody, so big and stiff and awkward I almost expected them to open their mouths with that monster's inarticulate cries.

Most of us go into the mental preparation phase, trying to concentrate and visualize our first lifts. Here's where your training partner really comes in: to keep your blood circulating through your arms once you're in your shirt, you have to keep them propped up. So competitors rest their arms on the shoulders of their partner before they start, and in between their lifts. A good partner will just stand there, silent, and let you concentrate. Billy waits for the weight of my arms without a word, and I prop them, try to clear my head and see myself getting the two plates up (two 45-pound plates on either side of the 45-pound bar totals 225). I think of faceless competitors who can press 250 when I'm only absolutely certain of 210. I think of Cindy last year with her 280. My hands are shaking a little, but when I reason it out, everyone's at such different levels, such different ages, bodyweights, range of experience, it makes no sense at all to compare us. When I used to run races in college, all of us were about the same age and equally trained. Each woman was a potential threat to every other woman's ranking and place. That's why my stomach is rumbling. But that mentality just has no place here. Powerlifting is a distinctly nonprofessional sport, not likely to get much newspaper ink, and it's occurred to me before that the crowd cheers for everyone just the same, that they don't even notice which lifter wins.

Still, my hands are starting to sweat. I'm really wondering if I can get over 220. I'd been doing 225 easily all summer and early fall, but the last couple of months, I'd only been able to get 220 when we practiced in the gym with the shirts. I thought I should open at 210, go to 215, then 220, but Billy said the nervous tension and yells of the crowd would boost me up that last five pounds and I should just go for the 225. I don't know. I can hear from the crowd the first lifters are about to start, and I head in.

Jean is first. She looks like anyone's grandmother, short and thin and really frail, a strange sight in this milling pack of Schwarzenegger brawn. She walks to the bench with her head up and a power to her steps that gives some solidity to the thinness of her arms. She's a pro: sits herself down, gives her chest a final stretch by pulling her elbows back, shakes her arms loose, and concentrates, looking straight ahead. Then she's down, her hands placed on the bar like clasps, and the weight's off the rack, down to her chest, and back up again, white light as the judges say, "Rack!" The crowd is rowdy and really gives her a yell, and she smiles, striding off to the announcers to report what her next attempt will be.

Tracy's right after her, and the crowd's really behind her, too. She's less certain of her movements and does everything a little fast, but she has no problem at all with her opening weight. When she racks it, several groups of people in the stands are on their feet. The crowd's voices echo off the gymnasium walls, and Tracy seems to grow taller as she jumps in excitement and runs to report her next lift.

Seventy-five years old, or thirteen, the girls are in the house today, and the crowd loves them. People are on their feet through each of Jean's and Tracy's lifts: boys in their late teens, their chests thick from lifting and football practice. Guys middle-aged, and graying, in nondescript windbreakers and Carhartt boots. Their wives, hair bleached and pulled back for the morning. Some girls in tight jeans, the girlfriends of the guys who will soon be pressing 425. Other girls in clusters, just watching. Old couples, parents, young kids, the rest of the competitors: "Nice! Nice! Way to go! Here we go now!"—Jean and Tracy are cheered like they're the state championship basketball team.

They both get their personal bests. They both look like they've been made Queen for a Day except prouder. They ruled today. They got their lifts. I smile and add my voice to the din. I drag my arms off Billy's shoulders and Frankenstein it on over to where they're changing, and I don't say anything but they see it in my eyes. They move up under my arms and we stand there with our arms around each other tight.

My arms around them, I feel the hammering in my chest, the edginess in my stomach, shift. I've linked arms with a woman who is seventy-five years old, and who has just bench-pressed the same weight as her age. With a girl the same age I was when I started to compete, who will learn who she is at least partly from this world and how men and women like me treat her here. I stop being scared and think it again: this isn't about first place.

"Deb Costanzas on deck, Leslie Heywood in the hole!" I watch Deb get her lift, 150, clean. My arms are propped again on Billy's shoulders, so it's hard to clap, but I yell really loud instead, so loud he covers his ears. When I first started doing these meets I never cheered for the other women, focusing, preparing myself for my own lifts instead. But cheering for my competitors, women showing their strength in public, I feel like I'm cheering for myself. As if the louder the cheers, the more it matters all of us are out here. So I'm still yelling for Deb even as the announcer is calling my name. "Settle down, champ," Billy says, walking me over to the chalk and smearing it over my back. "Down and up. Right off your chest. Let the shirt carry it." They announce my opening weight of 210 and the crowd starts to roar, but I'm thinking about setting myself under the bar just right. "Straight down, then up. Down, then up." And up it goes, like there was no weight on that bar at all. I get the white lights, run over to tell them my next lift's 215.

My arms are propped up until it's time to go again ten minutes later. The 215 is easy too. But on 225, my last try, the weight heads up but then hangs in the air three-quarters of the way, stopped dead. It's not going anywhere. The spotters grab it—red light. "Awww!" the crowd murmurs. But the announcer's upbeat. "Heywood out with 215—an enormous lift!" The crowd goes from disappointment to a rowdy cheer. I get up off the bench and wave. It's the best I've done in a contest. And winning? Yeah, I guess. But the crowd's cheered all of us. I'm not feeling like I'm flying because I lifted the most. I'm flying because I'm feeling respect for my competitors, my girls. The girl I murdered a long time ago within me. I feel her kicking in my chest: the girls were in the house today, girls and athletes both.

from *pilgrim* at *tinker* creek

ANNIE DILLARD

It is spring. I plan to try to control myself this year, to watch the progress of the season in a calm and orderly fashion. In spring I am prone to wretched excess. I abandon myself to flights and compulsions; I veer into various states of physical disarray. For the duration of one entire spring I played pinochle; another spring I played second base. One spring I missed because I had lobar pneumonia; one softball season I missed with bursitis; and every spring at just about the time the leaves first blur on the willows, I stop eating and pale, like a silver eel about to migrate. My mind wanders. Second base is a Broadway, a Hollywood and Vine; but oh, if I'm out in right field they can kiss me goodbye. As the sun sets, sundogs, which are mock suns—chunks of rainbow on either side of the sun but often very distant from it—appear over the pasture by Carvin's Creek. Wes Hillman is up in his biplane; the little Waco lords it over the stillness, cutting a fine silhouette. It might rain tomorrow, if those ice crystals find business. I have no idea how many outs there are; I luck through the left-handers, staring at rainbows. The field looks to me as it must look to Wes Hillman up in the biplane: everyone is running, and I can't hear a sound. The players look so thin on the green, and the shadows so long, and the ball a mystic thing, pale to invisibility . . . I'm better off in the infield.

contributors' notes

Deborah Abbott may often be found in and around water. On land, she is a psychotherapist and directs the Gay, Lesbian, Bi, Trans Resource Center at the University of California at Santa Cruz. Her writing has been widely anthologized; she also coedited *From Wedded Wife to Lesbian Life* (The Crossing Press, 1995).

Much-published poet, essayist, and naturalist **Diane Ackerman** is a devoted (okay, obsessive) cyclist and a recipient of the John Burroughs Nature Award and the Lavan Poetry Prize. Two of her recent books are *A Slender Thread* (nonfiction; Random House, 1997) and *I Praise My Destroyer* (poetry; Random House, 1998).

Anne Alexander is currently the editor in chief of *Prevention*, America's largest health magazine. She still rides her Bridgestone RB-1 bike and passes as many unsuspecting cyclists as possible.

Barbara Beckwith took up squash at the age of fifty-six and continues to play at age sixty-one. She lives in Cambridge, Massachusetts, where she works as a freelance writer and National Writers' Union activist.

Freelance journalist and creative-nonfiction teacher **Carol Bergman** lives in New York City. Her articles, essays, interviews, profiles, and short fiction pieces have appeared in numerous publications, including *The New York Times, Cosmopolitan*, and *Willow Review*.

Madeleine Blais is a Pulitzer Prize–winning journalist whose book about the Amherst High School girls' basketball team was a finalist for the National Book Critics Circle Award (1995) and chosen one of the Best Books for Young Adults 1996 by the American Library Association. Blais teaches at the University of Massachusetts–Amherst. Her son and her daughter belong to three soccer teams each.

Houston writer **Michelle Brockway**'s work has appeared in *Mother Jones, On the Issues, Houston Metropolitan Magazine, Texas Magazine, The Houston Press,* and *Comp and Rhetoric: A Writer's Guide with Readings.* Although she ran her first marathon in 1987, she's still working on hitting the cutoff.

Grace Butcher rode motorcycles for twenty years, making many long trips on her BMW R/90, racing motocross on a Suzuki TM125, and road racing a Yamaha RD250. She has also competed in track and field since 1949. From 1958 to 1961 she was U.S. 800 meter/880 yard champion; in 1996, she set a world indoor record in the mile for women age sixty to sixty-four. Her poetry has appeared in three collections and numerous magazines and anthologies.

Sandra J. Chu's work has appeared in the *Asian Pacific American Journal, The Washington Square Literary Review, The Chacalaca Review, The Cream City Review, Confluence,* and the anthology *Too Darn Hot: Writings about Sex since the Kinsey Report.* She is currently a vintner in Belle Mead, New Jersey, where she trains for triathlons and coaches crew at Princeton University.

Frances K. Conley is chief of staff at Veterans Affairs Palo Alto Health Care System and professor of neurosurgery at UCSF/Stanford Health Care Services. She lives in Woodside, California.

Ruth Conniff is the Washington editor of *The Progressive* magazine. She was a varsity runner at Yale University, and for six years coached girls' track and cross-country at East High School in Madison, Wisconsin, her own alma mater, where she holds records in the mile and 800 meters.

Sara Corbett traveled extensively with the U.S.A. Basketball Women's National Team before the 1996 Atlanta Olympics; her account of that experience is *Venus to the Hoop: A Gold Medal Year in Women's Basketball* (Anchor Books). Corbett's work has appeared in *Women Outside, Self, Women's Sports & Fitness,* and *Outside.*

Former Little Lassie League softball player **Barbara Crooker**'s poetry appears in such publications as *Yankee, The Christian Science Monitor,* and *Highlights for Children.* Her seven books include *In the Late Summer Garden* (H & H Press, 1998). Crooker now throws the ball around with her son, who participates in a Challenger league.

Betsy Crowfoot lives in Southern California with her seven-year-old daughter, Coco. A late bloomer who began sailing at age thirty-two, Crowfoot makes her living writing when not sailing on an all-women's team based in Long Beach. She particularly loves to race.

Barbara Davenport runs and rides her mountain bike north of San Diego, where she writes memoir and fiction. "Green Afternoons" is from her forthcoming memoir *Burning the Barn,* an account of her four-decade-long coming-out process, and an exploration of the heart's reasons for standing in the way of its own desires.

Debra Pennington Davis is an Alaskan writer and teacher newly transplanted to the Columbia River Gorge. Her work has appeared in *The Atlantic Monthly, The Muse Strikes Back* (Story Line Press, 1997), and other publications. A longtime runner and former cross-country coach, Davis now bikes, hikes, lifts weights, and attempts to practice yoga.

Carrie Dearborn learned to ski at the age of two. There is no scientific reason why she had a stroke; just luck, she guesses. Teaching skiing prepared her for her new career as a lesbian disabled stand-up comedian.

Rene Denfeld is an amateur boxer and author from Portland, Oregon.

The garage door **Annie Dillard** pitched against as a child stood in Pittsburgh, Pennsylvania, where she grew up. Her first book of essays, *Pilgrim at Tinker Creek* (most recently reissued by Harper-Collins in *Three by Annie Dillard*, 1990), won the Pulitzer Prize in 1975. Since then, she has published several books of poetry and non-fiction, as well as numerous essays and one novel, *The Living* (HarperCollins, 1993).

A freelance writer, lecturer, and licensed electrician, **Susan Eisenberg** wrote *We'll Call You If We Need You: Experiences of Women Working Construction* (Cornell, 1998) and *Pioneering: Poems from the Construction Site* (Cornell, 1998). She is currently on the faculty at the University of Massachusetts–Boston.

Sally Friedman is a scenic artist who has worked everywhere from Broadway to movie sets to *The Late Show*. She divides her time between Manhattan pools and the Adirondack lakes near Paradox, New York.

Ann Geracimos works as a feature writer for *The Washington Times* in Washington, D.C. She has continued her love affair with water, swimming regularly in ocean, lake, and pool.

Jewelle Gomez is a novelist, poet, and literary critic. Her novel *The Gilda Stories* (Firebrand Books, 1991) won two Lambda Literary Awards. Her new collection of short stories is *Don't Explain* (Firebrand Books, 1998). When accepting awards, Gomez always wears one of the four bracelets she received for being top swimmer at Breezy Meadows Camp.

Student **Leila Green** delivered a well-received speech, "The Outlook of Gymnastics," at Newcomb College's symposium on physical culture in 1899, from which her contribution was excerpted.

Gay Games participant (1990, 1994, and 1998) and former high school and college athlete and coach **Pat Griffin** is the author of *Strong Women, Deep Closets: Lesbians and Homophobia in Sport* (Human Kinetics, 1998). She is currently Professor of Social Justice Education at the University of Massachusetts–Amherst.

Leslie Heywood wrote *Pretty Good for a Girl: A Memoir* (The Free Press, 1998) and *Bodymakers: A Cultural Anatomy of Women's Bodybuilding* (Rutgers, 1998) and coedited *Third Wave Agenda: Being Feminist, Doing Feminism* (Minnesota, 1997). She ran track and cross-country in high school and college and today competes as a powerlifter and coaches Special Olympics lifters. Heywood directs the Nell Jackson Center for the Study of Female Athletes and serves as an associate professor at the State University of New York, Binghamton.

Shawn Hubler is a columnist for the *Los Angeles Times*, where she has earned a share in three Pulitzer Prizes as part of the metropolitan news staff. Thanks to the confidence her three daughters acquired from sports participation, her household now leads the neighborhood in spending on water polo gear, tennis rackets, cross-training shoes, weights, soccer gear, sweats, and sports camps.

Anna Seaton Huntington began rowing at Harvard College in 1983. After rowing in the Barcelona Olympics, she competed as a grinder with America3, the first women's team to sail for the America's Cup, and wrote *Making Waves* (The Summit Publishing Group, 1996) about her experience. She now lives in Kansas and writes about women's sports.

Amy Irvine has taught women's climbing clinics around the country. Her writing has appeared in *Climbing, Rock & Ice*, and numerous regional publications. She works as a grant writer for a grassroots environmental group known for raising hell.

Susan E. Johnson is the author of *When Women Played Hardball* (Seal Press, 1994). In October she becomes "Dr. Baseball," commenting on the major-league playoff season for an Anchorage, Alaska, classical-music radio station.

Maxine Kumin won the Pulitzer Prize for poetry in 1973. She has been a consultant in poetry to the Library of Congress, poet laureate of New Hampshire, and a chancellor of the Academy of Ameri-

Poets. Kumin is an ardent swimmer, and horses are her other passion. Her *Selected Poems 1960–1990* was published by Norton in 1997.

Teresa Leo's poetry and essays have appeared in *The Philadelphia Inquirer, The American Poetry Review*'s Philly Edition, *Painted Bride Quarterly*, and *CrossConnect*. She received an M.A. in Creative Writing from Temple University and currently works as a technical writer and Web editor at the University of Pennsylvania. Her best time in the two-mile was 11:40.

Linda Lewis discovered competitive rowing at the age of forty and retired from the sport at age forty-five. Ernestine Bayer, however, is still going strong—after more than fifty years on the water.

April Martin is a clinical psychologist and the author of *The Lesbian and Gay Parenting Handbook*. She and her partner of more than twenty years are joyfully raising their two donor-insemination children in New York City. Having weathered teenagers, menopause, bunions, and the rest of life's tribulations, Dr. Martin plans to keep skating at least until she's one hundred; who knows, by then she may even have her double jumps!

Poet and author **Colleen J. McElroy** is a professor of English and creative writing at the University of Washington. Having published more than a dozen books of poetry and prose, Dr. McElroy is the recipient of numerous honors, including the Before Columbus American Book Award, two Pushcart Prizes, and fellowship awards from the National Endowment of the Arts and the Rockefeller Foundation. She lives in Seattle, Washington.

Megan McNamer lives in Missoula, where she writes as a freelancer. She grew up in northern Montana watching high school basketball, and remains completely ignorant about college or professional sports.

Holly Morris's writing has appeared in several anthologies, as well as in literary journals and magazines including *The New York Times*

Book Review. She is the editor of two books, *Uncommon Waters: Women Write about Fishing* (Seal Press, 1991) and *A Different Angle: Fly Fishing Stories by Women* (Seal Press, 1995), and created and hosts the television travel series *Adventure Divas.* The daughter of two sportscasters, she has a very complex relationship to sport.

A former Stanford and pro basketball player, **Mariah Burton Nelson** wrote *Are We Winning Yet? How Women Are Changing Sports and Sports Are Changing Women* (Random House, 1991); *The Stronger Women Get, The More Men Love Football: Sexism and the American Culture of Sports* (Avon, 1995); and *Embracing Victory: Life Lessons in Competition and Compassion* (Morrow, 1998). The recipient of several national writing awards, Burton currently offers speeches to colleges and corporations, practices her golf game, and is writing a book about forgiveness.

Nancy Nerenberg is a freelance writer living in Los Gatos, California. Her published pieces are autobiographical in nature, although not all focus on her intense involvement in sport. On Tuesdays, Wednesdays, and Fridays, you can find her in the local gym, waiting for "next game."

Anne O'Hagan surveyed the state of U.S. women's sport in 1901 in a ten-page article for *Munsey Magazine.* She noted that in New York City, in addition to gymnasiums in all schools, in clubs for working women, and in YWCA branch buildings, six privately owned facilities opened their doors to women.

Joli Sandoz loves reading and writing about women's sport. She teaches at The Evergreen State College and is a Northwest Center for Research on Women Visiting Scholar at the University of Washington.

Kim Schaefer rides regularly and works with cyclists every day as a sports psychology consultant and bicycle mechanic. She feels blessed to be able to encourage other women to discover who they are while riding a bicycle.

Louise A. Smith lives in New York City and Los Angeles. She wrote *Mary Baker Eddy: Discoverer and Founder of Christian Science* and freelances as an editor and medical proofreader. Women's basketball is the subject of her second novel, *Rejection!*

Theodora Sohst wrote a regular column entitled "Women In Sport" for the New York *Herald Tribune* during the mid-1920s.

Alisa Solomon is a professor of English/journalism at Baruch College–City University of New York, and of English and theater at the CUNY Graduate Center. She is also a staff writer at the *Village Voice* and the author of *Re-Dressing the Canon: Essays on Theater and Gender* (Routledge, 1997). Solomon played varsity field hockey at the University of Michigan from 1974 to 1978 and has been practicing karate since 1984.

Helen Vozenilek feels lucky that when she was young, her older brother loved all sports and needed a playmate. As an adult, she continues to discover new athletic endeavors. Vozenilek works and plays in San Francisco.

Social justice activist and educator **Frances E. Willard** grew up on an isolated farm, where she nurtured the "pure natural love of adventure" which led her to learn to bicycle in 1892 at the then-outrageous age of fifty-three. One of the best-known U.S. women of her time, Willard campaigned for the eight-hour workday, public kindergartens, laws regulating child labor, pacifism, and equal rights and the vote for women; served as president of North Western Female College; and in 1879 became president of the largest women's organization in the country, the Women's Christian Temperance Union.

Wendy Patrice Williams now resides in California, and would have liked to play first base in a professional baseball league. She did play basketball for Barnard College in 1974. Her short story "Scheinman's Deck" appeared in the anthology *Shore Stories: Tales of the Jersey Shore* (Down the Shore, 1998).

Karen Zealand coedits *Nightsun* and works as a counseling therapist. Her poetry has been widely published in magazines and also appears in *The Carnegie Mellon Anthology of Poetry.* She wrote this poem for Christine Pihos, a discus thrower in the tradition of her father and her grandfather, who threw the discus in the Olympics.

permissions

acknowledgments

We are grateful to those women who have persisted in speaking their own truths about sport.

Sport and sportswomen fascinate, inspire, and delight us. We would like to acknowledge the strength we personally have found in the public stories of the greatest all-around athlete of our generation, Jackie Joyner Kersee; of sprinter Evelyn Ashford; of marathoner Joan Benoit; and of tennis champion and activist Martina Navratilova.

The essay "Coming Home" was written to honor the Humboldt State University women's track and field teams of 1977, 1978, and 1996, and the memory of Mary Ledford, who truly deserved to be Athlete of the Week.

We would be remiss if we did not mention our reliance on librarians near and far. Special thanks to Miko Francis, Don Edee, and the rest of the Interlibrary Loan and Reference staffs at The Evergreen State College Library; to the reference desk crew at Olympia Timberland Library; to Kokomo High School; and to librarians and archivists at the Kokomo-Howard County (Indiana) Public Library, the Free Library of Philadelphia, the New York Public Library, Urban Archives at Temple University, Bryn Mawr College, Smith College, Vassar College, Cornell University, the University of Chicago, the University of Puget Sound, the University of Oregon, and the University of Washington.

We are also grateful to professional colleagues for their encouragement and interest, especially Susan Preciso, whose patience never wavered, and Joyce Antler, whose interest and acknowledgments

kindness helped keep our faith in the significance of women's sport alive years ago and in trying circumstances. Thanks, too, to Helena Meyer-Knapp, Virginia Darney, Sarah Ryan, Jane Jervis, and Carole Oglesby. The work and talents of Elisabeth Kallick Dyssegaard and Elaine Blair at Farrar, Straus and Giroux made this a better book.

Our friends and families supported us in a myriad of ways as we researched and edited. Special thanks to Don, Helen, Doris, Tom, Kate, Douglas, and Donald Winans; Ann Strother Sandoz; and Alice Tunis.

Finally, we'd like to thank each other publicly. We did it!